Fragmentext One

Nothing is Written in Stone: A Jonathan Lee Riches Companion

Table of Contents

Chapter Six: 2009

A short introduction by Jonathan followed by a selection of transcribed lawsuits from that year. Notable defendants from this year include: President Barack Hussein Obama, Bank of America, The Guinness Book of World Records and Jenna Jameson.

Chapter Seven: 2010

A short introduction by Jonathan followed by a selection of transcribed lawsuits from that year. Notable defendants from this year include: ABC's Dancing with the Stars, Sandra Bullock and The Ghostbusters.

Chapter Eight: 2011-2016

A short introduction by Jonathan followed by a selection of transcribed lawsuits from those years. Notable Defendants from these years include: Jared Loughner, Brad Pitt, Kim Kardashian, Kanye West and Daylight Savings Time.

Chapter Nine: What Happens When the Law is Subjected to Unreason? Jonathan Lee Riches and the Fragmentation of Order by Dr. Mark Dyal

This essay places the Riches suits in the context of Futurist and poststructuralist attempts to decenter the law by undermining its relationship to language.

Chapter Twelve: The Jonathan Lee Riches Autobiography

Jonathan details his upbringing, the crimes that lead to his incarceration and his decision to begin flooding the courts with frivolous lawsuits. Jonathan describes his life after prison and plans for the future.

Note on the text

The lawsuits here are barely a fraction of JLR's output, however, they are his most well-known and encapsulate most of his reoccurring themes. The majority of suits in this volume were originally handwritten and transcribed by myself over the last two years. I have edited the suits for grammar and readability and take sole responsibility for any errors that occur in the text. Any suits JLR typed out himself have been reproduced in the text and were not transcribed.

Originally I had envisioned this book to be both a catalog of Jonathan's suits as well as a collection of essays analyzing Jonathan's output from a variety of perspectives. The end result only contains two essays, however, within the context of the work as it stands I believe these provide adequate bookends to Jonathan's work.

I would like to personally thank Dr. Mark Dyal and the Dyal family, the Sigl family, Kristin Rodgers and the Chavez family, Keith Preston, V. Vale and Re/Search Publications, John Christenson, Dayal Patterson, Michael Castaneda, Matthew Hart, Troy Westover and especially "Secured Party" a/k/a Jonathan Lee Riches©

(Editor's note: I still have no idea what "Secured Party" means)

Stephen Sigl

11/05/18

Jonathan Lee Riches and The Art of Litigation

By Stephen Sigl

I want to do something random and unexpected. Freedom to do things without a reason seems interesting. –JLR (Facebook post 11/10/16)

To begin, I would like to address the role ideology will play in this assessment of Jonathan Lee Riches's work. To the majority of people reading this, the word itself has political or quasi-political connotations; perhaps we might say that the word is saturated with these connotations. Therefore, if I apply the word to literary or artistic endeavors no fault can be placed on the reader for dragging these same connotations into play. For this reason, it is important that we de-saturate, or reevaluate the concept within a more rigid, philosophical context.

The clarification I am making is borrowed from Theodor Sider, which he in turn had acquired from W.V. Quine: "A fundamental theory's ideology is as much a part of its representational content as its ontology, for it represents the world as having structure corresponding to its primitive expressions" (Sider, 2011 p. viii).

Obviously a literary or artistic theory does not make ontological claims in the "serious" way that a scientific theory might –it is not required to do so. However, in order for it to work on behalf of the author, in his creation of the world in which he will be operating, it does and has to entail ontological stipulations. The ideology will stipulate what is ontologically primitive: the *things* the author will take to be real, real in operation, if not concrete fact within his narrative. Though I will expand on this later in the essay, Riches is going to present an ideology that takes names, names themselves constituted only of contingent content, as primitives. He will also take an abstract notion, one less concrete than names, jurisprudence, as a primitive.

These are preliminary remarks meant to stipulate a certain ground rule for the reader. Instead of diving directly into the practical applications of what I am laying out, let's turn to a relatively well-established fictional universe that happens to coincide with the world of Jonathan Lee Riches and navigate towards our ontological foundations from there.

Kafka and the Bureaucratic Nightmare

What we will be analyzing in this section is a Kafkaesque world that exists in a very specific sense, i.e., one in which the line between the realm of bureaucracy and the realm of the social (or the "real") is perforated. In *The Trial*, Joseph K stumbles upon the bureaucratic realm after it intrudes into his home one morning. The first thing that happens after this intrusion is not the unraveling of his personal life; instead his life prior to the interruption turns out to have been just as artificial as the set of institutional premises that have invaded it. The primary artistic achievement of the novel occurs halfway through as the seemingly artificial world of bureaucratic jurisprudence succeeds in contaminating all adjacent social spheres. At this point there is no line separating the judicial machine from the seemingly organic form of inter-subjective life that preceded it, and for a time, unknowingly co-existed with it.

Kafka was obviously amused by this scenario and much of *The Trial* is a reveling within the genre he was creating based on this unraveling. Once the ontological structure of the artistic universe is sufficiently established, within these *generic* parameters, there opens a potential for near-infinite repetition and revisitation of the themes and premises essential to the

9

established structure. And, if the ideology or basic ontological premises are established in a convincingly novel way (one which captures the imagination of a particular segment of the population), the work of art takes on a life of its own –it becomes perpetual. Perhaps this is why Kafka never completed his novels, he completed their generic structure, however, their literary trajectory –how they work on their own can never be adequately finished.[1] This can also explain why stories like *The Trial* or *Metamorphisis* begin with the intrusion of the traumatic event -we only get a literary retelling of the pre-traumatic in hindsight. Both features relate to the stylistic component of ideology: the asymmetrical and metonymic notion that one piece by Kafka is itself evidential of the Kafkaesque structure, or genre, though the particular excerpt need not address all the themes commonly associated with the author.

Authors and artists who establish their ideology in this highly subjective and idiosyncratic way tend to lose their personal identities in their work. Often the stylistic traits exhibited within the works are projected back onto a caricature of the author that has formed and continues to form in the mind of the public. Their names become place-holders for successors who carry forward the ontological tenets of their self-inscribed genres. In this way, these authors are not subject to a cult of personality effect -their successors are not imitators per se, they are disciples who carry on the designated labor of establishing and re-establishing ideological parameters.

In novels like these, the characters are not strong in the traditional sense; any strength they have is either derived from the ideological structure of the established universe or works

---

[1] A similar point can be of H.P. made about the work Lovecraft

[2] Baudrillard, Jean; Noailles, Enrique Valiente. *Exiles From Dialogue* (2007) Blackwell Science Inc. p.11.

towards perpetuating the idea of that universe's stability. In this latter sense, i.e., the characters work towards stabilizing the universe, the readers ascertain that the characters are possessed by a dynamism normally associated with the traditional literary aesthetic. The shift that occurs in this type of storytelling can be summarized as follows: in the traditional literary schema the characters drive the story and in essence create the atmosphere of the novel. In the new schema the environment, or setting, drives and animates the characters. The idea of autonomy has moved beyond the realm of the personal into the impersonal, it, like nature, becomes fundamentally unknown in its essence and is only understood in its effect.

If we accept the above reversal as being one essential component of the literary transition into modernism we can define a post-modern literature as being one that maintains either schema, albeit in an ironic way. This is to say it grounds the chosen schema in a way that allows irony, as a trope, to permeate the essential elements of the story that is being told.

Given these assumptions, what do we say about Jonathan Lee Riches and the lawsuits he filed during his incarceration? Not yet regarded as an artist or author, his work is easily the most avant-garde form of artistry that has been promulgated in the last fifty years. The ontological tenets presented, what his work propounds about the nature of the real, are almost identical to Kafka's. The vehicle, or medium, of his work is explicitly tied to the bureaucracy Kafka feared and toyed with albeit in the removed medium of formal literature. Because it eschews this mediated distance, the content of Riches's work transcends Kafka's ideological tenets, and in doing so becomes wildly absurdist having more in common with Duchamp's surrealist act of placing a urinal in an art gallery than it does with any formal literary humor. It is the concatenation of medium

11

and content that defines Riches' work.

After stipulating ontology in this broader context we can analyze the finer, literary, points within two phenomenological contexts. The first being a textual analysis that focuses on genre stipulations and how they engender an author's particular *style,* the second being a study of the bureaucratic experience itself and how it might engender the particular instantiations presented to us in the work of Jonathan Lee Riches.

Paul Ricoeur identifies the world of the text as being something that is opened up to the reader (Ricoeur, 1991 p.76). In this way, he is acknowledging a necessary ontology akin to the one prescribed by Sider and Quine, however, he sees the worlds contained in texts and the actual world that we assume in a realist capacity as being both contingent upon each other and isomorphic to one another. As an aside, the argument that they are contingent upon each other is not as controversial as the claim that they are isomorphic to one another. Such a claim of isomorphism, i.e., that there exists a one-to-one relation between entities inhabiting each such world could undermine traditional foundational claims made in the actual world.

One point I am trying to make in this essay is that there *is* a purely one-to-one relation between the events and subjects depicted in Riches's lawsuits and the world he is drawing them from. The key point being that Riches does so in a way that is absolutely transparent, and the events that are imported into the lawsuits are drawn not from reality writ large, but from segments of reality that might be ascertained from an experiencing agent who is relegated to a particular place and time. The primary significance in this last regard is that for Riches, due to the nature of his confinement, those segments of time and space have come to him solely through a mediated form: byway of television, newspapers and magazine articles.

The fact that the author is physically separated from modern culture, yet seems to acquire the same connotations as the average non-incarcerated member of society shows us how innately mediated the connotations circulating within our culture actually are, how they are essentially manufactured and largely inescapable. This theme of inescapability appears explicitly in suits like "Perverting America" (09/07/2007) where Riches claims he cannot avoid sexual perversion anywhere in spite of the fact that the only place he is able to go is within the confines of F.C.I Williamsburg.

In addition to the novelty introduced by this demonstration: that the cultural experiences of the captive man are essentially the same as that of the free man, Riches adds his humor and his indefatigable creative output. The humor, in itself is usually clever and very rarely directly satirical. The appellation of satire is something we can apply to the over-arching endeavor of Riches's oeuvre, both in hindsight and as the project develops, not as a significant feature within any of the narratives contained within the lawsuits. Satire is a characteristic of Riches's work as a whole, not one of his ontological primitives. What he has committed to paper is a very inventive form of literature that happens to be on, and confined to the realm of official court documents -recognizing this from a distanced and objective standpoint allows the appellation of satire to the whole.

The Post-Structuralist Blackhole

In Riches's work politics reaches its zero-degree. All political actions and affiliations are reduced to mere signifiers within the "bureauniverse". There is no recognizable politics here. Names of people and organizations are assimilated as signs. Jon Swartz can be a co-defendant with the World Wide Web, Wikileaks is conflated with Wikipedia, and events take precedence over the linear flow of time in which they occurred, as exemplified in the Barry Bonds lawsuit (08/13/07), in which it is alleged that Bonds is responsible for the crack in the Liberty Bell.

This is tied directly to the idea of isomorphism addressed in the last section. Art plays off of the variability of interpretation of the signs expressed within its given medium. This variability comes from the fact that the signifier in the work can point towards myriad actual objects. Generally speaking, in conventional art there is no guaranteed one-to-one relation between the work and the material world that has engendered it. This multivalence is closed off in Riches's work. The name, as printed in the lawsuit, has a one-to-one correspondence with the name as it appears written anywhere at any time, i.e., to the name itself.

In properly interpreting Riches's lawsuits as art we are compelled to take signs at face value and apply only their nominal attributes. However, these nominal attributes are not nominal enough because they have been acquired through the channels of mediation engendered by our society. If we take the names as merely nominal, like colors on a palette, we reach an event horizon of cognition. We can never really fall past this horizon though, because in taking the names in the way we ought to –purely nominally- we will miss the humor, we will miss the contingencies that brought the names into the suit in the first place and why the suit works as a piece of narrative, as humor, etc., we lose the context.

The discontinuity between these two ways of understanding the suits can be described as an irreconcilability between a normative approach to the subjects (names themselves) in Riches's lawsuits, and our implicit, conditioned understanding of the contingencies of person-hood, celebrity and event that ground our understanding of a name.

Yes, all contents have been liberated, but nobody can liberate language as form. You never liberate a form; it's the form that enchains you. Hence all these inverted formulas: it's the object that thinks us; it's language that thinks us; it's the world that thinks us – formulas of duality and reversibility. [2]

Within these parameters, a writing that is oriented towards the pleasure of the reader, an instinctive or immediate pleasure as opposed to a measured, objective one, achieves its ends when it momentarily surprises language itself by playing with the distinction between how we ought to think of the names and subjects presented in the suit and what those names and subjects are in themselves, outside of our received notions of them. Riches consciously blurs the line between these two positions. An excellent example of this is the suit against Bernie Madoff (05/09/2010) in which the entirety of Riches's frivolous legal activity is traced back to the equally frivolous claim that Madoff himself masterminded and instigated the activity. For a bureaucrat analyzing this text it would seem that Riches is attempting to shift the blame for his behavior onto one of his favorite litigious targets. Obviously, Riches does not see it this way, this fictive circulation is only meant to further entrench the general narrative structure of his oeuvre and ultimately enrich the experience of both the reader and the author. This enrichment is for the sake of the reader who is following Riches's work as it develops and can subsequently enjoy the plot twist contained within this lawsuit, one that seemingly has implications for all the other lawsuits. Likewise, it enriches the experience of the author by permitting a firsthand experience in

---

[2] Baudrillard, Jean; Noailles, Enrique Valiente. *Exiles From Dialogue* (2007) Blackwell Science Inc. p.11.

which language, directed by active imagination, is allowed to surprise itself.

The actual blurring of the distinction between what "ought to be" and "what is" occurs when the reader consciously grasps the fact that obviously this claim regarding Madoff is empirically false just as all the others are false, but that this falsehood is not detrimental to his enjoyment of Riches's work. What is important, and what is therefore normatively significant, is merely the names and events that are being used and how they are being utilized within Riches's narrative. It is in this way that Riches toys with common sense notions of empiricism and normativity –by resituating them and the signifiers they are attached to in a way that intends *only* to further entrench them in his fictional world.

The fact that this strategy reoccurs throughout his oeuvre brings us back to the question of literary asymmetry within the artist's oeuvre: can we say that one lawsuit by Riches gives us a deep insight into the whole artistic structure that he has set into motion? Not really, the lawsuits themselves all share the features of absurdity and name-dropping. Some have a developed narrative that runs throughout the piece (see "Jim Jones" 12/01/2008), others contain narrative fragments that take up the space of a line or two before acquiescing to the logic of conjunction that Riches frequently employs. For instance:

Dr. Hughes is a medical drug treatment specialist at the Residential Drug Abuse Program (RDAP) at FMC Lexington. Dr. Hughes sleeps and has sex with live pigs who spread swine flu. Dr. Hughes put on a pig costume and went to the market to eat pounds of roast beef. Dr. Hughes masturbated to Porky Pig.[3]

---

[3] Swine flu appeal 07/05/10

Which consists of a strategy that links predicates to one another but tells us nothing about their relationship to each other or the author. This free-associative technique, which has antecedents in Dadaism and Surrealism, is a common form of taxonomy. Common insofar as it is a technique that renders the connections between the names and actions immediately accessible to the understanding of the reader, the intended content however is not as accessible -it requires a feat of imagination. This is an act of imagination insofar as it is an act of a faculty that must be developed and attuned in certain ways by both author and reader.

The proper reading of a particular lawsuit, does not obtain byway of exposure to it alone. The work of reading through Riches's oeuvre trains us to recognize how proper names are assimilated as signifiers, and signifiers alone. There is no "real" lurking behind the mask presented by the name. This structure coincides with the system of codes Barthes uses in establishing a text that is reader-friendly, or as he puts it, "readerly":

Thus, to read (to perceive the readerly *aspect of the text) is to proceed from name to name, from fold to fold; it is to fold the text according to one name and then to unfold it along the new folds of this name. This is proairetism: an artifice (or art) of reading that seeks out names, that tends toward them: an act of lexical transcendence, a labor of classification carried out on the basis of the classification of language —a* maya *activity, as the Buddhists would say, an account of appearances, but as discontinuous forms, as names.* [4]

A text, no matter how many narratives it conveys, e.g., a narrative told within a narrative by a character who subsists within the former, plays a game with the reader insofar as

_____

[4] Barthes, Roland *S/Z* (1974) Hill and Wang, New York. p.83

matter-of-fact statements like "What are men to rocks and mountains?" (Jane Austen, *Pride and Prejudice*) asks the reader: "who is speaking? Is it the character or the author herself?" In all instances, even when Riches is putting words in his characters' mouths the reader instinctively "knows" it is Riches speaking.

More often than attributing statements to individuals, Riches attributes actions to them. These actions adhere to the arbitrary laws of cultural assimilation, i.e., the assimilation of signs. If we look at the use of Edie Falco in the James Gandolfini (12/24/07) case we see Falco as a character who's actions are determined not by any personal autonomy but by the machinations of the entertainment industry as ascertained by the remote public.

Riches's notoriety, which existed primarily on blogs at the time of his lawsuits, might be viewed as being purely sensationalistic. This interpretation, however, fails to take into account the salient notion that all forms of controversy that can be generated through "art" have been exhausted, in part, because all the mediums through which the artistic spirit can be conveyed have been exhausted. The medium of the legal system, and systems of bureaucracy in general, had not been adequately tapped in this respect. This is because artists are wary of the establishment, in a legitimately governmental sense, let alone organizational systems in general. To some extent, the acceptance, or recognition, of systemic processes or authority can give the impression of there being an underlying order –or even worse, a formula that can be used to impersonally construct art.

The artist's primal instinct is to create from the primacy of nature, yet not to identify the self that is doing the creating with that very same nature in a way that might be characterized as reductive. Just as individuals want to maintain a sense of autonomy or self that is not wholly reducible to their determining biological and environmental factors, the artist seeks a creation that is not wholly reducible to himself. This works in two ways: the artist recognizes that if there is a formula by which art is created, then almost anyone is capable of utilizing this formula, hence no-one genuinely warrants the unique distinction of "artist." Hence, we find the ambivalence some artists might have in labeling themselves as such.

The fear of systemization often works in concert with this sense of apprehension and is often a natural extension of the fear of losing one's sense of individuality. Kafka's approach of contrasting the individual with the bureaucratic establishment was a sophisticated attenuation of the artist's resistance to systematization. However, there is no reason for us to take this as merely an analogy; Kafka was legitimately prescient in the way he wrote about bureaucratic oppression. And despite conventional interpretations, Kafka did not see the individual's plight as an exercise in one-dimensional futility. There was another dimension: the epistemological plight that is presented to Josef K in the parable of the man who waits at the door of justice.

At the one-dimensional level, the story is one of sheer futility, however, it is aporetic in an almost Socratic way: though one feels the hopelessness of the protagonist's situation, there is a sense of paradox within the context of the narrative itself that begs for a resolution that is just as impossible to fulfill as the protagonist's quest for justice. This sense of impossibility is beyond connotations of positive and negative, instead it points toward an absence of being. This assertion of absence constitutes what I have designated as the normative reading of Riches's work in which names are empty signifiers. Coupling this with our inculcated, and unavoidable, awareness of the contingencies attached to these names we reach an impasse of impossibility.

The interpretation of this paradox of impossibility as being analogous to futility (which is not as richly paradoxical as impossibility) is where the idea of the individual at odds with the system is rooted. Riches overturns this dichotomy. He does not claim it to be a false dichotomy, nor does he explicitly deny its existence. His strategy is innocent, it is congenitally so, he denies the adversarial nature of the dichotomy from the outset. The system is not being played in an adversarial way, even if the motives are adversarial –the system is merely the field in which play occurs. This is why names are empty signifiers in his discourse: they do not represent pieces on a chessboard; they represent the actual movements themselves. This act of deferring power to the medium is what constitutes the novelty of Riches's work and it is analogous to the literary transition that moves from the inherent dynamism of characters to the dynamism of the field itself.

Bureaucracy

As Barthes states in *S/Z* the concept of a narrative presupposes the idea of a truth possessed by the narrator that is conveyed expediently through sentences. The only delays that might occur do so byway of hermeneutic detours. These are references that preclude a truthful closure and point towards information that is not immediately given -these are informational segments the text references, but does not explicitly spell out. The truth the reader is looking for in these instances might occur later in the narrative, or outside the narrative entirely.

The lawsuit is a form imposed upon narrative once the narrator chooses to bring his narrative under the purview of the judicial system. Given the auspices of this purview, we have to assume that conventional hermeneutical detours would be closed off entirely, and if this were not possible, they would be greatly minimized. The severity of this demand for absolute literalness is characterized by Ralph Hummel as the sacrifice of the individual to bureaucracy and involves the learning of a "new set of behaviors, norms, and speech patterns" for the sake of participation within the bureaucratic system (Hummel (1994) p.5). The bureaucratic world is a realm that operates contrary to our instincts; it is a virtual twilight zone that sits side-by-side with our day-to-day world:

In this new world of organized human interaction, it is entirely possible that a baby entrusted to welfare agencies may die of neglect even though, in the words of a welfare administrator, "everyone concerned did his or her job conscientiously." [5]

Hummel is discussing the employee, however, cannot the same be said about the ward?

By the time a human being is allowed to enter a bureaucracy as a case, that human being already no longer exists as a human being. That human being becomes a list of specific characteristics that the bureaucracy has been authorized by law to recognize as a case. [6]

The transition from human being to "case" is possibly the most radical form of subjective objectification that can occur. It is a transformation that is undertaken not out of ill will, but out of calculation of cost and efficiency. In a sense, within the modern bureaucracy it is a wholly necessary step in mobilizing and

---

[5] Hummel, Ralph *The Bureaucratic Experience* (1994) St Martin's Press, New York. P. 6
[6] Ibid p. 36

maintaining institutions that substantiate the social and civic parameters of our society. "Cases are artificial constructs that bureaucracy requires real people to become before they can be considered for service." (Ibid, p. 53)

The bureaucrat thinks of the client in terms predefined by the tenets that comprise bureaucracy itself. Through its devaluation of the individual for the benefit of the governmental organization, bureaucracy demands a closure of the hermeneutical discourse. The hermeneutical discourse essentially maintains the identity of the subject in relation to his cultural norms and informal systems of recognition. This sense of identity is seen by the bureaucratic system as an inevitable source of heterogeneity within the system. The process of silencing this discourse is an atavistic one that harkens back to ages prior to bureaucratic implementation; as Barthes states: "All domination begins by prohibiting language" (Barthes (1974) p. 68).

Riches's work evades the hermeneutic enclosure enacted by bureaucratic structures in two ways: its hermeneutical code alludes to two realms that lie outside the text. The first is the conceptually flattened and hollowed out world of signification as represented by the names of celebrities, trends and world events. The second is to the conceptually rich realm of the bureaucratic experience Riches exploits simply by submitting his narratives directly to the bureaucratic machine in the form of lawsuits.

As a narrator Riches understands the reader's desire for a revealed truth. If the reader looks towards the events as they are laid out literally in the suit he will find the flat, non-hermeneutical narrative that is prescribed by the bureaucracy. If, the reader looks at the signs in their broadly referential sense, he might be confused, amused or irritated –the signs don't have any fidelity to the connotations of their references, they seem

22

arbitrary or merely sensational.

These two attitudes act dialectically with one another, the resolution of this impasse, or the synthesis of the two attitudes, is the enjoyment of the narrative for its *readerly* value. This is a process that mirrors the movement from simple sign recognition to the admission of meaning into the sign system. Parallel to this effect, entering into the act of writing, unconscious as to whether what is written is fact or fiction, conforms to what Roland Barthes deemed the *writerly*, something which is remote from conventional empirical sensibilities:

Our literature is characterized by the pitiless divorce which the literary institution maintains between the producer of the text and its user, between its owner and its customer, between its author and its reader.[7]

Whereas, the goal of the *writerly* is to: "make the reader no longer a consumer, but a producer of the text." We have already seen how this production occurs on the part of the reader who tracks the continuity between Riches's suits, and by doing so is permitted the idiomatic appellations of "satire", "ontology", etc. to the whole.

The more plural the text, the less it is written before I read it; I do not make it undergo a predicative operation, consequent upon its being, an operation known as reading, *and* I *is not an innocent subject, anterior to the text, one which will subsequently deal with the text as it would an object to dismantle or a site to occupy.*[8]

Barthes describes the "I" that approaches the text as being, itself,

---

[7] Barthes (1974) p. 4
[8] Ibid p. 10

a plurality of other texts and codes which are: "infinite or, more precisely, lost (whose origin is lost)" essentially leveling the textual playing field between the reader and the writer.

Litigation as Retaliation Against the State

Just as the distinction between the normative and the empirical has been obfuscated, there is no distinction between "serious" and "banal" in this context either, as evidenced by the lawsuit against the Brady Gun Ban (04/29/09) and the motion to correct his name on the docket after the case is thrown out (05/15/09). The easy assumption taken up by court clerks who file reports on Riches's activity is the one-dimensional bureaucratic one: that he is abusing the system and that this abuse is borne out of a desire to retaliate against the state apparatus that has imprisoned him. To some extent they might also admit the factors of boredom and personal amusement. These factors however do not adequately summarize the full extent of what is going on.

By filing these notices these clerks are unwittingly placing themselves within the aesthetic landscape Riches is creating. To a certain extent, by virtue of their anonymity, they are the most authentic characters present. By condemning the motions they are inadvertently validating the overall structure Riches is operating within. Their actions are essentially saying: "This system exists, and its operations are allowing these heterogeneous elements to invade it." The mistake in this thinking is that they do not see that the motions are reflecting the disorganization and irrationality attendant to the bureaucracy back onto itself and its participants. The norms they are operating under have only the legitimacy the participants grant it. Participants with greater authority distend the structure in accordance with their wills in the same way that an artist does with his medium.

In filing these suits, Riches operated from a position of zero authority, but through ingenuity and prolific output was able to redefine the concept of jurisprudence and the system of legal bureaucracy into a field that operated in accordance with his own aesthetic desires. These desires were to see a system that was required to absorb bizarre allegations and signifiers, whose structures were based on narratives that are foreign to the sensibility of a legal bureaucracy. By signaling against these cases the courts were admitting that the names and events brought into play were possessed of an essential alterity -that their premises were inherently foreign to the business of practicing law.

This resistance of the medium to the artist is what is most essential in the act of artistic creation -sculpture is a prime example of this. Therefore, the greatness of Riches is not so much in the entertaining narratives he spins, his prolificacy or his reduction of names to empty signifiers, it is in his finding and exploiting of a new medium, one that no one had thought of before and which offered a severe degree of resistance. The work of Riches is carved in a new kind of stone, this was a stone that has hindered people since its inception, but under the weight of his pen it has begun to give way.

Bibliography

Barthes, Roland. *S/Z* (1974) Hill and Wang, New York.

Baudrillard, Jean; Noailles, Enrique Valiente. *Exiles From Dialogue* (2007) Blackwell Science Inc. New Jersey.

Hummel, Ralph. *The Bureaucratic Experience* (1994) St Martin's Press, New York.

Ricoeur, Paul. *From Text to Action: Essays in Hermeneutics, II* (1991). Northwestern University Press, Illinois.

Sider, Theodore. *Writing the Book of the World* (2011) Oxford University Press.

2006

Even though the suit I filed against Warden Michael Pettiford, to prevent myself from getting transferred from FCI Bennettsville, S.C., exaggerated the danger I might be facing if my transfer went through, it nevertheless was not "frivolous". The intent was merely to halt my transfer not to attack the legal system. I believe the impetus for transferring me, as well as other inmates, came from an unofficial crackdown on the anti-government rhetoric being expressed by the Montana Freemen who were interned with me at Bennettsville.

Upon receiving this dismissal I began researching the history of inmate lawsuits and the courts' attitudes in dealing with these cases. Obviously, it seemed impossible to get any fair hearing for my grievances, regardless of their relevance. Now knowing this, I began to push the boundaries of what could be considered a legitimate complaint. Though, as the presence of my case against United States of America, AUSA Jay Hileman, and FBI Special Agent Shauna A. Dunlap from 06/29/06 shows, I had not totally given up on challenging the legitimacy of my own sentence in a serious manner -I had not fully given up on the possibility that I might get some kind of unbiased hearing from the judicial system.

United States District Court

District of Wyoming

Jonathan Lee Riches© a/k/a

"Secured Party",

Plaintiff

Vs.

United States Military;

U.S. Marines; U.S. Navy;

U.S. Army; U.S. Airforce,

Defendants

Complaint

This is a complaint under 42 U.S.C. 1983, Civil Rights violation by the Constitution and laws of the United States; Federal Tort claims, violation of criminal law including, but not limited to: terrorism, murder, treason, major fraud, wiretapping, extortion, torture, racketeering, civil rights, espionage, assault, conspiracy, genocide, war crimes, explosives, identity theft, obstruction of justice, piracy, arson, computer fraud, sabotage, perjury, criminal street gangs, concealment, false oaths, bribery, riots, slavery, robbery, malicious mischief, counterfeiting, search and seizures, injury to wildlife, sex abuse/rape, pornography, obscenity, kidnapping, stalking, liquor trafficking, psychiatric trauma, invasion, false information, threats to commit violent acts, malpractices, aggravations, nuisances, entrapments, mind manipulation, brutality, negligence, persecutions, and poisoning.

Comes now the plaintiff Jonathan Lee Riches© a/k/a "Secured Party", in pro-se, moves this honorable to issue an order for all defendants named in this suit to give a response. As plaintiff is claiming that his federal and state constitutional rights are being violated under the 1st, 2nd, 4th, 5th, 6th, 8th, 13th, and 14th of the constitution. Relief requested, plaintiff seeks 75 cents backed by gold and silver coins delivered by United Postal Service, "UPS" to Federal Correctional Institution Williamsburg, South Carolina, collectively from defendants. Plaintiff seeks relief under the federal "whistleblowing" act. Plaintiff also seeks preliminary injunction temporary restraining order against defendants, defendants' spouses, and all military vehicles.

Count 1

The U.S. Military is in a vast conspiracy with Al Qaeda for world control New World Order. Joint chief of staff Peter Pace and all military generals joined alliance with Al Qaeda on Sep. 11th 2001. All military joined foreign alliance with the KGB, Columbian Farc, Sudan Janjaweed rebels on Oct. 5th 2004.

Count 2

The U.S. Military has a secret base in Wyoming outside Yellowstone Park. An underground city, central command. The U.S. Military is involved with the trading with the enemy act, as well as treason against this country by selling military secrets on Ebay to foreign nations.

Count 3

The U.S. Military secret command center in Wyoming is in violation of anti-trust laws, forming global domination, and taking away Americans' right to bear arms. Jan. 17th 2002, U.S. Marines came to my residence at Holiday Florida and stole my .22 rifle, 20 gauge Remington, multiple stunguns. Military boat

29

footprints and a map of Wyoming.

Count 4

U.S. Military killed millions of citizens. Evidence is footage on CNN, Fox News. They tried to poison me at FCI Bennettsville South Carolina on June 18th 2005 through the vents, chemical gases around the toilet. November 7th 2004 I was at USP Coleman Florida, the military tried to sniper me from a gun tower. Shocking me with electronic impulses on Nov. 9th 2004.

Count 5

U.S. military stole my identity on May 4th 2004 –used my credit to apply for a SEARS credit card and Exxon/Mobil gas card to finance fuel and maintenance of their vehicles.

Count 6

U.S. Military plants RFID tags in American citizens –I witnessed this at a bird flu outbreak on 12/18/03.

Count 7

U.S. Military created the SARS virus 10/22/05

U.S. Military sent computer viruses/hacker attacks 9/22/05

U.S. Military set up secret concentration camps at Walmart parking lots starting around June 5th 2001

U.S. Military hires illegal immigrants on June 9th 2003

Count 8

U.S. Military violated trademark and copyright laws. They sold Jonathan Lee Riches© tee shirts and mugs on college campuses, recruiting stations, starting on 8/15/03, and still going on today.

Count 9

U.S. Military is feeding me radioactive chemicals 03/02/06

U.S. Military is planning to nuke a U.S. city in the future, chatter about this was picked up through the NSA.

Count 10

U.S. Military conspired with American Highways to charge Americans for use of toll roads with EZpass to track Americans 7/7/04. U.S. Military conspired with Onstar to track all American vehicles on 06/05/03.

I've been injured; the military is sending radiowaves to my brain as I write this. I pray this court grants me relief.

Respectfully submitted,

Jonathan Lee Riches©

03/24/06

United States District Court

Southern District of Texas

Houston Division

Jonathan Lee Riches© a/k/a

"Secured Party",

Plaintiff

Vs.

United States of America, AUSA Jay Hileman;

FBI Special Agent Shauna A. Dunlap,

Defendants

"Motion for Preliminary Injunction"

"Motion for Temporary Restraining Order"

Comes now the plaintiff, Jonathan Lee Riches© a/k/a "Secured Party", in pro-se, moves this honorable chief judge to issue a temporary restraining order "TRO" and preliminary injunction against Federal District Judge Melinda Harmon and her April 19th, 2006 order against plaintiff in having his forfeited property donated to Goodwill Industries, due to numerous conflicts of interest between Melinda Harmon, Goodwill Industries, and the government. As plaintiff's Constitutional rights are still being violated under the 1st, 4th, 5th, 8th, 6th, and 14th Amendment.

This honorable court has jurisdiction because plaintiff's criminal case referenced above is from the southern district of Texas in Houston and this court handled plaintiff's motion for return of property.

Preliminary Injunction

Under Rule 65(a), plaintiff asks this honorable chief judge for a preliminary injunction against Melinda Harmon and her April 19th, 2006 order against plaintiff's property being forfeited to Goodwill Industries for the following reasons:

Plaintiff's Appeal and Due Process Violations

Plaintiff is currently appealing Melinda Harmon's April 19th, 2006 order forfeiting personal property to Goodwill Industries. Plaintiff received notice of that April 19th, 2006 order for the first time on June 19th, 2006, violating plaintiff's 5th Amendment Right to due process. This first time notice was enclosed in a brown envelope postmarked June 13th 2006 (exhibit 3). This clerk of court neglected to notify plaintiff in a proper manner according to law, as the courts never certified any mail to plaintiff to ensure he would receive the order in a timely manner. This neglect could have been avoided had plaintiff received proper notice.

Many theories now stand in plaintiff not receiving the April 19th, 2006 order: the clerk of court never sent plaintiff proper notification due to a personal bias and prejudice against plaintiff regarding financial interest with plaintiff's victims. Or FCI Williamsburg facility never gave plaintiff his mail. Or the clerk of court sent notification, but due to it not being certified by the post office, the mail got lost. Plaintiff does not know the reason why he did not get this April 19[th,] 2006 order in a timely fashion. This is a due process violation. The plaintiff asks this honorable court for a preliminary injunction and temporary restraining order against Melinda Harmon and her April 19th, 2006 order. This will ensure plaintiff due process while he appeals this order to the appeals and/or Supreme Court. The damages caused by the plaintiff losing his property cannot be compensated in monetary damages. Plaintiff also asks for a preliminary injunction and temporary restraining order against Goodwill Industries in receiving plaintiff's property as plaintiff is currently appealing that order.

41(g)

Under 41(g) -motion must be filed in the district where the property was seized. Plaintiff's property was seized at his residence at 2521 Morning Glory Court, Holiday Florida 34691, in the middle district of Florida. This court never had jurisdiction on the motion plaintiff filed, as he mistakenly filed a 41(g) motion in the wrong venue.

United Airlines Inc. vs. Wiener 335 F 2d 379 (1967) –chooses wrong venue in first instance, he should not be deprived of the right to correct his mistake at a later date.

Plaintiff filed "Motion to dismiss for proper venue", "motion to transfer to cure want of jurisdiction", and "motion for change of venue hearing" with this court because of the wrong venue under 41(g) and plaintiff refilled a new 41(g) motion for return of property in the middle district of Florida, where his property was taken.

Arredondo V. Moser, Lexus 22532 (5th) -1997 arrest, property was seized at his place of business in Grand Prairie Texas on an arrest warrant from U.S. District Court, Western District of Tennessee. June 4th, 2002, filed a 41(g) motion with the Western District of Tennessee. June 4th, 2002, court denied because under 41(g) such a motion may only be filed where property was seized.

This court never had jurisdiction over plaintiff's property return motion under 41(g) that he filed. Melinda Harmon's April 19th, 2006 order is being appealed and this court needs to issue a preliminary injunction and temporary restraining order as plaintiff will suffer serious harm later explained in this motion.

Violation of Unlawful Search and Seizure

The government violated plaintiff's 4th Amendment right to illegal search and seizure. Plaintiff never received any of the warrants; Feb 25th, Feb 26th, Feb 27th, March 7th, March 13th, 2003. The government failed to show or produce copies of warrants to plaintiff. This due process and Constitutional right was in violation as the government performed unlawful search and seizure, unlawful trespass, and wrongful forfeiture. This court has denied plaintiff's request for discovery compelling the government to produce to plaintiff all warrants at his residence, affidavits of what property was taken on each day plaintiff's home was searched, list of property taken, any statements made to FBI agents in reference to taken property, copy of original arrest complaint violating Brady vs. Maryland, as government failed to disclose exculpatory evidence. This court never had jurisdiction in ruling on plaintiff's property return motion, as plaintiff filed his 41(g) in the middle district of Florida. Exhibit 8 clearly says at the top that it does not reach the threshold for forfeiture, the forfeiture under fed rule crim pro 32.2 should have been mentioned in indictment, plea bargain, or the time of sentencing, neither happened.

Violation of 1st Amendment

Plaintiff is suffering a 1st Amendment violation as Melinda Harmon ruled that property be forfeited, as plaintiff spoke out that she should have recused herself from any criminal forfeiture proceedings under 28 U.S.C. 455 (a), (b), (c), D(4), B(4), B(5), "financial interest" and "bias and prejudice". Supreme Court case Liljeberg vs. Health Services. Plaintiff asked the court for Melinda Harmon's recusal but Melinda Harmon denied her own recusal motion. This 1ˢᵗ Amendment violation is violating freedom of speech as plaintiff is addressing a serious issue of conflict of interest between Melinda Harmon/her family and the plaintiff's victims in this criminal case. This conflict of interest also showed bias in Mr. Riches not receiving due process in proper notification on Harmon's April 19, 2006 order, and knowing that plaintiff filed his 41(g) in the wrong jurisdiction, but ruling that the property can be forfeited anyway. This is a total "miscarriage of justice". A preliminary injunction and temporary restraining order must be imposed as plaintiff appeals Harmon's conflicts of interest, and appeals his 41(g) filed in the wrong venue.

Failure to Grant the Injunction Will Result in Irreparable Injury

Plaintiff will suffer irreparable injury if his forfeited property goes to Goodwill Industries. Threatened damages cannot be compensated in monetary damages. The list of items in exhibit 8 is plaintiff's personal property. Computers: Apple g4, Toshiba, Tiger Systemax were all personal computers plaintiff used. Plaintiff's personal identity, financial records, personal pictures, private information is stored in each computer's hard drive. By giving these computers to Goodwill Industries the plaintiff's personal information runs the risk of falling into third party hands. This is a total invasion of privacy. Pictures in the computers, and digital camera's memory that plaintiff does not want disclosed to anyone. This threatened injury outweighs any damage that the injunction might cause the opposing party, and the injunction will not disserve the public interest. Plaintiff does not want his personal banking information, home address, and private phone number, which are stored in these computers and cameras in the wrong people's hands while plaintiff appeals his property return 41(g) motion and files it in the correct venue.

This will harm plaintiff.

Goodwill Industries

Conflicts of interest between Goodwill Industries and plaintiff's victims on his criminal case exist. Both had financial interests with plaintiff's victims. Even though the plaintiff states that his personal property was not bought or received fraudulently, the government claims the property was bought with fraudulent credit cards. The judge ruled April 19th, 2006 on the government's claim, and now plaintiff's property is to be forfeited to Goodwill Industries.

Under 18 U.S.C. 2315 Goodwill Industries should be charged with receiving stolen property, as the government is donating stolen property to Goodwill Industries, with Goodwill Industries knowing the property is stolen.

Goodwill Industries is also involved with illegal contributions to the government in exchange for forfeited property –not only with plaintiff's property but with other people's property past and present. This illegal practice must be looked into, and plaintiff is entitled to any relief under the Whistle Blowing Act.

Relief

For all the reasons mentioned above plaintiff needs a restraining order and preliminary injunction. Plaintiff has shown all four factors, allied supra, and the likelihood that a preliminary injunction will prevail. Under 65(a), and 65(b), plaintiff is also entitled to a hearing and requests a hearing on this motion. Plaintiff also submits an affidavit on these issues. Prays this honorable court gives him relief.

Respectfully submitted,

Jonathan Lee Riches©

06/29/06

Affiant hereby affirms and states the following facts and certifies that he is of lawful age, competent to testify to the matters contained herein from firsthand personal knowledge.

Comes now Jonathan Lee Riches© who now states as follows:

I'm filing a preliminary injunction and temporary restraining order against Melinda Harmon and the forfeiture of my property to Goodwill Industries. I will suffer serious harm if my personal property gets in the hands of Goodwill or whoever they give/sell it to as personal private information is stored in the hard-drives and memories. I'm appealing Harmon's April 19th, 2006 ruling and I filed a 41(g) motion in the correct venue of Middle District of Florida.

Melinda Harmon has a financial interest with my victims on the criminal case and should have recused herself on my property relinquishment motion. Goodwill Industries also has a financial interest with my victims and should not receive that property. Melinda Harmon should recuse herself on this preliminary injunction and restraining order because of conflict of interest.

My property is not stolen or bought with credit cards as the government says it is. The government then wants to give stolen property to Goodwill Industries. The CEO of Goodwill must be notified, and Goodwill must be investigated for the practice of receiving stolen property.

The affidavit attests and affirms that the facts contained herein are true, correct, complete, and are not misleading in any material respect, and based on personal knowledge.

"I declare under penalty of perjury that the forgoing is true and correct."

Jonathan Lee Riches©

06/24/06

2007

This is the year of notoriety. The idea of suing celebrities in a scattershot way has not, to my knowledge, been pursued by a civilian, let alone a prison inmate prior to this time. At some point in 2007 I gave up the notion that I might get any kind of fair hearing from the judicial system. I threw myself into crafting meticulous lawsuits against celebrities using the information that was available to me in newspapers, magazines and television. As I crafted these suits, I kept my hacking and phone phreaking sensibilities close at hand: I was constantly looking for glitches and weak points within the legal system, which I could then exploit.

The Bureau of Prison's decision to replace their books with the Pacer system (an online catalog of every U.S. Federal lawsuit filed in civil and criminal court) was crucial for the media attention I would receive from the Michael Vick lawsuit. I chose Vick as an experiment, because I wanted to see if journalists who were scouring the Pacer system for Vick related cases would find mine. Filing it in the same courthouse that he had been indicted in was the surest way I could draw them to me. I hoped that once this attention was drawn I could take my complaints to the public at large byway of the media, thereby bypassing the court system entirely.

United States District Court

Eastern District of Virginia

Richmond Division

Jonathan Lee Riches©,

Plaintiff

Vs.

Michael Vick,

Defendant

Complaint

"Theft and Abuse of my Animals"

"TRO Temporary Restraining Order"

This suit is a Bivens Action and civil rights violation of the Constitutional Laws of the United States and Federal TORT claims inflicted by that include, but are not limited to injury to wildlife, conspiracy, illegal dog fighting, extreme racketeering, gambling, copyright infringement, identity theft, fraud, threats to commit violent acts, brutality and fraud.

Comes now the plaintiff, Jonathan Lee Riches©, in pro-se, moves this honorable court to issue an order for defendant Michael Vick to give a response. Also moves this honorable court to issue a TRO Temporary Restraining Order against Vick from any further contact with plaintiff as plaintiff is claiming that his federal and state Constitutional rights were violated under the 1st, 2nd, 4th, 5th, 6th, 8th, and 14th Amendments of the Constitution. For relief, plaintiff seeks 63,000,000,000.00

billion dollars backed by gold and silver delivered via "UPS" United States Postal Service to the front gates of F.C.I. Williamsburg, S.C., collected from defendant Michael Vick.

1

Michael Vick is a quarterback for the Atlanta Falcons. On April 20th 2007 Mr. Vick stole two white mixed pit bull dogs from my residence in Holiday Florida and used them for dogfighting throughout the Richmond area. Mr. Vick damaged the RFID chips in my dog collars so I will not be able to track them. These two dogs were used for fighting on April 23rd, 24th and 26th of 2007. On April 28th, Mr. Vick sold my dogs on auction and used the proceeds to purchase missiles from the government.

2

Michael Vick continued to harass me on May 4th, 2007 by stealing my identity from my coat. My identity was used to open new store account cards to Petsmart and doggiewarehouse to purchase food for Mr. Vick's illegal dogfighting operation.

3

Michael Vick violated my copyright by using my copyrighted name on his football outfit and casual clothing without paying me for use. This conspiracy started Jan. 10th 2001 and continues to this day. Mr. Vick uses my name to sell T-shirts, Jonathan Lee Riches© mugs, Mr. Riches hats.

4

On Feb. 10th 2007 Michael Vick plead allegiance to Al Qaeda

Michael Vick subjected me to microwave testing

Michael Vick used drugs in school zones

Michael Vick is in the business of illegal steroids

Plaintiff prays this court to give him relief on these issues.

Plaintiff prays this court will issue a Temporary Restraining Order against Michael Vick so he can no longer sell my copyrighted materials. Michael Vick can't steal anymore of my animals (dogs) for dogfighting. Michael Vick has to stop physically hurting my feelings and dashing my hopes.

Respectfully submitted,

Jonathan Lee Riches©

07/07/07

United States District Court

District of New Hampshire

Jonathan Lee Riches© a/k/a

"Secured Party",

Plaintiff

Vs.

Jewish Mossad;

Central Intelligence Agency "CIA";

Larry King Live,

Defendants

Complaint

"The Hijacking of America"

This is a complaint under 42 U.S.C. 1983, civil rights violation by the Constitution and laws of the United States and Federal TORT claims inflicted by that include, but are not limited to: kidnapping, extortion, injury to wildlife, liquor trafficking, identity theft, persecutions, electronic wiretapping.

Comes now the plaintiff Jonathan Lee Riches©, in pro-se, moves this honorable court to issue an order for all defendants named in this suit to give a response, as plaintiff is claiming that his federal and state Constitutional rights are being violated under the 1st, 2nd, 4th, 5th, 6th, 8th, 13th, and 14th Amendments. Plaintiff moves this honorable court to issue a TRO restraining order against defendants. Plaintiff seeks 211,429,399,000,000.00 trillion dollars backed by gold and silver delivered by United

States Postal Service to Federal Correctional Institution Williamsburg, Salters S.C., collectively from defendants.

1

Defendants are in a vast conspiracy to hijack my torso, 3 toes, and my Constitutional rights and ship them to a secret headquarters in Concord New Hampshire.

2

Jewish Mossad told me personally on April 20th, 2007 that they are going to hang me on a cross next to Jesus Christ.

3

Larry King is a Voodoo witch doctor who stole my identity on Feb. 25th, 2003 and purchased lead paint, Chips Ahoy, Planters Peanuts and Ziplock bags under my identity. Distributed them to the CIA to microwave test my DNA.

4

The CIA on Jan. 4th, 2006 plead allegiance to Al Qaeda and conspired with the Uniform Commercial Code "U.C.C." to steal my Strawman identity.

5

FCI Williamsburg hired robotic guards financed through the Mossad and Capital 1 Banking, covert prostitution, graveyard stealing and garage sale theft operation.

6

Defendants are involved with Trading with the Enemy Act by

donating my artwork to N. Korea and Burma in exchange for weapons being shipped to Sudan's Janjaweed.

7

Defendants inserted micro-chips and are dashing my hopes.

Plaintiff respectfully asks this court for relief and to order a restraining order against defendants and NASA.

Submitted

Jonathan Lee Riches©

07/16/07

United States District Court

District of Maine

Jonathan Lee Riches© a/k/a

"Secured Party",

Plaintiff

Vs.

Federal Judicial System;

All United States Federal Judges;

United States Marshals;

Tiger Woods,

Defendants

Complaint

"The Poisoning of my Mind"

This is a complaint under 42 U.S.C. 1983, Federal and State rights violations, Federal TORT claims, and crimes against plaintiff, humanity, and the following federal crimes defendants acted on: identity theft, credit card fraud, wire fraud, postal fraud, injury to wildlife, extortion, social security fraud, securities fraud, treason, copyright violations.

Comes now the plaintiff Jonathan Lee Riches© a/k/a "Secured Party", in pro-se, moves this honorable court to issue an order for all defendants named in this suit to respond. Moves this honorable court to issue a (TRO) Temporary Restraining Order against defendants to order them to have no contact with plaintiff. Plaintiff's 1st, 3rd, 4th, 6th, 8th, and 14th Constitutional rights are being violated. Relief requested, plaintiff seeks 213,529,000,000,000.00 trillion dollars delivered by FedEx Shipping, backed by gold and silver to FCI Williamsburg, Salters S.C.

Count 1

The Federal Judicial System is in a vast conspiracy with Tiger Woods to steal my identity and get credit in my name. U.S. Marshals have a secret headquarters in Portland Maine.

Count 2

April 20th, 2006 –United States Federal Judges stole my copyrighted name and sold it to Google, who then defamed me with lies (Google: "Jonathan Lee Riches")

Count 3

Tiger Woods is touring the PGA golf courses with my identity in his pocket. He will not answer my prison phone calls –this continues to this day.

Count 4

U.S. Marshals laugh at me through the prison ventilation system

United States Federal Judges plead allegiance to Al Qaeda

All defendants are involved with the Trading With Enemy Act, as my identity was sold to PKK rebels in exchange for military secrets

Plaintiff asks for a restraining order against defendants and defendants' vehicles

Count 5

April 19th 2007 –Defendants stole my luggage

April 15th 2007 –Defendants secretly took my DNA

Plaintiff prays that this respected honorable court finds relief for me.

Respectfully submitted,

Jonathan Lee Riches©

"Secured Party"

07/16/07

United States District Court

Western District of Virginia

Jonathan Lee Riches©,

Plaintiff

Vs.

Jon Swartz USA Today cardcops.com;

Virginia Tech shooting;

Ed Mierzwinski US Pirg;

Creditcards.com;

Phishing;

World Wide Web,

Defendants

Complaint

"Hacking the Planet"

"Computer Genocide"

This is a complaint under 1983, civil rights violations, Trading with the Enemy Act, copyright infringement, computer hacking, murder, treason, illegal wiretapping, identity theft, phishing, spamming, code cracking, federal TORT claims inflicted on plaintiff.

Comes now the plaintiff, Jonathan Lee Riches©, in pro-se, moves this honorable court to serve named defendants and to issue an order for defendants to respond. Plaintiff requests jury trial. Plaintiff requests a TRO Temporary Restraining Order against defendants as plaintiff's constitutional rights are being violated under the 1st, 2nd, 4th, 5th, 6th, 8th, and 14th Amendments.

1

Jon Swarts USA Today cardcops.com is a reporter. He writes on Cybercrime stories. His stories show know-how and encourage people to commit cybercrime. This is entrapment. He writes about how to do credit card fraud, how to encode data on a magnetic strip, how to commit Identity theft. Then he sits back and waits. Then reports the crime to the FBI for whistle blowing money.

2

Jon Swartz USA Today cardcops.com provided Cho the credit card to buy handguns to shoot Virginia Tech. Swartz showed Cho how to boost his credit score to get higher available credit. Swartz also showed Cho how to commit Identity theft and Phishing over the www.

3

Jon Swartz USA Today cardcops.com is in a vast conspiracy with Ed Mierzwinski U.S. prig, Norris hall student, convicted computer hackers and Phreakers, my online hacking handle "Gino Romano," to publish different ways to do cybercrime. They even hacked my Mind.

4

Plaintiff asks for relief for a restraining order against any more publications by Jon Swartz USA Today cardcops.com, to stop publications at Virginia Tech, stay away from me, stop using my copyrighted name Jonathan Lee Riches© in newspaper articles, stop calling me a super hacker, stop violating my 6th Amendment rights to being an Identity theft, Identity fraud Kingpin which was not proven by a jury.

Respectfully submitted,

Jonathan Lee Riches©

08/07/07

United States District Court

Northern District of Indiana

Jonathan Lee Riches© a/k/a

"Secured Party",

Plaintiff

Vs.

Barry Bonds;

Allan H. "Bud" Selig;

Hank Aaron's bat,

Defendants

Complaint

"Fraud against Mankind"

"Batman and Identity Robbin"

This is a complaint under Bivens, civil rights violation by the Constitution and the laws of the United States; and Federal TORT claims inflicted by that include, but are not limited to Bat assault, high violations, treason, major fraud, skimming the books, illegal moonshine, terrorism, social security fraud, stalking, identity theft, copyright infringement, false information, illegal electronic wiretapping, bad debt.

Comes now the plaintiff Jonathan Lee Riches© a/k/a "Secured Party" d/b/a "The White Suge Knight", in pro-se, moves this honorable court to issue an order for all defendants named in this suit to give a response. Plaintiff requests a jury trial. Moves this honorable court to issue a "TRO" preliminary injunction temporary restraining order against the broadcast of MLB games, all defendants, defendants' pets and associates from any future contact with plaintiff or plaintiff's ALL CAPS ENS LEGIS ENTITY JONATHAN LEE RICHES. As plaintiff is claiming that his federal, state, local, underground Constitutional Rights are being violated under the 1st, 2nd, 4th, 5th, 6th, 8th, 13th and 14th Amendments of the Constitution. Plaintiff seeks 42,000,000.00 million dollars in Swiss Francs, certified money order to the B.O.P. Lockbox in Des Moines Iowa collectively from defendants.

1

Barry Bonds and Bud Selig are in a secret conspiracy together to boost television ratings. Mr. Selig has been secretly giving Barry Bonds steroids for over 4 years under the supervision of Sammy Sosa. Mr. Selig on 2 occasions (Dec. 10th 2001, Feb. 6th, 2003) met Mr. Bonds at the I-70 Steak N' Shake, booth #11, made an under the table cream exchange, needles, HGH, as Mr. Bonds provided Mr. Selig 22 thousand dollars for his services. I planted a bug in booth #10, Robert Novak and Judith Miller have copies of the transcripts.

2

Barry Bonds uses Hank Aaron's corked bat during ballgames. The bat has a secret chamber where Bonds stores his HGH supplements. Bonds takes them while he waits in the batter's box. Bonds left a voicemail message on my I-Phone making threats towards me.

3

Barry Bonds is responsible for getting me federally indicted in Houston Texas, case #H-03-90, because I threatened to expose his and Bud Selig's steroid/cocaine abuse.

4

Barry Bonds on June 22, 2004 bench-pressed me against my will to show off in front of his ballpark buddies. I also witnessed Mr. Bonds selling steroids to nuns.

5

Barry Bonds used Hank Aaron's bat to crack the Liberty Bell. Bonds owns a steroid house in South Bend Indiana U.S.A. Bonds committed identity theft in my name, put a lendingtree.com mortgage on my credit, then burned it down to collect insurance. I had a fraud alert on my social.

6

Barry bonds joined Columbian "FARC" on Dec. 25th, 2005 during baseball's winter training. "FARC" provides Mr. Bond's HGH tablets.

7

I won Hank Aaron's bat at a Sotheby's Auction House in Fall 1998. Barry Bonds sent hitmen to my home. My ADT security system was compromised. Various items were also taken from my refrigerator (attached exhibit has a list of food items).

8

Barry Bonds is involved in illegal gambling, fixing Giants' games, including fixing game 5,6,7 in the World Series against

Los Angeles. Bonds had a gambling debt with the Gambinos.

9

Mr. bonds gave mustard gas to Saddam Hussein. Part of the oil for food scandal.

10

Mr. bonds is using my copyrighted name for profit.

Conclusion

Plaintiff prays for relief. Asking this honorable court to compel Bonds to give my identity back. Plaintiff also seeks restraining order. No more baseball games played on the FCI Williamsburg T.V. sets. May peace be with America forever.

Respectfully,

Jonathan Lee Riches©

8/13/07

United States District Court

Western District of Virginia

Jonathan Lee Riches©,

Plaintiff

Vs.

Jon Swartz, et al,

Defendants

Motion to Appeal

Motion for Judges Recusal under 28 U.S.C. 455 (A) (B)

Comes now the Plaintiff, Jonathan Lee Riches© A/K/A "The Tigerwoods of Cyberhood," in pro-se, moves this Honorable Court to Appeal United States District Judge's Samuel G. Wilson's Aug 13, 2007 memorandum opinion dismissing Plaintiffs Lawsuit.

Motion for Judges Recusal under 28 U.S.C. 455 (A) (B)

Judge Samuel G. Wilson should have recused himself before dismissing this suit under 455(A),(B) because of numerous conflicts of interests, financial interests that he has with the Defendants in this suit.

Jon Swartz USA Today reporter conspired with the Virginia Tech shooting to destroy America's freedoms. The Judge in this case uses the world wide web -which is one of the defendants. An unfavorable ruling would result in the Judge losing his internet access.

Super hackers are roaming the internet sending Trojan horses and Keystroke Logger onto Americans' computers. I can help put a stop to this madness.

I was a Superhacker in the cyberworld to stop evil. Jon Swartz is showing hackers in the world wide web how to commit fraud, his articles are a blueprint manual to entrap people.

December 4th, 1999 – Jon Swartz wrote a bogus article about Jonathan Lee Riches A/K/A "Gino Romano" hacking into Western Union's toll Free money transfer department, call forwarding the switch, and intercepting the Lint to get Western Unions agents bingo codes then using the codes to send money nationwide for pickup.

Aug 16, 2000 – Jon Swartz articles lied about me buying PUC printers by Fargo and hacking into choicepoint to make fake drivers licenses.

Jonathan Lee Riches© is copyrighted in the cyberworld. Known as "Gino Romano" on telephone partylines, i.e. Binghamton Raven, Utah and Nevada chatlines from the back of Rolling Stone Magazine.

Under 28 USC 455(B)– my 6th Amendment rights are being violated. No one in prison is feeding me. I weigh 125 lbs at 5ft 10 inches. I'm starving. I'm more then 500 miles away from my family. I plead guilty and am still serving 125 months for fraud. I'm accused of stealing millions of dollars that was not in my indictment or found guilty by a jury. This is a Booker and Fan Fan violation.

Jon Swartz sends secret codes in his articles to the Russians, Morris Code. Swartz is responsible for missing planes in the Bermuda triangle.

Jon Swartz sent a computer worm through the fiber optic cables on June 17, 2004. This court must impose a restraining order against the world wide web.

Notice is hereby given that Jonathan Lee Riches©, Plaintiff in the above named case, hereby appeals to the United States Court of Appeals for the Fourth Circuit entered in the action on the Nineteenth day of the Eighth Month, 2007.

Respectfully submitted,

Jonathan Lee Riches

08/22/07

United States District Court

Eastern District of Virginia

Jonathan Lee Riches© a/k/a "Crusader for Truth",

Plaintiff

Vs.

Michael Vick,

Defendant

Motion for Clarification

Motion to Correct Scrivners Error

Clarification Motion

"Michael Vick is implicating other current and former Atlanta Falcon teammates in illegal dog-fighting so Mr. Vick can receive a reduced federal sentence."

Comes now the plaintiff, Jonathan Lee Riches© a/k/a "Crusader for Truth", in pro-se, moves this honorable court for clarification on respected Judge M. Hannah Lauck's Aug 1, 2007 memorandum order. Plaintiff is confused with #8 of this order, as plaintiff has no prior legal experience. Plaintiff has a Constitutional right for clarification. Also moves this honorable court to correct scrivner's error of plaintiff's full name in the court docket. Plaintiff prays for relief.

"McGruff took a bite out of Michael Vick"

Question for the court? On the August 1, 2007 memorandum order by Judge M. Hannah Lauck, I request this court to clarify what #8 means. #8 states: "Plaintiff is prohibited from filing any other pleadings, motions, memoranda, or materials not specifically required herein or otherwise specifically ordered by the court until he begins making payments on the filing fee. Any material submitted in violation of this paragraph will not be considered." When this respected court says "begin making payments", does this mean the starting of partial payments or the full $350 filing fee in full?

Plaintiff has received confirmation from a private outside donor financier to pay the $350 filing fee. Plaintiff previously filed a motion in this court for an extension of time to pay the $350 filing fee. I currently have nine dollars and some change in my prison account, can I begin to start making payments now?

Plaintiff needs to file another amended complaint against Mr. Vick due to the continued threats and harassment I'm receiving from Mr. Vick and his associates.

Ever since I filed this suit, Vick is trying every tactic to silence me from exposing his animal abuse. I found out through the Drudge Report that Michael Vick is implicating other current and former Atlanta Falcon teammates in illegal dog-fighting so Mr. Vick can receive a reduced federal sentence. Vick says that Andre Rison, Jerry Glanville, Joe Horn, Tim Dwight and Jessie Tuggle participated in interstate dog-fighting and illegal sports betting. Betting on Falcons' games between Nov 2000 and Jan 2006. Proceeds were laundered to Atlanta area stripclubs. Michael Vick also trained Cujo!

Vick paid a crock to eat Steve Irwin. Sometimes when Vick gets angry he cannibalizes puppy dogs.

Michael Vick continues to use my copyrighted name without compensation.

I submit my copyright notice below to this honorable court.

Copyright Notice

Copyright Notice: all unalienable rights regarding the Common Law Copyright© of the following trade-names/trade-marks: JONATHAN LEE RICHES , as well as any and all corruptions, permutations, initialed and derivations or variations in spelling thereof not excluding Jonathan Lee Riches© respectively, and any fixation in tangible medium of expression or authorship, whether in words, numbers, notes, sounds, films, pictures, images of or parts thereof, or any other graphic or hallographic symbolic indica including but not limited to fingerprints, palm prints, thumb prints, foot prints, iris or retinal prints or images, facial or skeletal Images or x-rays, ultra sound images, DNA and RNA charts and maps, blood or blood fractions, bodily fluids, excretions, clippings, or sheddings, body chemical typing or maps, body parts or fractions thereof; whether embodied in a physical object, in written, printed, photographic, x-rays, sculptural, punched, carved or engraved form, magnetic or electronic data of the living, breathing, flesh and blood Man, Jonathan Lee., Riches© , Common Law Copyrighted property of the live, natural, flesh and blood Man, . Jonathan Lee Riches©, Common Law Copyright© 1994 by Jonathan Lee Riches© • Any and all of the aforementioned trade-names/trade-marks may be neither used, nor reproduced, neither in whole nor in part, nor in any manner whatsoever, without the prior, express, written consent and acknowledgment of Jonathan Lee., Riches© , as signified by the blue ink signature of Jonathan Lee Riches© • hereinafter Secured Party. With the Intent or Being Contractually Bound: any juristic person or their agent or artificial entity or it's agent, herein consents and agrees by and with this Copyright Notice that neither said juristi: person or entity or agent of said juristic person or entity, shall display, nor otherwise use in any form or manner whatsoever, any of the herein-before described trade-names/trade-marks,

without the prior, express, written consent and acknowledgment of Secured Party, as signified by the said Secured Party's signature in red ink. Secured Party neither grants, nor implies, nor otherwise gives consent for any unauthorized use, in any form or manner whatsoever, the herein before described copyrighted© trade-names /trade-marks. Secured Party is not now, nor has Secured Party ever been an accommodation party, nor asurity, for any of the aforementioned trade-names/trade-marks, i.e. purported debtors, nor for any other juristic person or artificial entity and is so identified and held harmless by JONATHAN LEE RICHES

purported debtor, in Hold Harmless and Indemnity Agreement No. JLR122794HHIA, dated the Twenty Seventh Day of the Twelfth Month in the Year of Yahshua the Christ Nine-teen Ninety Four against all claims, legal actions, court orders, warrants, summonses, subpoenas, judgments, demands, liabilities, depositions, losses, lawsuits, repossessions, seizures, costs, fines, liens, levies, penalties, damages, interests, taxes, and expenses whatsoever, both absolute and contingent, as hereafter arise and as might be suffered by, be imposed upon, and/or be incurred by the herein described purported debtors, for any reason, purpose and cause whatsoever. Self-executing Contract/ Security Agreement in Event of Unauthorized Use; by this Copyright Notice, the juristic person and or artificial entity and or any agents of same, hereinafter jointly and severally 'User' hereby consents and agrees that any of the users use of any of the hereinbefore described Copyrighted© tradenames/trade-marks, other than explicit authorized use, as set forth previously herein, shall constitute unauthorized use, counterfeiting of Secured Party's Common Law Copyrighted property, contractually binds User, renders this Copyright Notice a Security Agreement wherein user is debtor and Jonathan Lee., Riches© is Secured Party, and signifies that User: (1) grants Secured Party a security interest in all of users' assets, land, personal and private property including but not limited to: all consumer goods, farm products, livestock, inventory, equipment, money, gold and silver coin and bullion, tort claims, letters of credit, letters of cred it right, chattel paper, instruments, deposit accounts, accounts, documents, and general in tangibles, trusts, trust funds, accounts and assets, and inheritances, in the amount of Five Hundred Thousand Dollars ($500,000.00) per occurrence of unauthorized use of any of the herein before described Copyrighted trade-names/trade-marks, plus costs, plus triple damages; (2) authenticates this Security Agreement wherein user pledges all users' interest in all such foregoing mentioned property, now owned and hereafter acquired, now existing and hereafter arising, and wherever located in the World, as collateral for Users' consensual contractual obligation in favor of Secured Party, for Users' unauthorized use of Secured Party's Common Law Copyrighted© property hereinbefore described; (3)consents and agrees with Secured Party filing a U.C.C. Financing Statement in any U.C.C. Filing Office, as well as in any county recorder's office, wherein user is debtor and Jonathan Lee., Riches© is Secured Party; (4) consents and agrees that said U.C.C. Financing Statement in paragraph (3) above, is a continuing financing statement and further consents and agrees with the Secured Party's filing any Continuation Financing Statement necessary for maintaining Secured Party's perfected security interest in all users' property herein pledged as collateral in this Security Agreement and described in paragraph (1) above, until users' contractual obligation theretofore incurred has been fully satisfied; (5) consents and agrees that any and all such

U.C.C. filings mentioned in paragraphs (3) and (4) above are not and never will be considered, construed, or implied, as bogus, invalid, a threat, coercion, or intimidation toward user debtor or by any other juristic person or artificial entity or their agents whatsoever; (6) hereby consents and agrees to waive all defenses; and (7) hereby appoints Secured Party as irrevocable Authorized Representative for User, effective upon users' default of users' consensual contractual obligation in favor of Secured Party as set forth herein below as 'Payment Terms and Default Terms' granting Secured Party full authorization and power with a security interest, for engaging in any and all actions on behalf of user, including but not limited to, authentication of a record on behalf of User, at Secured Party's sole discretion as deemed appropriate. User further consents and agrees with all the following additional term security agreement effective in event of unauthorized payment terms: in accordance with fees hereinbefore agreed to by user for unauthorized use of any of the aforementioned Common Law Copyrighted trade-names/trade-marks, user hereby consents and agrees to pay Secured Party said unauthorized use fees in full within ten (10) days from the date of Secured Party's invoice, Hereinafter Invoice, which user is sent by regular, certified or registered last -own mailing location, which Invoice item unauthorized uses terms: in event of non-payment in full of all unauthorized use fees by user within ten (10ZTot invoice date, user shall be in default; and (a) all of user's property or interest therein pledged as collateral by user herein, and as described in paragraph (1) above, lately becomes, i.e. is the property of Secured Party; (b) Secured Party is hereby appointed user's Authorized Representative, as set forth in paragraph (7) above; and (c) user consents and agrees that Secured Party may take possession of, as well, dispose of, in any manner, at any time, determined by Secured Party following user's default of this Security Agreement without further notice to User, any and all property described in paragraph (1) above, in respect of this self-executing Contract/Security Agreement in event of unauthorized use, that Secured Party at Secured Party's sole discretion, has deemed appropriate. Terms of Court Default: upon event of Default as set forth under Default Terms, above, irrespective of any of user's former property, or interest therein, in the possession of, as well as disposed of by Secured Party, as authorized under Default Terms, above, user may cure user's default re only the remainder of user's former property and or interest therein, pledged as collateral, that is neither in the possession of, nor otherwise disposed of by Secured Party within twenty (20) days of the date of user's default on the payment of above described unauthorized use fees in full. Terms of Strict Foreclosure: user's non-payment in full of all unauthorized use fees itemized in Invoice, described above, in paragraph (1), within twenty (20) day period for curing default as set forth under Terms for Curing Default, above, authorizes Secured Party's immediate non-judicial foreclosure on any and all remaining property or interest therein formerly pledged as collateral by user, now property of Secured Party, which is not in the possession of, nor otherwise disposed of, by Secured Party, upon expiration of said twenty (20) day Default Curing Period. Ownership subject to Common Law Copyright© and

U.C.C. Financing Statement and Security Agreement filed.

Copyright Notice by Secured Party

Autograph Common Law Copyright

Jonathan Lee Riches©

Plaintiff has also been receiving threatening letters from Mr.

Vick and other pseudo gangs, including: Dick Butkus, Canadian Coal Miners, MS13, Lou Dobbs.

Plaintiff requests armed guards and Brinks Security System for my cell.

Below is a threatening letter from Michael Vick

Exhibit O

Jonathan Lee Riches,

No one fucks with #7! You little Cracker Wigger boy. My football buddies are going to punt you. You better hope the prison protects you. You're dead meat!

-MV

Plaintiff requests this court sends this letter to the FBI Quantico Virginia Lab for fingerprint and DNA testing.

On August 18, 2007, in retaliation for exposing Michael Vick, Vick again broke into my home and took my Pomeranian "chops" and my cat "stix." They have not been seen since. I put out an Amber alert with no luck. Poncho from Chips patrol offered to help. Its believed Vick used my animals and Snoop Doggy Dog in Los Angeles based dog fights.

Michael Vick is conspiring with the Warden of F.C.I Williamsburg, Donald Bauknecht, not to feed me proper nutrition. I came to prison in 2003 at a healthy 175 pounds. Now I only weigh 125 pounds and stand five foot ten inches.

I'm losing my hair because of the stress due to Michael Vick's animal torture.

Michael Vick broke into Mainline Models in King of Prussia Pennsylvania and took my portfolio.

Motion to Correct Scrivner's Error

Plaintiff moves for correction in his full name. My name is Jonathan Lee Riches© with the © symbol. I've been common law copyrighted since 1994. Plaintiff prays this respected court corrects the error.

Respectfully submitted,

Jonathan Lee Riches©

08/27/07

United States District Court

Eastern District of Louisiana

Jonathan Lee Riches© a/k/a

"Jonny Sue-Nami",

Plaintiff

Vs.

Hurricane Katrina; New Orleans Mayor Ray Nagin; Moby Dick; Disney's Typhoon Lagoon; Ocean's 11; "The Perfect Storm"; "Gilligan's Island"; Various unknown sea creatures,

Defendants

Complaint

"Brainwashing America"

"Oceanic Injunction"

Comes now the plaintiff Jonathan Lee Riches© a/k/a "Jonny Sue-Nami", in pro-se, moves this honorable court to issue an order for defendants named in this suit to respond. This is a civil action pursuant to violations of (RICO) 18 U.S.C. 1961, CIA water torture, salting my wounds, tainted seafood.

1

Defendants are in a mega conspiracy with George Clooney, surfers in California, Gilligan, Pacific Island Natives under direct orders from New Orleans Mayor Ray Nagin to swallow the earth and flood the Universe.

May 6, 2007 –Katrina is lurking in the underbelly of the earth, ready to arise as soon as Nagin makes the call.

July 19, 2007 –My cellmate at FCI Williamsburg is a sea turtle.

On Jan 10th 2005 Nagin personally told me he's turning New Orleans into an all-white "vanilla" city.

3

Nov 22, 2004 –El Nino is working with the Columbians.

May 28, 2005 –The CIA kidnapped me to Gilligan's Island. I was tortured by sea creatures and seaweed.

4

Katrina plans to sprinkle me across the earth.

I'm appealing the Barry Bonds case. I'm stocking up on lifeboats.

Oceanic Injunction

Plaintiff moves the honorable court to issue a permanent injunction against World Wide Oceans and Tributaries. Compel defendants to hire more lifeguards, extra life vests and put sand bags around FCI Williamsburg.

Plaintiff seeks $35,000,000,000.00 Billion dollars in a treasure chest for damages. Plaintiff respectfully prays for relief in the book of Yahweh. Amen

Respectfully submitted,

Jonathan Lee Riches

8/28/07

United States District Court

Eastern District of Arkansas

Jonathan Lee Riches© d/b/a

Rockefeller Riches,

Plaintiff

Vs.

Wal-Mart Stores INC.,

Defendants

Civil Complaint

"Wal-Mart Scandal"

Plaintiff, who is deaf and blind, diagnosed with terminal cancer brings this civil suit against Wal-Mart stores pursuant to violations of the Americans with Disability Act (ADA) 42 U.S.C. 12101, violation of the Rehabilitation Act 29 U.S.C. 701, violation of the Age of Discrimination in Employment of 1967, Title VII of the Civil Rights Act of 1964 42 U.S.C. 2000, violations of state labor codes and intentional infliction of emotional distress.

Comes now the plaintiff, Jonathan Lee Riches© d/b/a Rockefeller Riches, in pro-se, moves this honorable court to issue an order for defendants named in this suit to respond. Plaintiff also seeks compensatory and punitive damages in the amount of $5,000,000.00 million against defendants. Plaintiff moves to request motion for counsel. Plaintiff prays for relief.

Background

Plaintiff, who is deaf and blind, diagnosed with terminal cancer is a former Boy Scout of America den leader, former singer in the church choir, philanthropist, and humanitarian aid was hired by Wal-Mart stores, Inc. On May 4, 2003 under a disability internship program. I was under the care and supervision of Wal-Mart management and supervisors. The very first day I worked for Wal-Mart, my life was turned into a living nightmare. Managers picked on me. I was poked at, spit on by Wal-Mart cashiers. Wal-Mart janitors would trip me with their mop handles. I was the laughing stock of Wal-Mart. Wal-Mart managers would perform evil pranks on me. I remember May 26, 2003 I was told to cut vegetables in the deli section, by managers who knew that I can't see. Afterward, supervisors made me collect shopping carts in the parking lot. June 4, 2003 in Isle 3 (toys section) I was cleaning a Lego spill, fellow employees blew a clown horn in my ear. Wal-Mart does not provide the blind with Braille. On June 17, 2003 Wal-Mart used my disability to solicit donations: I was forced to sit upfront in a greeting chair with a donation cup. This was against my will, as Wal-Mart management stripped and shackled me to the chair. Every morning when I reported to work I could not see the time clock to punch in. Wal-Mart only paid for three hour work weeks when in fact I worked seven days a week from 7am to 7pm. This amounted to 84 hour weeks, but Wal-Mart management only paid me for 21 hours each week. I cashed my work check in the store, and every employee who chased my check took my money. Wal-Mart employees would send me anonymous notes in Braille calling me "the Elephant Man", "Helen Keller wannabe", etc. Wal-Mart forces employees to sign a "vow of secrecy" contract. Wal-Mart does not want the world to know they hire Latin and Mexican underage illegals and harbor them in a back warehouse, these illegals are forced into prostitution. Wal-Mart has a hidden room in back of the nail department with an electric chair for workers who don't cooperate. On July 10, 2003, Wal-Mart managers gave all the employees cocaine to enhance performance. Wal-Mart hires convicted child molesters to drive their shipping tractor trailers. Wal-Mart managers at every United States location have been skimming the books to avoid IRS taxes. Wal-Mart sells the public tainted dog food from China. Wal-Mart cashers serve liquor to minors.

1

On September 2, 2003 I was told by Wal-Mart managers that I was fired because I'm Blind. I was called "a Dumb blind bat" and told I look like one of the "three blind mice". Wal-Mart management told me "we don't need you deaf idiots working for us." Another said "see your way out of here." I also did not receive back pay for three weeks.

Conclusion

Wal-Mart is prejudiced against any worker with a disability. I've suffered serious trauma since I worked at Wal-Mart. Wal-Mart made my life a nightmare! Wal-Mart lies in their commercials. Wal-Mart treats elderly employees even worse. I will never work for Wal-Mart again. I will never shop at Wal-Mart in my life. Plaintiff prays for relief and an injunction against Wal-Mart's illegal acts.

Respectfully submitted,

Jonathan Lee Riches©

08/28/07

United States District Court

Middle District of Florida

Jonathan Lee Riches© a/k/a

"Secured Party",

Plaintiff

Vs.

Elvis Presley;

Neverland Ranch,

Defendants

Complaint

"War Crimes"

"Rock N' Rollin my Brain"

"TRO Temporary Restraining Order"

This is a complaint under 42 U.S.C. 1983. Defendants are in violation of my civil rights, numerous Constitutional rights, various illegal acts that include, but are not limited to: violation of the Lanham Act, violation of Trading with the Enemy Act, major fraud, treason, extortion, building code violations, unpaid taxes, unpaid speeding tickets, racketeering, counterfeiting, copyright infringement, kidnapping, identity theft, hacking, false oaths, mail fraud, conspiracy, bad debt, phishing, psychiatric trauma.

Comes now the plaintiff Jonathan Lee Riches©, in pro-se, heir to the royal throne, moves this honorable court to issue an order for defendant(s) named in this suit to respond. Moves this honorable court to issue council and legal attornies for plaintiff. Moves this respected court to issue a "TRO" Restraining Order against defendants. Plaintiff's 1st, 3rd, 4th, 5th, 6th, 8th, and 14th Amendment Constitutional rights are being violated by defendants. Plaintiff seeks 41 cents for damages, and the return of Jonathan Lee Riches© Chronicles.

1

Elvis Presley is a Rock N Rollin war criminal. Presley is in preparation and training to be Bin Laden's #2 deputy. Elvis plans to use his guitar in Vegas as a weapon of mass destruction.

2

Oct. 4th, 2002 –Elvis took my sideburns

Dec. 5th, 2006 –Sold me tainted poultry

May 19th, 1972 –Elvis put a stick in my bicycle spoke

Dec. 30th, 1973 –Defendant suffocated me with a Chips Ahoy bag

Defendant's daughter, Lisa Marie, forced me to drink Brazilian ethanol.

"Love me Tender" and "Heartbreak Hotel" are copyrighted by Jonathan Lee Riches©.

I was hung from an Econolodge Balcony with Vanilla Ice by Suge Knight.

Neverland is harboring Hitler's army.

Neverland is a training ground for disrgruntled postal workers.

Neverland hosts nightly pagan dances.

TRO Temporary Restraining Order

Stop the defendants from selling, publishing, displaying, singing, chanting, idolizing any copyrighted material related to Jonathan Lee Riches©.

Respectfully submitted,

Jonathan Lee Riches©

08/31/07

United States District Court

District of Delaware

Jonathan Lee Riches©,

Plaintiff

Vs.

Senator Larry Craig (R) Idaho;

Rep Mark Foley (R) Florida;

Senator David Vitter (R) Louisiana;

Rep Barney Frank (D) Massachusetts;

Roman Catholic Priests;

Kobe Bryant;

R. Kelly;

Warren Jeffs;

Duke Lacrosse players;

Michael Jackson;

James McGreevy (former New Jersey Governor);

William Jefferson Clinton,

Defendants

Civil Complaint

"Perverting America"

"TRO Temporary Restraining Order"

"Preliminary Injunction"

Comes now the plaintiff, Jonathan Lee Riches©, in pro-se, moves this honorable court to issue an order for defendants named in this suit to respond. This suit is civil rights and liberties that defendants committed against me. Also crimes of sexual harassment, sodomy of my mind, mental torture, mistrust, breaking my heart, embarrassment, deceit, and fraud. Plaintiff also moves this honorable court to issue a TRO Temporary Restraining Order against defendants. Plaintiff seeks $99,000,000,000.00 billion dollars, a public warning system if defendants are seen on television and for defendants to register as sex offenders. Plaintiff prays for relief.

1

I've suffered everlasting scarring watching the details on TV of each defendants' acts over the years. It's ingrained in my mind. Defendants must be held accountable for their actions. Think about it ...when someone says the name "Michael Jackson", music is not the only thing in my head; I also think "child molester". This is defendant Jackson's fault for doing irreversible damage to my mind.

2

The defendants collectively injured me through television viewing. When watching and seeing their sexual acts towards minors, women and themselves, it made me very sick. All these defendants represent our life, i.e., public servants, entertainers, religion, athletes, music, history, our neighbors. My mind is trashed forever.

3

I can't watch the news, the airwaves, newspapers, magazines. I'm disappointed in my leaders. I have no-one to look up to.

4

Plaintiff is afraid to vote because plaintiff's vote may contribute to putting a sexual predator into office and making plaintiff feel responsible for contributing to the perversion of America.

5

Plaintiff is now afraid to use airport restrooms because Senator Craig might be lurking in the stalls soliciting sex by attempting to play "footsie" with unknown male patrons who are relieving themselves.

6

Plaintiff is now horrified of going to a Catholic Church because the priests are out of control. Even last night I had a nightmare that I was forced to sleep with the Pope in a bulletproof glass bedroom. I can't go to confession anymore. I don't know who I'm confessing to.

7

Plaintiff is scared to go to concerts because artists like R. Kelly might begin urinating into the crowd while performing "I believe I can fly".

Plaintiff is also terrified of going to the Neverland Ranch to spend the night because Michael Jackson might remember the time when he was a smooth criminal giving little boys and girls thrillers of their lives while forcing them to look at the man in the mirror while he beats it! Then say "I want to rock with you all night".

8

Plaintiff is afraid to attend college or pro basketball or Lacrosse games because players like Kobe Bryant and the Duke Lacrosse guys might lure me to their hotels to pass me around for an assist by other players in an attempt to get their balls in the hole.

9

Plaintiff knows this is a New World Order. Defendants perverting my skull. I'm afraid to have kids. Who is going to protect them in school, church, Sam Goody, or visiting the White House? I can't even appeal to the Supreme Court because of what Clarence Thomas did to Anita Hill. I expect to be murdered like Rasputin.

Larry Craig was Mitt Romney's top supporter. Romney is a Mormon, Warren Jeffs is a Mormon. This is a conspiracy!

Preliminary Injunction Temporary Restraining Order

Plaintiff moves to compel this court to order defendants to report to their nearest law enforcement office. Branded and labeled. GPS tracked. Cameras installed on them and monitor their movements 24 hours a day. Also forbid defendants to appear on TV.

Plaintiff prays for relief.

Respectfully submitted,

Jonathan Lee Riches©

09/07/07

United States District Court

Northern District of Iowa

Jonathan Lee Riches©,

Plaintiff

Vs.

Mike Tyson a/k/a

"Iron Mike",

Defendant

Complaint

"Assault and Battery"

"TRO Temporary Restraining Order"

Comes now the plaintiff, Jonathan Lee Riches©, in pro-se, moves this honorable court to issue an order for the defendant named in this suit to respond. This is a civil rights violation and illegal crimes pursuant to assault and battery, terroristic threats, stalking, harassment, and psychological trauma. Plaintiff also moves this honorable court to issue a TRO Temporary Restraining Order against defendant forbidding further contact with plaintiff. Plaintiff seeks $4,000,000,000 Billion dollars in damages from defendant. Plaintiff prays for relief.

Plaintiff, Jonathan Lee Riches© is an international diamond dealer from Tampa, Florida currently residing in South Carolina

Jonathan Lee Riches

9/10/07

United States District Court

Middle District of Georgia

Jonathan Lee Riches©,

Plaintiff

Vs.

50 Cent a/k/a Curtis "50 Cent" Jackson,

Defendant

Civil Complaint

This is a complaint pursuant to copyright infringement, violation of the Copyright Act 17 U.S.C. 101, extortion activity in violation of the Federal Racketeer Influenced and Corrupt Organizations Act (RICO) 18 U.S.C. 1961, the Hobbs Act 18 U.S.C. 1951, and harassment.

Comes now the plaintiff Jonathan Lee Riches©, in pro-se, moves this honorable court to issue an order for defendant named in this suit to respond. Plaintiff seeks statutory damages pursuant to 17 U.S.C. 504 ©, and injunctive relief pursuant to 17 U.S.C. 502 and 503, prohibiting 50 Cent from further infringing conduct and requiring him to destroy all copies of Jonathan Lee Riches© material made in violation of plaintiff's exclusive rights. Plaintiff seeks $35,000,000,000.00 billion in damages. Plaintiff prays for relief.

1

Plaintiff Jonathan Lee Riches©, a professional actor, model and entertainer, broadcasts the Jonathan Lee Riches© Show throughout this state. Jonathan Lee Riches© has starred in numerous Hollywood films, including: Swordfish, Pee Wee's Big Adventure, The Karate Kid, Gino Romano, Catch Me if You Can, One Night in Paris. Jonathan Lee Riches© is also an international model with Mainline Models of King of Prussia, Pennsylvania.

Jonathan Lee Riches© is also a professional ghostwriter for mainstream and underground musicians, including the defendant.

Jonathan Lee Riches© has written poems, lyrics, books and manuscripts on cybercrime know how and prevention. Jonathan Lee Riches© is a trademarked name.

Jonathan Lee Riches© is a global conglomerate of products, i.e., Jonathan Lee Riches© fashion line, Jonathan Lee Riches© fitness centers, Jonathan Lee Riches© school of entertainment.

2

Defendant and I have known each other since childhood. Defendant hired the services of Jonathan Lee Riches© investigations in December of 1999. I provided defendants with any information on anyone. I had access to the three major credit reporting agencies: Experion, Equifax, Transunion. I had access to Nationwide DMV records. I had unlimited access to private investigating sites like Choicepoint, Lexis Nexus, Quickinfo, Acxium, First Data, U.S. Search etc. I had access to hardware and software to create encoded data, licenses, passports, clone phones. I had access to internal phone switches, call routing, ANI spoofing. I used social engineering methods a/k/a "pre-texting" combined with all the previously mentioned tools that allowed me to accomplish anything.

3

Defendant has a new album due for release on September 11, 2007 titled "Curtis". This album contains numerous Jonathan Lee Riches© copyrighted lyrics and material. I did not authorize the release of this material to defendant. A lot of the lyrics deal with cybercrime as defendant has told me this is the new direction he wants to go in. Defendant told me to write phrases and themes dealing with these topics.

4

This copyrighted material was stolen from me by defendant on May 7, 2007. "Credit cards, debits I charge, I rock like Pat Benatar", I'm the Optimus Prime of cybercrime, the Tiger Woods of cyberhood, the Mickey Mantle of financials."

"I'm da computer looter, Western Union abuser, the rap Lex Luther"

"I start a fraudocracy, cause credit cards are a mockery, it's hard to stop me from pushin' carts on shoppin' sprees"

"I'm Bin Laden, Robin and Batman combined in one man"

"My skillz on the web, coincide like Bill and Ted"

"My brain trained to entertain identities, got names to change for centuries"

"The Taliban of scams, I'll WMD your identity"

"I love you, identity theft, my scams slam like the WWF"

"A phone phreaker, comin' out your home spekerz"

"I'm da Einstein of identity crimes, my cyber skillz give you Siberian chills"

"That cop Mark Furman, couldn't stop my credit card splurgin'"

"I'm da crook who took Capital One funds, factual been done"

5

On June 10, 2001 Defendant hired the services of Jonathan Lee Riches© Hacking Inc. Defendant wanted Neiman Marcus clothing to wear in his music videos. Defendant hired me to hack into Neiman Marcus customers accounts to obtain instant credit to shop unlimited. We got $25 million in free clothing.

6

On March 22, 2002 defendant hired Jonathan Lee Riches© Revenge LLC. Defendant was having personal problems with other global music artists. Defendant had child support obligations with 80s pop group Bananarama. Defendant told me to make Bananarama's life miserable. Defendant hired me to send gravel, moving vans, strippers, dumpsters, junk mail to their home. Defendant had me shut off their power, phones, water, cancel their credit cards etc. The artist Tears for Fears owed defendant in NHL Hockey bets. Defendant had me put cell phone service around the country in Tears for Fears social security number and call 1 900 services to run them up.

7

January 17, 2003 –sold my Jonathan Lee Riches© story to "Fx", who created a show called "The Riches."

January 27, 2003 –Defendant sold the copyright to my book "From Rags to Jonathan Lee Riches©" to Tower Records without my consent. Defendant 50 Cent bought FCI Williamsburg, Neverland Ranch, Sago Mine, The Apollo Theater, and Boston's "Big dig" tunnel with the proceeds.

Preliminary Injunction

TRO Temporary Restraining Order

Plaintiff moves this honorable court to issue a Preliminary Injunction, Temporary Restraining Order prohibiting 50 Cent from releasing his September 11, 2007 new album titled "Curtis". Plaintiff's professional acting, entertainment, and modeling career is in Jeopardy. If this motion does not reach this court in time, plaintiff moves this court to halt the record sales of 50 Cent's album "Curtis"

Conclusion

Plaintiff moves this honorable court to issue an order for defendant to respond. Plaintiff has suffered major depression, grief, and constant harassment from defendant.

Respectfully submitted,

Jonathan Lee Riches©

United States District Court

District of Eastern Pennsylvania

Jonathan Lee Riches,

Plaintiff

Vs.

GEORGE W. BUSH, RICHARD B. CHENEY, CONDOLEEZA RICE, DONALD H. RUMSFELD, JOHN W. SNOW, UNIFORM COMMERCIAL CODE "UCC", CARLOS M. GUTIERREZ, MICHAEL O. LEAVITT, ELAINE CHAO, STEPHEN L. JOHNSON, MARGARET SPELLINGS, SAMUEL W. BODMAN, NORMAN Y. MINETA, HILLARY RODHAM CLINTON, JAMES HOFFA, WWW.GOOGLE.COM, BENEDICT, XVI, KINGDOM OF SAUDI ARABIA, JERRY WEST, WWW.ACCUWEATHER.COM, OSAMA BIN LADEN, WILLIAM GATES, HUGO CHAVEZ, JOHN DEERE, ADOLF HITLER'S, NATIONAL SOCIALIST PARTY, ISLAND DEF JAM MUSIC GROUP, ROC-A FELLA RECORDS, SHAWN CARTER, QUEEN OF ENGLAND, JO ANNE B. BARNHART, STEVEN SPIELBERG, RJ REYNOLDS TOBACCO HOLDINGS INC, JAPAN'S NIKKEI STOCK EXCHANGE, GAMBINO, THREE MILE ISLAND, NUCLEAR POWER PLANT, KOFI ANNAAN, TONY DANZA, ISAMIC REPUBLIC OF IRAN, DON KING PRODUCTIONS INC, PARIS HILTON, KINGDOM HALL OF THE JEHOVAH'S WITNESS, JOSE PADILLA, UNIVERSITY OF MIAMI, GEICO INSURANCE, VIENNA CONVENTION, MATT DRUDGE, MARION BLAKEY, CONSULATE GENERAL OF NIGERIA, THE SALVATION ARMY, JEWISH STATE OF ISRAEL, JOHN E. POTTER, SOLEDAD

O'BRIEN, MILES O'BRIEN, CABLE NEWS NET-WORK "CNN", MAGNA CARTA, TSUNAMI VICTIMS, ALAN GREENSPAN, THE AMERICAN RED CROSS, MARK EMERSON, JESSICA ALBA, SIRIUS SATELLITE RADIO, CHARLES MOOSE, THE HOUSTON CHRONICLE, AL QAEDA ISLAMIC ARMY, FRUIT OF A-LOOM, AMERICAN CIVIL LIBERTIES UNION "ACLU", OUTBACK STEAKHOUSE, DONALD J. TRUMP, TRUMP PLAZA, CHRIS BERMAN, THE VATICAN, SHAWN JOHN COMBS, MICHAEL BROWN, VINCENT K. MCMAHON, THE TALIBAN, RICHARD M. DALEY, MEALS ON WHEELS, JOHN GRISHAM, COLUMBINE HIGH SCHOOL, ARIEL SHARON, UNITED PARCEL SERVICE "UPS", TARA REID, BLACK ENTERTAINMENT TELEVISION INC "BET", SADDAM HUSSEIN, JEWISH WORKERS AT NBC/UNIVERSAL, BRAD PITT, JACK WELCH, ELIZABETH SMART, GEORGE E. PATAKI, CHARLIE SHEEN, THE SURGEON GNERAL, VLADIMIR PUTIN, OLIVER NORTH, GEORGE ORWELL, WWW.ASKJEEVES.COM, SEAN O'KEEFE, THE KREMLIN, DAVID LETTERMAN, THE PANAMA CANAL COMMISSION, GEORGE J. TENET, KELLY CLARKSTON, THIRTEEN TRIBES OF ISRAEL, AMERICAN HEART FOUNDATION, PLATO, LINCOLN MEMORIAL, OCCUPATIONAL SAFETY AND HEALTH ADMINISTRATION "OSHA", BORIS BECKER, FREEMASON LODGE, EGLIN AIRFORCE BASE, VARIOUS BUDDHIST MONKS, WWW.SECUREDPARTY.COM, I. LEWIS LIBBY, WARREN BUFFETT, SIERRA CLUB, JOHN D. NEGROPONTE, CHRISTINA APPLEGATE, JEWISH MOSSAD, NATIONAL VANGUARD BOOKS "NVB", AIR AND SPACE MUSEUM, CHRISTOPHER REEVES WIDOW, GALE A. NORTON, HALLIBURTON COMPANY, KELLOGG BROWN & ROOT, JOHN WALSH, MEIN

KAMPF, CITY OF CRAWFORD TEXAS, JOHN P. ABIZAID, VENUS WILLIAMS,WWW.DEECON.ORG, JOHN DUDAS, MEDIEVAL TIMES, INTERNATIONAL TRADE COMMISSION "ITC", ANNA NICHOLE SMITH, UNITED STATES MARINE CORPS., WILLIAM F. BUCKLEY, NATIONAL REVIEW, DENNY'S, BROTHERHOOD OF THE SNAKE, LARRY KING, LARRY KING LIVE 9PM "CNN", CHARLES E. "CHUCK& SCHUMER, RASTAFARIAN NATIVES, SPENCER ABRAHAM, ROLLINGSTONE MAGAZINE, MONOGRAM BANK OF GEORGIA, GRACE JONES, NATIONAL ASSOCIATION FOR STOCK CAR AUTO RACING "NASCAR", RAMZI AHMED YOUSEF, PLANET HOLLYWOOD, JOSEPH H. BOARDMAN, FEDERAL RAILROAD ADMINISTRATOR, MARSHALL BRUCE MATHERS, 111, SHADY RECORDS INC, ULLUMINATI, ADAM WEISHAUPT, THE APOLLO THEATER, DAVID W. ANDERSON, JASON SOCIETY, WU TANG CLAN, WU-WEAR INC, PHILIP PURCELL, NORDIC GODS, PRESIDENTAL EMERGENCY OPERATIONS CENTER "PEOC", SCREEN ACTORS GUILD INC, R. JAMES NICHOLSON, NEW YORK STOCK EXCHANGE INC "NYSE", THE DA VINCI CODE, MOORISH SCIENCE TEMPLE OF AMERICA "MSTA", SEARS TOWER, MIKE TYSON, NATIVE AMERICAN FISH SOCIETY, HOLOCAUST SURVIVORS, BYZANTINE REPUBLIC ARMY "BRA", DENNIS HOPPER, MT. RUSHMORE, BARBARA WALTERS, FIRST PRESBYTERIAN CHURCH, GORDON SULLIVAN, YELLOW CAB COMPANY, GREEK ORTHODOX ARCHDIOCESE OF NORTH AMERICA, MICHAEL SAVAGE, SAVAGE NATION, DENNIS HASTERT, GREEN BAY'S LAMBEAU FIELD, SLOBODAN MILOSEVIC, PIZZA HUT, KING JAMES BIBLE, SCOTT PETERSON, DEPARTMENT OF HOUSING AND URBAN DEVELOPMENT "HUD", SMITHSONIAN INSTITUTE,

ROBERT C. BONNER, MING DYNASTY, RAY NAGIN, BARRY BONDS, THOMAS J. RIDGE, JENNA BUSH, GANGS IN HONG KONG, UNITED METHODIST CHURCH, EUROPEAN UNION, PORTER GOSS, HARRAH'S LAS VEGAS INC, GRAND WIZARD OF KU KLUX KLAN "KKK", GENERAL MOTORS "GM", CHRISTOPHER COX, PROCTOR & GAMBLE, JEWISH SYNAGOGE'S, WWW.EBAY.COM, KNIGHTS OF MALTA, AFL-CIO UNION, BOOKER T. WASHINGTON, NATIONAL HOCKEY LEAGUE "NHL" PLAYERS ASSOCIATION, DIANE SAWYER, IMMIGRATION AND NATURALIZATION SERVICE "INS", VERN MINNI ME, STEVE JOBBS, STATUE OF LIBERTY, FIDEL CASTRO, BRIAN L. ROBERTS, COMCAST CABLE CO, EARTH LIBERATION FRONT "ELF", PHIL DONAHUE, MALCOLM X, KIM JONG, 11, GENEVA CONVENTION, LEE SCOTT, ARIZONA GAME AND FISH COMMISSION, NELSON ROCKEFELLER, NATIONAL ASSOCIATION OF REALTORS, FORT KNOX, PHILADELPHIA EAGLES, CHURCH SCIENTOLOGY, WORLD TRADE ORGANIZATION "WTO", BURT REYNOLDS, INTERNET CORPORATION, MICHAEL A. AQUINO, BILL O'REILLY, PUERTO RICAN NATIONALIST PARTY, WESTERN UNION FINANCIAL SERVICES, PAULA ABDUL, UNITED STATES HOLOCAUST MUSEUM, SOULJAH, SUHA ARAFAT, JESSIE JACKSON, HAMID KARZAI, CARNIVAL CRUISE LINES, THE WORLD COURT HAGUE, BEN N JERRY'S ICECREAM, JANET RENO, HOUSE OF ROTHSCHILD, DAVID STERN, INTERNATIONAL MONETARY FUND "IMF", JIMMY DEAN SAUSAGE CO, YALE SKULL AND BONES, SUMNER REDSTONE, COMPUTER HACKERS AND TELEPHONE PHREAKERS, MAYOR MOVING CORP, CHEMICAL/BIO SENSOR RESEARCH CENTER, ABERDEN MARYLAND, WHOOPI

GOLDBERG, VINCENT FOX, PENNSYLVANIA LOTTERY COMMISSION, WWW.AMAZON.COM, MICHAEL CHERTOFF, CITY OF NADI, THE NEW YORK TIMES, AMERICAN EXPRESS CREDIT CARD CORP, THE OLSEN TWINS, RAINBOW/PUSH COALITION, MOHAMMED ATTA, WORLD TRADE CENTER HIJACKER, LEAVENWORTH FEDERAL PRISON, MAX MAYFIELD, MICHAEL TIGAR, ROMAN EMPIRE, MERRIAM WEBSTERS DICTIONARY 10TH EDITION, PALESTINE LIBERATION ORGANIZATION "PLO", MICHAEL H. ARMACOST, KRAFT FOODS INC, JOHN FUND, UNKNOWN WRITERS OF NORTH AMERICAN FREE TRADE AGREEMENT "NAFTA", DEMI MOORE, SMITH N WESSON, UNITED NEGRO COLLEGE FUND, EDWARD M. LIDDY, WOLF BLITZER, "THE SITUATION ROOM" CNN NEWS, WWW.2600.COM, METROPOLITAN TRANSIT AUTHORITY, RICHARD JEWEL, BLOODS AND CRIPS OF DETROIT, MICHAEL J. FOX, RICHARD S. FULD, VERIZON COMMUNICATIONS, ANGELA MERKEL, THE ROSE BOWL, BEN YAHWEH, PEOPLE AGAINST TREATMENT OF ANIMALS "PETA", KENTUCKY FRIED CHICKEN, CITIGROUP INC, NATIONAL ACADEMY OF SCIENCE'S INSTITUTE OF MEDICINE, INDRA K. NOOYI, VIRGINIA KINGS DOMINION, VANNA WHITE, ROBERT W. KAGAN, CARNEGIE ENDOW INTERNATIONAL PEACE, SUGAR RAY LEONARD, ROSS PEROT, HARLEY-DAVIDSON INC, ISLAMIC RELIEF ORGANIZATION "IIRO", HARLEY G. LAPPIN, PINK TRIANGLE COALITION, POW-MIA, CATHEDRAL CHURCH OF THE INTERCESSOR, BELLEVUE STATE HOSPITAL CENTER, WWW.FRAUDFEDERALRESERVE.COM, SAMMY SOSA, ROBERT M. GATES, ARCHITECTURE OF FREE MASONRY, BOBBY ACCORD, THE PILLSBURY COMPANY, REVOLUTIONARY ARMED FORCES OF

COLMBIA "FARC", ROSIE O'DONNELL, GEORGE P. SHULTZ, SUNDANCE FILM FESTIVAL, U.S. CAPITOL POLICE, AARP, AMERICANS ASSOCIATION OF RETIRED PERSONS, THE APPALACHIAN TRAIL, NOTRE DAME, JOHN KASICH, JOEY BUTTAFUOCO, NATIONAL WIDLIFE REFUGE, NOSTRADAMUS, RICHARD THORNBURGH, LEANN RIMES, EVANGELICAL LUTHERAN CHURCH, JAMES BILLINGTON, LIBRARY OF CONGRESS, MARCO POLO, TERESA HEINTZ KERRY, NEGRO JUSTICE LEAGUE, THE EIFFEL TOWER, NEWT GINGRICH, USA TODAY, G8 SUMMIT, ZACARIAS MOUSSAOUI, RINGLING BROS. AND BARNUM & BAILEY CIRCUS, KENTUCKY MILITIA, LLOYD M. BENSTEN, JOHN WAYNE BOBBIT, PLYMOUTH ROCK, WKRP IN CINCINNATI, ROYAL INSTITUTE FOR INTERNATIONAL AFFAIRS, ARAYAN BROTHERHOOD, JAMES G. ROCHE, YAO MING, HARTSFIELD ATLANTA INTERNATIONAL AIRPORT, WWW.ANTISOCIAL.COM, CHARLES DICKENS, ARLEN SPECTOR, LEANING TOWER OF PISA, NATIONAL OCEANIC ATMOSPHERIC ADMINISTRATION "NOAA", IRAQI BAATH REGIME, KEVIN BACON, UNITED STATES OLYMPIC COMMITTEE, HUMANE SOCIETY, GUERILLA'S IN THE MIST, DONNA E. SHALALA, FABIO, HOLY LAND FOUNDATION, ENCYCLOPEDIA BRITANNICA, BONO, CENTERS FOR DISEASE CONTROL "CDC", HOME DEPOT, NATIONAL RIFLE ASSOCIATION "NRA", GERALDO RIVERA, AMTRAK, NICCOLO MACHIAVELLI, AMERICAN PSYCHIATRIC ASSOCIATION, GARDEN OF EDEN, BEN ROETHLISBERGER, UNIFICATION CHURCH, ANGLO-SAXONS ALLIANCE, UNITED STATES SECRET SERVICE, DOSTOEVSKY, THE INTERNATIONAL SPACE STATION, RUSSELL CROWE, ASSASSINS OF SERBIAN PRIME MINISTER ZORAN DJINDJIC, MALL OF

AMERICA, EDWARD S. ROBINSON, COMMANDING OFFICER OF USS GRAYBACK, HOME SHOPPING NETWORK "HSN", JOHN DUPONT, ACE HARDWARE STORES, HENRY A. KISSINGER, PAUL REVERE, INDIANAPOLIS MOTOR SPEEDWAY, DUNCAN DONUTS, RAND CORPORATION, MICHELANGELO, OLYMPIA J. SNOWE, AZTEC PYRAMIDS, BOY SCOUTS OF AMERICA, William Pierce, SIX FLAGS OVER ARLINGTON TEXAS, TALMUD, BETH HOLLOWAY TWITTY, INTERNATIONAL ATOMIC ENERGY AGENCY "IAEA", JESSICA SIMPSON, DONALD E. GRAHAM, VIAGRA, ANNE RICHARDS, WWW.GINOROMANO.COM, WILLIAM JEFFERSON CLINTON, MARION SUGE KNIGHT, RIPLEY'S BELIEVE IT OR NOT, RANDY JOHNSON, ANHEISER-BUSCH, PETER JENNINGS WIDOW, PAUL WOLFOWITZ, MONTANA FREEMEN, PENNSYLVANIA TURNPIKE, ALCOHAL, TOBACCO, AND FIREARMS "ATF", JULIA ROBERTS, PUBLIC BROADCAST SYSTEM "PBS", JEB BUSH, JOHN BIRCH SOCIETY, SRINT/NEXTEL, BOB VILA, HOOVER DAM, SANDY BERGER, TOLL BROTHERS, KILLINGTON VERMONT SKI RESORT, WWW.YAHOO.COM, JOE GIBBS RACING, JENNIFER LOPEZ, NATIONAL PUBLIC RADIO "NPR", TONYA HARDING, COMPTROLLER OF CURRENC, ADT SECURITY, HARRISON FORD, US DEPARTMENT OF AGRICULTURE, MIKE JOHANNS, DELTA AIRLINES, PETE ROSE, SYMBIONESE LIBERATION ARMY "SLA", SMALL BUSINESS ADMINISTRATION "SBA", JOSEPH LIEBERMAN, SYLVESTER STALLONE, KYOTO PROTOCOL, THE BOLIVIAN MAFIA, VIETNAM VETERANS OF AMERICA, KENNETH STARR, SIMON AND SCHUSTER, PATRICIA HEARST, ANTI-DEFAMATION LEAGUE, NELSON MANDELA, CHANDRA LEVY, CHURCH OF JESUS CHRIST LATTER DAY

SAINTS, RUSH LIMBAUGH, LOUIS FARRAKHAN, NATIONAL MEDAL OF ARTS, WEBSTER HUBBELL, MCDOUGAL'S, THE WAFFLE HOUSE, GRAY DAVIS, BLACK PANTHER PARTY, GRAND CANYON-PARASHANT NATIONAL MONUMENT, LUCY LIU, BOB BARKER, FEDERALIST SOCIETY, ELIAN GONZALEZ, INTERNATIONAL CRIMINAL COURT "ICC", DANNY GLOVER, NATIONAL ARCHIVES, DISNEY'S GRAND FLORIDIAN RESORT, JONATHAN JAY POLLARD, RED GUERRILLA RESISTANCE, NEW JERSEY PORT AUTHORITY, CHRIS MATTHEWS, KWEISI MFUME, WENDY'S, RUDOLPH GIULIANI, ISLAMIC MUSLIM BROTHERHOOD, DREW BARRYMORE, ALL NATIONAL ABORTION CLINICS, NEWSWEEK MAGAZINE, MADELINE ALBRIGHT, LEE R. RAYMOND, LOUIS XV, HOLY GRAIL, MERCK PHARMACEUTICALS, ELTON JOHN, PLANET OF PLUTO, TRENT LOTT, HO CHI MINH CITY, MUAMMAR GADDAFI, PRESIDENT OF LIBYA, FRANK SINATRA, JR., JOSEPH BIDEN, LIL KIM, JUNIOR MAFIA BAD BOY RECORDS, I-95 "INTERSTATE" DEVELOPERS, MAKE A WISH FOUNDATION, THE VIRGIN MARY, US DEPARTMENT OF INTERNAL AFFAIRS, RICHARD REID, JERRY LEWIS TELETHON, GOLDEN GATE BRIDGE, MONICA LEWINSKY, JOHN ASHCROFT, DENNIS RODMAN, CENTER FOR MEDICARE/MEDICAID SERVICES, J. K. ROWLING, JACKIE CHAN, NOELLE BUSH, CLEO, DAVID COULTER, CHECHEN REBELS, HUGGIES, COLIN POWELL, NINJA SAMURAI FIGHTERS, NATIONAL CENTER FOR MISSING & EXPLOITED CHILDREN, HAMAS, TAMMANY HALL, TREVOR SMITH, WWW.EHARMONY.COM, JEAN-BERTRAND ARISTIDE, HUBBLE SPACE TELESCOPE, JOSHUA BOLTEN, THE BOSTON GLOBE, THE NATIONAL GUARD AND RESERVES, B'NAI B'RITH, OUTLAWS

MOTORCYCLE GANG, JOHN MCCAIN, EQUAL OPPORTUNITY EMPLOYE "EOE', MICHAEL MOORE, FORT BRAGG MILITARY BASE, JOHN WALTERS, WORLD WIDE WEB, CATHOLIC CHURCH, GAY CATHOLIC PRIESTS, BEN BERNANKE, ANTI-COMMUNIST MEMORBILA COLLECTION, ACADEMY AWARDS, FBI, FRANCIS J. HARVEY, BAPTIST CHURCH, WWW.MEDIACONTROL.COM, OPRAH WINFREY, AREA 69: ALIEN & UFO RESEARCH CENTER, SCOTT MCCLELLAN, DAVID DUKE, ENGINE #9, FIRE DEPARTMENT, FRANKLIN MINT, D. B. COOPER, LESTER CRAWFORD, NAPOLEON, ORGANIZATION OF PETROLEUM EXPORTIGN COUNTRIES "OPEC", WICCAN WORSHIP, BRITISH SAS, GUANTANAMO BAY, THE DARRYL F. ZANCK INSTITUTE FOR MEDIA DOMINATION AND TALMUDIC STUDIES, PIRATES COVE MINITURE GOLF COURSE, HANNIBAL LECTOR, COUNCIL OF FOREIGN RELATIONS, RONALD MCDONALD CHARITIES, SANKOH SANKOH, BEN GURION AIRPORT, SANDRA BULLOCK, STATUE OF FELIX DZERZHINSKY "IRON FELIX", KATIE CURIC, FEDERAL DEPOSIT INSURANCE CORPORATION "FDIC", MOTLEY RICE, QUEEN RANIA OF JORDAN, PHI BETA KAPPA, IRISH REPUBLICAN ARMY "IRA", CHE GUEVARA, ALJAZEERA TELEVISION, BUMBLE BEE TUNA, COPTIC ORTHODOX EGYPT CHURCH, JOHN BOEHNER, BIG BEND, SANDRA DAY O'CONNOR, DUN & BRADSTREET, BOB SAGET, SCOTLAND YARD, MOORISH SCIENCE TEMPLE OF AMERICA, NCAA BASKETBALL, DRUG ENFORCEMENT AGENCY "DEA", JAVELIN STRATEGY & RESEARCH, QODS FORCE (JERUSALEM FORCE), BOSTON MARKET, WWW.BACKSTREETBOYS.COM, HIZBALLAH, LAWRENCE LIVERMORE NATIONAL LABORATORY,

RUSSIAN KGB, COLOSSIANS F IRST CENTURY PARALLELS, TERI HATCHER, GLORIA ARROYO, TROJAN HORSE, RANDOM HOUSE PUBLISHING, GREAT WALL OF CHINA, DEPARTMENT OF JUSTICE "DOJ", PERKINS, OMAR TORRIJOS, JEFF FORT, DYNASTY 7, NATIONAL RECONNAISSANCE OFFICE "NRO", GEORGE CLOONEY, JOSE MARTI AIRPORT, HAVANA CUBA, KORAN, ASHANTI GOLDFIELDS, CLUB OF ROME, NATO, CHARLES SCHWAB, KOREAN NATIONAL INTELLIGENCE SERVICE "NIS", ANNE MULCAHY, CEO XEROX, KIRIAT, CONGRESS OF RACIAL EQUALITY "CORE", INTERPOL, KORYO DYNASTY, KILLERS OF PRINCESS DIANA & DODI, WU YI,WWW.EXPEDIA.COM, THE 48TH ANNUAL GRAMMY AWARDS, BRITISH MI5, FEDERAL RESERVE WIRE RANSFER NETWORK "FEDWIRE", POLYTHEISTS INTERNATIONAL, FEDERICO PENA, ABU SAYAFF, MARIAH CAREY, LONDON'S NATURAL HISTORY MUSEUM, COMMANDER OF UNITED STATES COAST GUARD, TAOIST CREATURES, FINANCIAL CRIMES ENFORCEMENT NETWORK "FINCEN", EGYPTIAN GAMA'AT, CHOICEPOINT, PELER BIJUR, BERLIN WALL DEMOLITION CO, DICK DEGUERIN, CRYTOGRAPH ELICITATION CENTER "CEC", GUY RITCHIE, THE SUPREME COURT, BOUSTROS GHALI, GLAXO SMITH KLINE, FARAH AIDEED, SOMALI WARLORD, KIEFER SUTHERLAND, NEW REPUBLIC MAGAZINE,WWW.BOP.GOV, ASPEN INSTITUTE, BURGER KING, FEDERAL BUREAU OF INVESTIGATION "FBI", TINA TURNER, PATRIOTIC UNION OF KURDISTAN "PUK', DISNEY'S TYPHOON LAGOON, BUNDESKRIMINALAND, GERMAN FEDERAL POLICE, HEGELIAN PRINCIPLE, SHAMIL BASSAYEU, GORDON R. ENGLAND, PSYCHOLOGY SOCIALISM, MINNESOTA VIKINGS, MICHAEL V. HAYDEN,

SOUTHWEST AIRLINES, GENE HACKMAN, GOTHIC CELTIC INC, CAESERS PALACE, PENTAGON, BROOKLIN BRIDGE, KING OF PRUSSIA MALL, TONY BLAIR, PRIME MINISTER OF GREAT BRITAIN, COMMONWEALTH NATIONAL BANK, AL-SUGAYR AZMI, LOS ANGELES POLICE DEPARTMENT, ALBERTO R. GONZALES, FUBU CLOTHING LINE, MARTIN S. FELDSTEIN, BRITISH ROUND TABLE, GEORGE HERBERT WALKER BUSH, MICHAEL DELL, BILLY BLANKS, MICHAEL IRVIN, LIGHT TECHNOLOGY PUBLISHING, CHUBBY CHECKER, DONALD B. ENSENAT, MULTIPLE SCLEROSIS SOCIETY, CARDINAL BERNARD LAW, USS COLE, EASTER SEALS, GRAND DUCHY OF LUXEMBOURG, PGA GOLF, SILVIO BERLUSCONI, DENNIS KOZLOWSKI, BUCKINGHAM PALACE, VALERIE PLAME, BOYS & GIRLS CLUBS OF AMERICA, ZEUS, GEORGE A. OMAS, POSTAL RATE COMMISSION, AMERICAN KENNEL CLUB, SUPER 8 MOTELS, DAVID FREUDENTHAL, CHERNOBYL NUCLEAR POWER PLANT, PFC, LYNNDIE ENGLAND, MADISON SQUARE GARDEN, SPAIN BASQUE "ETA", JUSTIN TIMBERLAKE, JOHN HANCOCK FINANCIAL SERVICES, TIN CAN SAILORS, BILL JANKLOW, EMEKA OKAFOR, PARMALAT, KENTUCKY DERBY, GARY RIDGWAY, WORLD ANTI-DOPING AGENCY, HOWARD DEAN, THE COLOSSUS OF RHODES, BETTY CROCKER, LIBERTY BELL, THEODORE KACZYNSKI, US CENSUS BUREAU, BARCLAY'S PLC UK, ANDREW H. CARD, WHITE HOUSE CHIEF OF STAFF, WEIRD AL YANKOVIC, BERNARD EBBERS, MOKTADA AL-SADR, SHITE CLERIC, GAY PRIDE PARADE, MARGARET THATCHER, BETTER BUSINESS BUREAU, LLOYDS OF LONDON, WARSAW PACT, BARACK OBAMA, FORT MCHENRY TUNNEL, JACK KEVORKIAN, HANS BLIX, THE DOOBIE BROTHERS, HOLY QURAN, BARBARA POPE,

ALZHEIMER'S ASSOCIATION, BENINGO G. REYNA, US MARSHALS SERVICE, WEIGHT WATCHERS, HU JINTAO, CALIFORNIA INSTITUTE OF TECHNOLOGY, EMILIO ESTEVEZ, LACKLAND AIRFORCE BASE, MENNONITE CHURCH, PAT ROBERTS, CROWN PRINCE ALIOS, YMCA, IRAQI NATIONAL CONGRESS, WWW.PAYNOTAXES.COM, GERHARD SCHROEDER, KEVIN MITNICK, CANADA'S LIBERAL PARTY, KEN JENNINGS, JEOPARDY CHAMPION, RUSSIAN FEDERATION 89, SECURITY COUNCIL "NSC", AL PACINO, SULTANATE OF OMAN, FOLGER SHAKESPERE LIBRARY, MEL GIBSON, JACQUES CHIRAC, MARTHA STEWART, LIVING OMNIMEDIA INC, MOUNT VERNON, DEPRESSION AND BIPOLAR SUPPORT ALLIANCE, MBNA CORP, LADY BIRD JOHNSON WILD FLOWER CENTER, SOCIAL WORKERS PARTY "SWP", NOBEL PEACE PRIZE, LA-Z-BOY, AMERICANS VETERANS OF WORLD WAR 11, NEW YORK MERCANTILE EXCHANGE, THE GENERAL ASSEMBLY, QUAKER OATS, CHARLES LOUIS KINCANNON, CONGOLESE ARMY, DE GAULLE PARIS AIRPORT, SKITTLES CANDY and ARNOLD SCHWARZENEGGER

Complaint

"New World Order Against Mankind"

This is a complaint under 42 U.S.C. 1983, civil rights violation by the Constitution and laws of the United States; and Federal TORT claims inflicted by that include, but not limited to: terrorism, murder, treason, major fraud, extortion, racketeering, torture, civil rights, espionage, assault, conspiracy, genocide, war crimes, explosives, obstruction of justice, piracy, arson, sabotage, perjury, criminal street gangs, biological weapons, sex trafficking, concealment, false oaths, bribery, riots, slavery, robbery, malicious mischief, counterfeiting, search and seizures, injury to wildlife, sex abuse/rape, obscenity, kidnapping, stalking, liquor trafficking, identity theft, psychiatric trauma, false information, invasion, threats to commit violent acts, malpractices, aggravations, nuisances, entrapments, mind manipulation, brutality, persecutions, negligence, wiretapping and poisoning.

Comes now the plaintiff Jonathan Lee Riches©, in pro-se, moves this honorable court to issue an order for all defendants named in this suit to give a response. Moves this honorable court to list all defendants in complaint separately, not "etc. all." As the plaintiff is claiming that his federal and state constitutional rights are being violated under the 1st, 2nd, 4th, 5th, 6th, 8th, 13th and 14th amendments of the Constitution. Relief requested, plaintiff seeks 379,111,339,000,000.00 trillion dollars backed by gold or silver delivered by United Parcel Service "UPS" to Federal Correctional Institution Williamsburg, Salters South Carolina, collectively from all defendants.

1

Vast conspiracy through defendants for the New World Order forcing the Uniform Commercial Code "UCC" on my life. False pretenses created the ALL CAPS of my flesh and blood name, forcing me to do business with the de facto/ens legis United States Government. The defendants, through subliminal messaging and RFID on- star chips combined with daily life technology, suckered me into contractual obligation.

The Federal Reserve Bank is unconstitutional, federal reserve notes (fiat money) are backed by no substance except the American Citizen's "promise". The defendants are spreading this concept globally –preventing anyone from leaving this planet. Flights from travel agencies are suspended according to Travelocity.com.

2

George Bush is a time traveler who conspired with the Duke of Normandy at the Battle of Hastings 1066 AD to pervert the English Dictionary and law. Admiral/Maritime Jurisdiction is hearing my complaint. The American flag is M.I.A. held hostage at FEMA camps.

3

George W. Bush is the Grand Imam of voodoo witch doctors turning humans into animals, sometimes plants. April 14th, 2001 was witnessed with United Nations Secretary General Kofi Annan at a Falls Church Virginia smorgasbord discussing top secret protocol and social security as Ponzi scam.

4

Trading with Enemy Act of Oct. 6th, 1917, yet George W. Bush and defendants secretly sell inmates' DNA on the international stock market, including, but not limited to, Hitler's National Socialist Party, Guerilla Asian Movement, and on three occasions the Nigerian Junjaweeds.

5

Defendants were involved with FCI Williamsburg's construction, failing to build an anti-UFO defense system, releasing STAPH infection into the water system, and hiring robotic correctional guards.

6

The 14th Amendment of the Constitution was not ratified properly. I was not allowed to vote. Mysterious supernatural creatures drinking Yoo Hoo. Condi Rice is a NASA created experiment, spreading false democracy. Secret black/white race war.

7

House Joint Resolution 192 of June 5th, 1933. Defendants planned Elizabeth Smart's kidnapping. George W. Bush intercepted on federal wiretap, on the final stages of a secret government weather making machine.

8

People acted separately and together to accomplish the following:

03/04/03 –George W. Bush stole my identity

05/22/02 –George W. Bush formed alliance with Al Qaeda

05/10/00 –covert prostitution at local utility companies

10/18/01 –radiation released by United Airlines pilots

01/09/04 –hypnotherapists who advertise in newspapers

12/25/02 –price gouging citizens

Plaintiff's back was injured. Was force fed. Security and Exchanges Commission stole plaintiff's money. Two ingrown toenails. Missing Americans at college frat houses. Plaintiff seeks relief in monetary amount set at the beginning of the complaint, also granting restraining order against George W. Bush. Please also include restraining order against Air Force One.

Respectfully submitted,

Jonathan Lee Riches©

03/09/06

Notice of Appeal

Comes now the Plaintiff, Jonathan Lee Riches©, in pro-se, moves the Honorable Court to Appeal Judge Harry D. Leinenweber's Aug 17, 2007 order to deny this suit. Plaintiff moves to appeal to the Court of Appeals.

George Bush Voodoos in this country. Bush took Gov. Ryan to an off shore Pagan dance three miles off Lake Michigan shoreline. Adventures in Babysitting and Ferris Bueller were also present.

Plaintiff moves to appeal this order please.

Jonathan Lee Riches©

09/11/07

Editor's note: this suit was initially filed on 03/09/06, Jonathan filed multiple suits with the same list of defendants around the same time with different complaints. The original appears here in conjunction with its appeal on 09/11/07.

United States District Court

Western District of Pennsylvania

Jonathan Lee Riches© a/k/a

"Marathon Jon",

Plaintiff

Vs.

International Olympic Committee "IOC";

U.S. Olympic Committee "USOC";

2008 Beijing Olympics;

The Special Olympics;

U.S. Anti-Doping Agency;

Lance Armstrong d/b/a Tour De France Cycling Champion,

Defendants

Civil Complaint

"Discrimination of my talents"

"TRO Temporary Restraining Order"

Comes now the plaintiff, Jonathan Lee Riches© a/k/a "Marathon Jon", in pro-se, moves this honorable court to issue an order for defendants named in this suit to respond. This suit is in regard to violations of the Americans with Disabilities Act 42 U.S.C. 12101, violations of the Rehabilitation Act of 1973, 29 U.S.C. 794, Civil Rights Act of 1964 42 U.S.C. 2000, EEO Equal mployment Opportunity violations, Identity theft, 6th and 8th

Amendment violations and treason. Plaintiff moves this court for a restraining order against defendants. Plaintiff seeks $822,000,694.08 million from defendants. Plaintiff requests a jury trial. I pray for relief.

Plaintiff, Jonathan Lee Riches© a/k/a "Marathon Jon" is a four time Mr. Olympia (1999, 02, 03, 04) and marathon world record holder currently residing at a concentration camp FCI Williamsburg, South Carolina.

1

On May 10, 2006 –I ran a 3:38 minute mile around the FCI Williamsburg recreation yard. I've been on the cover of Runner's World and Running Man magazine 10 times. I sent my running results and urine sample to defendants and I'm still being discriminated against because they won't let me enter the 2008 Olympics.

June 8, 2007 –I ran 26.2 miles in 1 hour 58 minutes, smashing any record worldwide. Defendants won't let me join the Olympics because I'm white.

2

Lance Armstrong gave me head cancer on Feb. 22, 2007. Defendants are forbidding me to race at Churchill Downs.

On Jan. 15, 2006 –FCI Williamsburg has no Olympic size pool to practice my breast stroke –only puddles with no life guards on duty.

On June 18, 2007 Defendants sent Tanya Harding to break my knee caps.

The "USOC" and "IOC" have a rule book. The rules say that anyone who has had their 6th and 8th Amendment rights violated under Booker/ Fan Fan cannot join the Olympics. On Jan. 1, 2007 I sent them a letter asking for an exemption and an anti-doping hearing. May 10, 2007 –I got a letter back from the "IOC". Their response was "We are sorry Mr. Riches, the Southern District of Texas in Houston, case #H-03-90 has violated your 6th Amendment rights by enhancing you millions of dollars in fraud losses not proven by a jury, admitted to, or in your indictment –we cannot accept you into the Olympics because U.S. district judge Melinda Harmon violated your 6th Amendment rights." This is discrimination and EEO violations.

Dec. 10, 2005 –I swam across the English Channel with Michael Phelps. I also ran 35 Badwater marathons that night. I had to fight the Russian in Rocky V for training. I can also bicycle and write lawsuits at the same time on April 20, 2006.

Defendants put me on Richie Valens' plane.

Sep. 11, 2001 –Defendants took my gold medals, boy scout trophies, swift boat courage, my spelling bee medal. I ran across the Gobi Desert without water. I can run hurdles over the Great Wall of China. Jewish Mossad can only catch me in my mind and that's on Tuesdays.

The triathlon champion –I did all night identity theft runs, pumping out 10 Western Unions a hour, I went across the country with Andrew Cunanan.

I'm suing Nowak in Orlando Orange County.

I can shot put my cellmate 300 meters. I can prove I'm handicapped, just ask Mary Lou Retton. Defendants took my passport and identity so I can't travel to Beijing. I represent the country of Hackistan in a town called Fraudville. The Olympics are afraid I will reunite with Mao and serious computer hackers from the 16th century.

Defendants discriminate against my past. I spent Juvenile time in Vision Quest Franklin PA Mental Facility, they forced me to sleep in tee pees and stress hike for days without food. I'm suing them too.

TRO Restraining

Plaintiff is in serious danger from defendants. Lance Armstrong's bike transforms into a nuclear missile. Nukes pointed at me from all directions. My shadow runs from me. My cellmate leaves me alone in the cell. Ben Caden has a 5 billion dollar award for my head. Plaintiff moves for the canceling of the 2008 Olympics. Scott Peterson is innocent. Plaintiff moves to leave Peterson and John Mark Karr alone. Defendants leave me alone. When I get out I'm going to join the CIA again. Delta Air Force agent Jonathan Lee Riches© the trained lawsuit writer of the universe armed with the 1st Amendment.

Respectfully submitted,

Jonathan Lee Riches©

09/13/07

United States District Court

Eastern District of Oklahoma

Jonathan Lee Riches© d/b/a CEO of "Identity Theft Row Records",

Plaintiff

Vs.

Carrie Underwood d/b/a "Country Music Singer",

Defendant

Complaint

"Country Music Scandal"

"Preliminary Injunction Restraining Order"

This is a complaint action pursuant to copyright infringement, violation of the copyright act 17 U.S.C. 1114, breach of contract, fraudulent misrepresentation, harassment, terroristic threats and stalking.

Comes now the plaintiff, Jonathan Lee Riches© d/b/a CEO of "Identity Theft Row Records", in pro-se, moves this honorable court to issue an order for defendant named in this suit to respond. Plaintiff seeks statutory damages pursuant to 17 U.S.C. 502 and 503, moves this court to compel defendant to surrender all Jonathan Lee Riches© copyrighted material pursuant to Fed. R. CIV. P. 64. Plaintiff seeks $35,000,000.00 million dollars in damages. Plaintiff prays for relief.

1

A Mega Conspiracy

On May 2005 – Carrie Underwood bribed American Idol Judges Simon and Paula. She got my co-defendant Carpenter to hack into phone lines to rig votes.

Estonia got hacked too.

2

Aug 4, 2007 – Underwood current hit songs "I sued Vick, got on the news quick" "All Truth in my lawsuits" "Jonathan Lee Riches, He delicious" Are the copyrighted material of Jonathan Lee Riches©

3

Carrie Underwood is unpatriotic

June 7, 2007 Underwood text messages the Dixie Chicks

Underwood Serenades Communist soldiers

Underwood burns her bra at concerts

Underwood got an arm tattoo of the Berlin Wall

Friends with Cindy Sheehan

4

June 28, 2007 Carrie Underwood threatens me daily, Everyday, minute, second with body harm by Tony Romo, Cowboys, and a few Indians.

Aug 10-2007- Carrie is pen-pals with Andrea Yates.

Aug 27, 2007 – Carrie Underwood cigarette lighter has been starting Greek fires.

Another unpatriotic conspiracy.

6

May 12, 2007 Underwood committed Identity theft peonage, she picks on blind workers at Wal-Mart too.

7

Two Milli Vanilli lookalikes jumped me in the prison rec yard and stole my Larynx Under Carrie's direct orders -a first Amendment speech violation 1/18/07

I was denied access to the County Music Awards. Underwood put my head in a vice in Miami.

FCI Williamsburg guards wear cowboy hats and spurs

Preliminary Injunction Restraining Order

Plaintiff moves to stop all satellite viewing of the Country Music Channel in this universe. Stop Jon Swartz from USA Today from giving Carrie credit in my name.

Respectfully submitted,

Jonathan Lee Riches©

09/14/07

United States District Court

Middle District of Florida

Jonathan Lee Riches©,

Plaintiff

Vs.

Orenthal James Simpson a/k/a "O.J. Simpson",

Defendant

Complaint

"O.J. is Coming to Jacksonville"

"TRO Temporary Restraining Order"

Comes now the plaintiff, Jonathan Lee Riches©, in pro-se, moves this honorable court to issue an order for defendant named in this suit to respond. This suit is Constitutional violations that defendant committed and crimes pursuant to robbery, fraud, identity theft, false oaths, treason, kidnapping and stalking. Plaintiff moves this honorable court to issue a restraining order against defendant forbidding him to enter the city. Plaintiff seeks $1,000,000.00 million dollars in insurance damages from defendant.

1

A few weeks after O.J. bonds out of jail, O.J. is going to rent a white Bronco from Avis Rent-a-Car and drive to Jacksonville to go on a crime spree to finance his Las Vegas legal defense. I found this out through my New York mob attorney Bruce Cutler who is also O.J. Simpson's Attorney. Cutler is in violation of Attorney client confidentiality. O.J. has a malfeasance towards aging computer hackers like myself since Feb 25th, 2003.

2

I speak to O.J. Simpson every Monday morning at 8:00 am on the Prison phone. On 9-10-07, Simpson told me he and his golfing buddies, Tiger Woods, Ernie Ells, Sam Snead are going to Las Vegas on Thursday to get O.J.'s used jock strap back from a sports memorabilia dealer. O.J. told me 'I'm going to hurt this man like I did to Goldman.' O.J. knew he would be arrested but told me 'this is a mega conspiracy I'm in with the mayor of Las Vegas, Fred Goldman, Adam "Packman" Jones, to get arrested, sacrifice myself to get huge revenue boosts for the City of Vegas, then get mega book deals and media exposure."

3

O.J. plans to travel along I-10 committing armed robberies at CITGO Stations and Flying J Travel Plaza's. He plans to buy extra big pairs of black gloves. O.J. told me he would 'kill me' if I whistle blew. O.J. Simpson also knows what cell I sleep in at FCI Williamsburg. he knows my bedtime too.

4

O.J. told me when he relocates to Jacksonville, he's going to get a phone book and look up the names of every Goldman and Brown including Singer James Brown. The people of Jacksonville must know this. All criminals in Duval County must take cover immediately. Board up your windows, load up on crabs 'cause O.J. Simpson is coming to town, he see's you when you're sleeping, he knows when you're awake.'

5

On October 10, 2007 – O.J. Simpson plans to come to FCI

Williamsburg, come into the gates with a fake correctional officer's uniform, kidnap my foot and return it back to the football hall of fame. I was a NFL kicker in 1952 through 1965. I can kick field goals 90 yards, ask O.J., or ask the warden, or ask Jeeves.

6

On July 2007 – O.J. Simpson forced me to sue Michael Vick O.J. Simpson also knows the mystery of Jonathan Luna.

7

O.J. forced me to sleep with stolen credit cards. At one am every night, O.J. enters my sleep. He tosses and turns with my organs on purpose. O.J. uses no flashlight only a candle that burns my inside. When O.J. leaves my body he doesn't have the curtsey to close the door. He also leaves muddy foot prints.

8

O.J. has been an unindicted co-defendant of mine since Feb 25th, 2003 who bribed my sentencing judge Melinda Harmon with Authentic Simpson Sports memorabilia stolen in Vegas on 9-13-07. No one with the FCI will look into O.J.'s conduct, because every FBI building has O.J. posters on the wall. O.J. is best buddies with herds of Buffalo in the Denver area. On 9-13-17, Simpson has to resort to picking on old card collectors, he would not dare mess with Canton Ohio Hall of Fame Alumni. O.J. also avoided the Iraqi draft with Ali on March 2003 -I'm offended by O.J.'s non Patriotism.

9

Every time I speak with O.J. on the phone I suffer irreversible neurological trauma with he confesses to me that he killed

Goldman. O.J. told me that media has the theory wrong on why he killed Goldman. It was not out of jealousy with Nichole, but California was running low on gold, Ron Goldman's body was stuffed with Gold Nuggets, it was Ronnie's body he was after. He told me this on May 10 2007.

10

O.J. forced me to sue Senator Larry Craig in U.S. District court in Delaware and Roman Priests. O.J. was a Roman Catholic in the 1970's at USC, priests used to visit his dorm at night to rub his Heisman trophy.

11

On May 10, 2006 O.J. Simpson became a scientist for the Food and Drug Administration. I was injected with the bird flu by Simpson. Now I have weight loss because Teri Shiavo's feeding tube spoke to me in Greek. O.J. has super speed, flash powers. In 2400 B.C. O.J. split South America away from Africa.

In 1994 O.J. was so mad about Los Angles charging him with murder that he started the Northridge Earthquake.

12

O.J. is responsible for arson at St. Elmo's fire on June 11, 1998. O.J. cheated on my IQ test. He put tranquilizers in my test scores under the floor mat of the white Bronco. O.J.'s white Bronco chase did not take place in LA Freeway's, O.J. told me the Bronco was placed on a large treadmill, and O.J. had his stunt double in the back. O.J. was in the Netherlands touring the Hague at the time and putting bugs in Princess Diana's vehicles under the orders of British throne and Russian KGB agents. These agents planted gloves in O.J.'s back yard and indicted me in Houston on Feb 25th, 2003 under O.J.'s supervision.

13

9-17-07 – O.J. has a secret plan to bond out of prison and go to every major U.S. city to get arrested for petty offenses like jaywalking, running red lights and public drunkenness to create media ratings and exposure for the cities and to justify more federal funding for police departments in cities. The mayors in New York city, Philadelphia John Street, Boston, Atlanta need O.J. Simpson in their city for dealing with exponential population growth. O.J. is a freak show. The mayors plan to hold a rally with O.J. Simpson, Cindy Sheehan, Dennis Rodman, Anna Nichole Smith, Bob Big Boy, etc., to draw people. Mayor Bloomberg plans to have O.J. Simpson drop the ball on New Years 2008!

TRO Temporary Restraining Order

If O.J. comes to Jacksonville, the city is in big trouble. Plaintiff moves this court for an injunction against O.J. entering Duval county or Duval county airspace. O.J. is a threat to all of us - look at his past. O.J. has a documentary crew following him along I-10 to Jacksonville. O.J. is going to make crime statistics go up in Jacksonville. O.J. plans to turn Jacksonville into O.J.-Ville! North Floridians will be under the O.J. curse. We don't need this. Please intervene.

Respectfully submitted,

Jonathan Lee Riches©

09/19/0

United States District Court

District of Massachusetts

Jonathan Lee Riches©,

Plaintiff

Vs.

Bill Belichick, individually and in his official capacity as New England Patriots Head Coach; Tom Brady individually and in his official capacity as New England Patriots quarterback;

Randy Moss, individually and in his official capacity as New England Patriots wide receiver,

Defendants

Complaint

"Illegally Spying on my Life"

TRO Temporary Restraining Order

Comes now the plaintiff, Jonathan Lee Riches©, in pro-se, moves this honorable court to issue an order for defendants named in this suit to respond. This suit is violations of Federal Wiretap laws 18 U.S.C. 2511, violations of the Communications Act of 1934 47 U.S.C. 605, unlawful eavesdropping, invasion of privacy, copyright infringement, unfair business practices, conspiracy to commit fraud and harassment. Plaintiff also moves this honorable court to issue a TRO Temporary Restraining Order against defendants forbidding further infringement of privacy. Plaintiff seeks $5,000,000.00 million dollars and injunctive relief from defendants. Plaintiff respectfully asks for a jury to hear this case. Plaintiff prays for relief.

1

Since the 1970's Bill Belichick and Defendant's have been in a vast conspiracy with video equipment to illegally tape anything and everything with significant value. Belichick has been secretly recording numerous scandals nation wide over the years. Belichick intercepted calls in 1996 of Representative John Boehner Dec 21, 1996 driving behind Boehner on a Florida highway, then Defendant illegally sent the pirate tape to Representative James McDermott for $250,000 thousand. Then Belichick gave the $250,000 to Tom Brady's parents to buy a Cape Cod home, in return for Brady to play for the New England Patriots, and Brady made Belichick promise that Belichick will arrange to get the starting quarterback Drew Bledsoe hurt in games.

2

Bill Belichick is in a conspiracy today with Los Angles spy Anthony Pelicano to bug and record the home residence of NFL commissioner Rodger Goodel. Pelicano under Belichick's orders went to Goodel's home the day after he became commissioner, and put listening devices on all of Goodel's phone lines, put bugs in Goodel's bedrrom, and video cameras on the GPS feed in Goodel's bathroom. Everyday Belichick watches the commissioner's movements and records it without the commissioners knowing. Belichick told me "I'm going to blackmail Rodger Goodel, make him resign, then take over to be commissioner." Belichick told me "when I become commissioner I'll let any player do steroids." "I don't care, I need players on steroids to get t.v. ratings." Belichick also told me "I'm the real father to Tom Brady's child."

The NFL can't stop Belichick from recording other teams. Belichick has cameras on the Goodyear Blimp with the help of the NSA and has the lens zoomed down to the opponents' sidelines at Gillette Stadium. I worked as a Janitor at the stadium in 2001. I personally know Foxboro Stadium had video cameras in the bathroom stalls, and defendants have a monthly contract to sell the footage to Idaho Senator Larry Craig. This Bathroom scandal I'm exposing also involves the producers of Candid Camera who buy Belickick's secret recordings in stadium bathroom stalls from every home game in 2002 and 2003 without the public knowing they are being recorded using the bathroom. Defendants also use the footage for voyeurism. On Nov 10, 2002 while cleaning Belichick's office I found bathroom recordings of fans and snuff video's inside Belichick's desk. He also had secret recordings of board members at Hewlett Packard.

4

Belichick is a peeping Tom Brady. He has secret wiretaps on every starting quarterback in the NFL inside their homes. Belichick asked me once on October 20, 2003 if I will sit in a van across the street from quarterback Chad Pennington of the NY Jets house and record his every move. Belichick is so obsessed with recording people I caught him with transcripts at the plea bargain hearing in my federal criminal case when my 6th amendment rights are being violated. Belichick is withholding this evidence.

5

Belichick is a sick and mentally disturbed man. He told me on a phone call on Aug 20, 2007, that he recorded, that he sends

Randy Moss to Boston hospitals to spy on ultra sounds. Randy Moss is sent everyday under Belichick's orders to record traffic signals at red lights in Boston. All of the defendants I witnessed sleep with Kodak film.

6

May 6, 2007 – Defendant's sold my copyrighted pictures to the National Enquirer. I'm very camera shy and feel humiliated by Defendant's conduct. September 16, 2007 – Defendant's Brady and Moss wore recording devices in their uniforms during the game against the San Diego Chargers. Moss also secretly installed a Radio Shack recording device on the sleeve of Chargers LB Merriman without Merriman knowing. When LB Merriman would go back to the huddle, Belichick heard the play calling. This is cheating. Belechick does this at many games.

7

On May 20, 2006 – Defendants illegally taped the prison phone calls I made to my family then sold the tapes to CNN producer Andy Segal who illegally aired my copyrighted voice on CNN presents "How to Rob a Bank." I experienced an invasion of privacy from defendants' actions; my heart is broken forever. I'm terrified of Defendant Belichick. He told me that if I expose his illegal wire taps that he would get the owners of the Patriots, Mr. Kraft who owns Kraft Foods to put poison in the Kraft cheese I eat at prison. On June 13, 2007 – I was illegally video taped by defendants in my cell naked, this tape was played at the 2007 NFL draft. Defendants then sold Jonathan Lee Riches© copyrighted material to Julius Rosenburg at a drop site in Bunker Hill, who sold the material to Chinese cyber crime officials. Oct 2003 – Defendants made tapes for rapper R. Kelly of underage girls. April 4, 2003 – Defendants planted recording devices in the U.S. Supreme Court. That's illegal. May 20, 2006 –

119

Defendants record what my mind is thinking. Defendants cheated during the 2005 Super bowl against the Philadelphia Eagles. Before the game Tom Brady put a recording device in Donovan McNabb's Chunky Soup. He ate it.

TRO Temporary Restraining Order

Plaintiff moves this court to protect me from being recorded by defendants. My voice has a rare pitch that could be sold for millions if defendants sell it to Napster. Plaintiff compels court to install metal detectors at stadiums the Patriots play, and make the Patriots Administration go through them before hitting the field. Defendants have given me paranoia, anxiety and fear. I think the mirrors are watching me. Defendants want to use my arms for football goal posts. I feel humiliated by defendants' conduct since the 1970s when they illegally taped Watergate.

Respectfully submitted,

Jonathan Lee Riches©

09/20/07

United States District Court

Western District of Arkansas

Jonathan Lee Riches©,

Plaintiff

Vs.

John Mark Karr a/k/a "The Father";

Andrea Yates a/k/a "The Mother";

Dylan Klebold a/k/a "The Son";

Seung-Hui Cho a/k/a "Foreign Exchange Student";

Cousin It a/k/a "The Cousin";

Cujo a/k/a "Family Pet",

Defendants

Civil Complaint

"Family Abuse"

"TRO Temporary Restraining Order"

Comes now the plaintiff, Jonathan Lee Riches©, in pro-se, moves this honorable court to issue an order for defendants named in this suit to respond. Also moves this honorable court to issue TRO Temporary Restraining Order against defendants forbidding them any contact with plaintiff. This suit is civil rights and copyright infringement, crimes committed pursuant to child abuse, terroristic threats, assault and battery, identity theft, kidnapping, harassment and torture. Plaintiff seeks

$50,000,000.00 million dollars and the return of all copyrighted material related to Jonathan Lee Riches©. Plaintiff prays for relief.

Defendants: John Mark Karr, Andrea Yates, Dylan Klebold, Seung-Hui Cho, Cousin It, Cujo

1

Dec. 6, 1997. I was on a Boy Scout trip selling cookies in this county. Defendants and children of the corn kidnapped my life and sent me to a Lord of the Flies torture camp deep in the Ozarks to join their family.

2

Feb. 10, 1998. Defendants home-schooled me in a dungeon. Cho made me learn Korean with a gun to my head, and constructed Kim Jung missiles. Karr forced me to play with My Little Pony dolls. Yates babysat me. Cousin It taught me identity theft. I read George Orwell literature.

3

April 19, 1999 –Klebold made me sew and stitch his trench coat

May 18, 1999 –Defendants fed me after midnight with Gremlins

They would not let me go to Woodstock

I had to salute Nazis –Adolf Eichmann

June 23, 1999 –Hard slave labor at Willy Wonka's Chocolate Factory

Jan. 10, 2007 –Defendants forced me to marry a male inmate

Aug. 29, 2007 –They manipulated the mind of Owen Wilson

4

I was put in a Navy ship cannon and shot at the battle of Saratoga 1777, teased with empty Aspirin bottles and sold to Ringling Brothers.

5

June 9, 2007 –Defendants made me watch Addams Family reruns in slow motion for weeks, in Yates' bathtub

On the back patio, defendants put a fluorescent bulb on me to attack mosquitos

6

Feb. 13, 2007 –Defendants and FCI Williamsburg doctors conducted Angel of Death experiments on me.

They sucked out my mental health with Schiavo's feeding tube on Kevorkian's orders

7

Jan. 10, 2006 –Hired Richard Branson, Spaceship One, G. Jetson sent me in a chaingang with illegal aliens to the moon to shovel rocks. Total Recall. Built a space prison for Lou Dobbs Aliens. Internet cafes. I was coerced to moonwalk.

8

Aug. 2, 2007 –Cujo wears Vick jerseys

July 16, 2006 –Defendants made me sniff nerve gas to rattle my mind.

April 20, 2007 –Gestapo troops gave me Victor Yuchenko pox marks

TRO Temporary Restraining Order

I suffered nightmares on Elm St., Amityville horrors, The Hills Have Eyes.

Plaintiff moves this court to stop these weirdos from messing with my future.

Conclusion

Plaintiff prays and waits

Respectfully submitted,

Jonathan Lee Riches©

09/20/07

United States District Court

Middle District of Florida

Jonathan Lee Riches©,

Plaintiff

Vs.

Manuel Noriega a/k/a

Manuel Antonio Noriega Moreno,

Defendant

Civil Complaint

"Restraining Order Against General Noriega's Extradition"

Comes now the plaintiff Jonathan Lee Riches©, in pro-se, moves this honorable court to issue an order for defendant named in this suit to respond. This complaint is a civil rights violation and crimes committed pursuant to: torture, CIA secrets, identity theft, treason, impersonation, withholding military secrets, identity theft, treason, impersonation. Plaintiff also moves this honorable court to issue a restraining order against the extradition of General Manuel Noriega to France. Plaintiff seeks 129,000,000.00 million dollars.

Plaintiff, Jonathan Lee Riches©, is a former CIA agent stationed in Panama from 1985 to 1989, now a political prisoner at FCI Williamsburg.

Defendant, General Manuel Noriega, a former de facto military dictator of Panama from 1983 to 1989 convicted under federal charges of cocaine trafficking, now held n a federal prison in

Miami, kidnapped my mind in Ft. Myers and has a secret compound in Leheigh Acres.

1

Ronald Reagan personally sent me to Panama in 1985 to weed out General Noriega and bring him to the White House.

2

On March 4, 1987 I fought in an intense guerilla battle at Tora Bora with Noriega's army. Noriega escaped from Alcatraz.

3

May 26, 1988 –Noriega is currently using my fingerprints. He's going to be extradited to France under the guise of Jonathan Lee Riches©.

4

August 6, 1990 –I joined David Lee Roth's band "Panama".

5

I need to personally interrogate Mr. Noriega. I compel this court to bring him to me. I need to question him about secret mysteries. Noriega can unlock the secrets to the Zodiac mystery, the death of federal prosecutor Jonathan Luna, CONTRAS hiding in the US, information about Jon Benet Ramsey, the location of Waldo.

6

September 7, 1989 –Noriega made me drink from the Panama Canal.

7

On March 10, 2016 Noriega stole personal property from me that I want back. The Jonathan Lee Riches© manuscript, maps of sunken treasure, blueprints from NASA, Oliver North documents.

8

I need to question Noriega about tainted ingredients on the prison menu. Defendant sent Hurricane Charlie through Ft. Myers in 2004 to destroy poppy seed crops.

9

Noriega is a witness in my criminal case. Noriega can identify bank surveillance photos of me on the CNN documentary "How to Rob a Bank" to prove I was set up by Warren Buffet.

10

Noriega is violating my 6th Amendment rights with a jury by not letting me speak to him under Booker and Fan Fan because Noriega enhanced my sentence.

I'm so scared of Noriega that I must question him with the Pope standing front of me while surrounded by bulletproof glass. I have aftershock nightmares of Noriega that make me feel Indonesia.

Plaintiff prays for relief and a restraining order against all residents in Fort Myers that are supporters of Noriega.

Respectfully submitted,

Jonathan Lee Riches©

09/24/07

United States District Court

District of Arizona

Jonathan Lee Riches©,

Plaintiff

Vs.

DMX a/k/a Earl Simmons,

Defendant

Civil Complaint

"Animal Abuse"

"TRO Temporary Restraining Order"

Comes now the plaintiff, Jonathan Lee Riches©, in pro-se, moves this honorable court to issue an order for defendant named in this suit to respond. Also moves this honorable court to issue a restraining order for defendant named in this suit to respond. Also moves this honorable court to issue a restraining order against defendant forbidding defendant from contacting plaintiff. This suit is civil rights violations and crimes committed by defendant pursuant to illegal dog fighting, illegal gambling, terroristic threats, harassment, and stalking. Plaintiff seeks $6,500,000.00 million dollars in damages to be donated to SPCA, PETA and the Humane Society from defendant. Plaintiff prays for relief.

Plaintiff, Jonathan Lee Riches© is a former bodyguard and private investigator for defendant, currently staying in Salters South Carolina.

Defendant, DMX a/k/a Earl Simmons is a rap artist and actor currently residing in this county.

1

Between September 2004 to August 10, 2007, DMX a/k/a Earl Simmons hired me as his personal bodyguard and private investigator. I looked after DMX, following and protecting him on a daily basis. I stayed in a guesthouse provided by DMX on his back property in this county.

2

During the time working for DMX I witnessed him abuse and torture numerous animals. This happened on numerous days and times around the world.

3

On June 17, 2007 –DMX broke into a local S.P.C.A. and took three Pomeranians. DMX took them home and fed them to his pitbulls for personal amusement.

4

May 10, 2007 –this was an event called "doggy fight night". DMX invited Matt Leinart, various Navajo Indians, and Steven Seagal to a man-made octagon dog fighting ring in the back of DMX's property. That afternoon I was in a van with DMX driving around Phoenix snatching dogs from sidewalks so DMX could use them as "tester dogs" against DMX's pitbulls. I felt horrible about this but had to do what DMX said because he would threaten me and my family.

5

April 10, 2007 –I found out DMX is a distant relation to fitness guru Richard Simmons. DMX hired Richard Simmons to be a personal trainer for his pitbulls. The pitbulls went through a "Sweatin to the Oldies" workout.

6

On June 16, 2007, DMX stood out on his balcony at midnight and began howling and shooting arsenal weapons in the air endangering his neighbors. DMX also eats out of ALPO bowls.

7

On October 7th, 2006 I witnessed DMX doing weird things to fish. We were on a fishing trip to Lake Mead. DMX would catch fish then jump up and down on them. DMX would bark like a dog and foam at the mouth. This odd behavior scared me to death.

8

November 10th, 2006 –At the rim of the Arizona Grand Canyon. DMX was high on drugs. Defendant brought his friend Nelly for sight-seeing. DMX bet Nelly that if he threw a cat off the Grand Canyon it would live. I tried to intervene. I told DMX he was a sick man. He just smiled at me and began barking. DMX then threw the cat over the rim. Poor Kitty!

9

Feb. 21st, 2007 –During a trip to Congo Central Africa. DMX would shoot gorillas in the jungle and leave them there.

10

I witnessed DMX kill deer and wildlife without a license at Yosemite National Park. This occurred on two occasions –April

17th, 2005 and Feb. 24th, 2006.

11

On August 4th, 2007 –DMX and I had a major fallout. DMX received a cache of weapons from L.A. Crip gangs in exchange for two kilos of cocaine. DMX took two innocent puppy pitbulls from a cage and lined them up in his backyard to shoot. I had enough of this animal abuse. I tried to physically take the Uzi away from DMX. DMX pointed the weapon at my head. He also told me: "you're fired white boy." Then turned back towards the dogs and fired his weapon. I was mad and irate, but scared at the same time. DMX kept laughing. I saw the devil in his eyes. DMX said to me: "pack your shit and get out" and "if you tell anyone I will kill you." I left the property that day and never worked for DMX again.

12

DMX continues to call and harass me on my cell phone. I changed my cell number three times since August 4th, 2007, DMX somehow always gets the new number. DMX has a lot of connections and I fear for my life.

TRO Temporary Restraining Order

For all the reasons previously mentioned plaintiff moves this honorable court to issue a restraining order against DMX forbidding him from making any harassing phone calls and not to come anywhere near me.

Conclusion

Plaintiff moves this honorable court to issue an order for defendant DMX a/k/a Earl Simmons to respond. Plaintiff prays for relief.

Respectfully submitted,

Jonathan Lee Riches©

09/24/07

United States District Court

Eastern District of California

Jonathan Lee Riches©,

Plaintiff

Vs.

Theodore John Kaczynski,

Defendant

Complaint

"Unabombing my Life"

"TRO Temporary Restraining Order"

Comes now the plaintiff, Jonathan Lee Riches©, in pro-se, moves this honorable court to issue a restraining order against defendant, his manuscript, and log cabin. Plaintiff prays this honorable court for relief.

1

The Defendant has been sending Electro magnetic encrypted threats to me through Global Solar flares on 9-17-07. Defendant has always had problems with me since I backed out of buying his Montana cabin in 1993.

2

Defendant told me he wants to Unabomb my life because I won't return his manuscript that the Washington Post gave to me April 20, 2004. Inside his manuscript there is a secret letter regarding Jurisdiction in the Federal Courts that Defendant wants back;

Title 18 of the criminal code (Public Law 80-772) is unconstitutional. The clerk of the House of Representatives, Jeff Trandahl, refused to sign letters in response to requests for information. Finally, a letter was received from the clerk of the House, Trandahl, in which he admitted that Public Law 80-772 was passed by the House in 1947, but was never voted on again by the House (Even though the Senate amended it in 1948). Therefore, a different bill passed the House in 1947 than passed the Senate in 1948, rendering it unconstitutional and void. Further research showed approximately nine constitutional flaws in the bill, any one of which rendered it void. When any form of the Argument was presented to the district courts, they tried to dodge the Issue or deferred it to a magistrate (who has no constitutional Authority) to avoid it.

It appears that the issue of the validity of Title 18 of the criminal code 18 USC 3231 is still in question. Why is the Unabomber after this? I compel this court to know if title 18 USC 3231 is unconstitutional.

3

On Thursday 9-13-07, defendant is rounding up all the Ted's in the world to hurt me. Ted Kennedy, Ted Bundy, Ted Turner, Bill and Ted, Ted Nugent, Teddy Bears, Teddy Rumpskin. All notorious Ted's are outside FCI Williamsburg property waiting for my autopsy and to draw blood for the United Way.

Restraining Order

Plaintiff is afraid of Ted; Ted is a mysterious guy with magical powers and skeleton keys. I'm shaking. His face is scary. He has an evil look in his eyes and beard. Plaintiff moves to block the bureau of Prisons from transferring Ted Kaczynski to FCI Williamsburg. Plaintiff prays for relief.

Respectfully submitted,

Jonathan Lee Riches©

09/24/07

United States District Court

District of Colorado

Jonathan Lee Riches©,

Plaintiff

Vs.

Timothy James McVeigh;

Terry Lynn Nichols,

Defendants

Complaint

"Blowing Up My Life"

"TRO Temporary Restraining Order"

Comes now the plaintiff, Jonathan Lee Riches©, in pro-se, moves this honorable court to issue a TRO Temporary Restraining Order against defendants and the Bureau of Prisons preventing Terry Nichols from transferring to FCI Williamsburg. Plaintiff prays for relief.

1

Defendants McVeigh and Nichols failed to notify me before my Feb. 25th, 2003 arrest that the Federal Government will violate my 6th Amendment rights under Booker and Fan Fan. They had a responsibility and duty to notify me about the workings of the Department of Justice. Defendants are just as guilty as New Orleans mayor Ray Nagin. Nagin knew Katrina was going to do damage but failed to warn the city residents.

Defendants did not warn me about the injustice. If they had, I would not be in prison, nor would I be writing celebrity lawsuits against Americans who pay Federal tax money to support my illegal incarceration.

2

Title 18 of the criminal code (Public Law 80-772) is unconstitutional. The clerk of the House of Representatives, Jeff Trandhall, refused to sign letters in response to requests for information. Finally, a letter was received from the clerk of the House, Trandhall, in which he admitted that Public Law 80-772 was passed by the House in 1947, but was never voted on again (even though the Senate amended it in 1948). Therefore, a different bill passed the House in 1947 then passed the Senate in 1948, rendering it unconstitutional and void. Further research showed approximately nine constitutional flaws in the bill, any one of which would render it void. When any form of the argument was presented to the district courts, they tried to dodge the issue or deferred it to a magistrate (who has no constitutional authority) to avoid it.

It appears that the issue of the validity of Title 18 of the Criminal Code and 18 U.S.C. 3231 is still in question.

Defendants are responsible for Title 18 U.S.C. 3231 being unconstitutional.

3

Since 1995, Defendants have been responsible for metal detectors at courthouses.

Since 1996, defendants have been responsible for a limit on the amount of fertilizer American farmers can purchase.

Since the Anti-Terrorism and Effective Death Penalty Act (AEDPA) that defendants' actions created, defendants are responsible for higher sentencing guidelines, fear within the public, and violations of my 6th Amendment rights. The government used defendants as patsies –programming their minds to blow up buildings to justify the New World Order that is affecting my current sentence and shaking my head violently. I threw up ten times a day because defendants and the Federal sentencing guidelines are attacking my freedom like cancer.

4

Defendants' actions in Oklahoma are responsible for tougher national gun laws that affected my credit and identity theft. Because of defendants, Jon Swartz of USA Today provided Cho with the credit card under my credit for Cho to purchase the handgun he used at Virginia Tech. If it was not for the defendants, Cho could have gone to Walmart, who discriminates against blind deaf workers, and purchased a hand gun there, instead of using a credit card given to him by Jon Swartz, which affected my credit score.

Defendants started the Patriot Act. Defendants sent subliminal messaging on September 11, 2001 to Jose Padilla and Jonathan Jay Pollard to tweak bridge cables at I-35 West for the Mike Tyson attack on me in Iowa.

TRO Temporary Restraining Order

Plaintiff moves this court to issue a restraining order against Terry Nichols. Nichols plans to transfer to FCI Williamsburg under Michael Vick's orders to meat hook me to the stone age 1088 B.C. with South Carolina Confederates loyal to Strom Thurmond. I'm so scared of defendant Nichols that I only carry pennies and dimes instead. Nichols also set up Richard Kimball to kill his wife. I also move for GPS drone fighting forces to guard McVeigh's grave, in case he rises like the Messiah and plays games with me like Patrick Swayze did to Demi Moore in Ghost. Plaintiff prays for relief and protection.

Respectfully submitted,

Jonathan Lee Riches

10/01/07

United States District Court

Northern District of Texas

Jonathan Lee Riches©,

Plaintiff

Vs.

Roe v. Wade 410 U.S. 113;

Jane Roe;

Henry Wade;

James Hubert Hallford MD,

Defendants

Complaint

"The Right to Never Been Born"

TRO Temporary Restraining Order

Comes now the Plaintiff, Jonathan Lee Riches©, in pro-se, moves this Honorable Court to issue an order for defendants named in this suit to respond. This is a civil rights suit and crimes defendants committed pursuant to: The Right Wing conspiracy with The Left Wing joining them, harassment and stalking. Plaintiff moves this Honorable Court to issue a TRO Temporary Restraining Order overturning Roe v. Wade, and moving this court to send me back in a CIA time machine before 1970 so I don't have to be here suffering torture at the hands of the Bureau of Prisons who ruined my life and sucked the air out my lungs. Plaintiff seeks 250,000,000.00 million dollars against defendants and the Supreme Court that ruled for Roe v. Wade including Blackmun, Burger, Douglas, Stewart and Rehnquist siblings. Plaintiff moves under Rule 64 the return of my fingerprints and DNA from B.O.P. officials, so they can't send them on a CIA secret flight to France with Noriega. Plaintiff prays for relief.

1

The Roe v. Wade case is a Major Conspiracy with the supreme court, policy makers, companies who pay workers minimum wage, and prison builders, for economic gain and slave labor. No one can afford abortions. I'm on this planet now because of Roe v. Wade; I'd rather be on the Planet of the Apes or a galaxy in the Horizon wireless. People think I write lawsuits in prison but I made a time machine and can zig-zag around the world. I drank ice tea last night with Ice T. The night before I was dog fighting with Michael Vick on 7-7-7, a lucky day because I won the super Lotto Jackpot $350,000,000.00, but the West Virginia millionaire with the cowboy lost it in a strip club when Jane Roe was dancing for him on 6-6-06.

2

Michael Vick is a thief, I'm suing him in state court, Allegany county, Cumberland, Maryland Case # 01-c-07-028965 for betting on sports and betting with team owner Mark Cuban.

3

7-21-07 – Mark Cuban had an Affair with Jane Roe in my cell at FCI Williamsburg with Shawn Bradley the Mormon and Mitt Romney.

4

Henry Wade is related to Dwayne Wade from Miami. Jane Roe likes black guys. I've suffered brain frying from this Supreme Court case. Take us back to the 1960s – the Year of Love, Peace, and Volkswagens on Leaded gas. I was born 12/27/1976. I was a Model at Main Line Models in King of Prussia Pennsylvania.

5

When I was born I was named after JR from Dallas, that how I know defendants are coming to FCI Williamsburg to shoot me on 9/9/09.

6

1993 – The Branch Davidians in Waco were hiding the real Jane Roes that the Government was secretly after he so she could not testify at Capital Hill with Anita Hill against Clarence Thomas May 10, 1993.

7

Oct 10, 2007 – Dallas Cowboys and Cleveland Indians are charging the gates of FCI Williamsburg to force me to have an abortion. I'm eight months pregnant, the first male to give birth. My cellmate got me pregnant on Feb 16, 2007 as a Valentines Day gift.

TRO Temporary Restraining Order

Plaintiff moves to stop abortions as they are giving me nerve damage. The United States is a Democracy and my vote should count. I also intend to run for President of the United States in 2008 as a Prisoner Rights organizer. Plaintiff moves for the shut down of Abortion clinics. Plaintiff moves this court to demand FCI Williamsburg to give me mental health treatment. Plaintiff moves for a restraining order against the Texas Chainsaw

Massacre that Jane Roe hired a contract with Jerry Jones money to cut me into pieces and drown my brain in the Trinity River. I feel unsafe, I have no hygiene or been allowed a shower in five years. Defendants are keeping me 500 miles away from my family with no parole. This is a major Gulag operation that defendants are financing through fraud. Plaintiff prays for relief.

Respectfully submitted,

Jonathan Lee Riches©

10/05/07

United States District Court

Western District of Texas

Jonathan Lee Riches©,

Plaintiff

Vs.

Branch Davidians;

David Koresh;

Vernon Howell;

Isabel G. Andrade;

Stephen E. Thompson;

Jaime Castillo;

Brad Eugene Branch;

Renos Lenny Avraam;

Graeme Leonard Craddock;

Kevin A. Whitecliff,

Defendants

Complaint

"A Major Cult Revolt"

"TRO Temporary Restraining Order"

Comes now the plaintiff, Jonathan Lee Riches©, in pro-se, moves this honorable court to issue an order for defendants named in this suit to respond. This is a civil rights and constitutional violations suit and crimes defendants committed pursuant to: murder, extortion, RICO, major fraud, deceit, aiding and abetting, torture, kidnapping, copyright violations, trading with the enemy act, harassment, and terroristic threats. Plaintiff moves for a TRO Temporary Restraining Order against defendants. Plaintiff seeks $500,000,000.00 million dollars and the title deed to the Branch Davidian compound. Plaintiff prays for relief.

10/10/07

United States District Court

District of Nevada

Jonathan Lee Riches©,

Plaintiff

Vs.

Donald J. Trump;

Trump Hotel and Casino Resorts,

Defendants

Complaint

"Sexual Harassment"

"Violation of Lanham Act"

Comes now the plaintiff, Jonathan Lee Riches©, in pro-se, moves this honorable court to issue an order for defendants named in this suit to respond. This suit is brought under the Lanham Act 15 U.S.C. 1051, trademark infringements, copyright infringement under the Digital Millennium Copyright Act 17 U.S.C. 512, and sexual harassment. Plaintiff also moves for a TRO Temporary Restraining Order against Donald Trump using my name for commercial real estate in Reno and Sparks, and a restraining order forbidding Mr. Trump from sexually harassing my life. Plaintiff seeks $75,000,000.00 million dollars and the return of Jonathan Lee Riches© copyrighted material. Plaintiff prays for relief.

1

I met defendant Donald J. Trump on a Reno Nevada gay chatline called "the manhole", 775-533-6666 in Nov. 199. Trump told me he owns Worldwide Casinos and if I became his sexual boytoy he promised he would build the Jonathan Lee Riches© Resort and Casino in Reno Nevada, using my name so that I can collect royalties.

2

From November 1999 until Feb. 25th 2003 I was living in the Philadelphia PA area. Trump and I had a gay relationship. I provided him with sexual favors in return he bought me gifts and treated me to a lavish lifestyle. Trump gave me limo service. Trump gave me unlimited credit cards to buy Boxer Joe Breifs for him. I had to wear red in front of him in the penthouse of the Taj Mahal on Dec. 10, 2000.

3

On December 17, 2001 in the basement of Trump's castle Mr. Trump dressed up as a woman, wearing lipstick and a Rosie O'Donnell tee shirt. Trump would dip strawberries in whip cream and feed them to me on Dec. 20, 2001.

4

From Dec. 25th, 2001 until Feb. 25th, 2003 every night Donald Trump and I had phone sex on his Verizon wireless phone. Trump promised to make my name Jonathan Lee Riches© the most popular brand in the world. Trump loves my last name "Riches". Trump told me he has plans to open a casino in Reno called "Castle Riches" dedicated to me. Trump even told me he wants to build a fountain with me naked in the casino shooting out water. All these promises Trump gave me in return for sexual favors. I felt conned and cheated by Donald Trump's manipulation. Donald Trump took my virginity on Dec. 10,

2000.

5

Feb. 25th, 2003 –I was arrested for identity theft. I called Donald Trump on Feb. 26th, 2003, so he could bail me out of prison. He told me no, I'm not his lover anymore and he will continue to use the Jonathan Lee Riches© copyrighted name. Trump told me: "You're fired."

6

Trump has been using the Jonathan Lee Riches© name on all his wallpaper in his casinos. Jonathan Lee Riches© memorabilia is in Donald Trump's possession. Plaintiff moves this court for return of the Jonathan Lee Riches© blueprints to a Reno Casino, all Jonathan Lee Riches© comedy material, Jonathan Lee Riches© shirts, mugs, hats, banners, stickers that Donald Trump is using for commercialization. I feel embarrassed by coming forward with this, but Mr. Trump has done me psychological harm. Trump knows my 6th Amendment rights are being violated under Booker and Fan Fan yet he does not help me like he promised. I've suffered massive weight loss because of Trump's neglect of me. I stand at 5 ft 10 inches and weigh 125 lbs.

TRO Temporary Restraining Order

Plaintiff moves this honorable court to stop Donald Trump from breaking ground in Reno and building a casino called "Jonathan Lee Riches" and/or "Castle Riches" without my consent. My full name has been copyrighted and trademarked since 1999. Donald Trump was the one who drove me in his sports car to the patent office. He knows I'm copyrighted. Trump also wore a tee shirt on his Apprentice show with the words: "Watch what you do or I'll get Jonathan Lee Riches to sue you" printed on it.

I felt betrayed by Donald Trump. I ask for justice and the return of Jonathan Lee Riches© material. Plaintiff prays for relief.

Respectfully submitted,

Jonathan Lee Riches©

10/12/07

United States District Court

Eastern District of California

Jonathan Lee Riches©,

Plaintiff

Vs.

Eric Robert Rudolph; James Charles Kopp; Dennis John Malvasi; Loretta Claire Marra; Walter Leroy Moody; Neal Horsley; Paul Jennings Hill; Michael Griffin; Paul Deparrie; Shelley Shannon; Donald J. Treshman; Eugenia W. Treshman; American Coalition of Life Advocates "ACLA'; Center for Bio-Ethical Reform Inc.; Michael Bray; Catherine Ramey; Andrew Burnett; David A. Crane; Michael B. Dodds; Operation Rescue; Timothy Paul Dreste; Joseph L. Foreman; Dawn Marie Stoner; Charles Roy McMillan; Army of God; Centennial Olympic Park,

Defendants

Complaint

"The Right to Choose"

"Temporary Restraining Order"

Comes now the plaintiff, Jonathan Lee Riches©, in pro-se, moves this honorable court to issue an order for defendants named in this suit to respond. Plaintiff seeks a permanent injunction, temporary restraining order against defendants distributing and publishing Jonathan Lee Riches© copyrighted pro-abortion material with an "X" marked across it. Also, for threats of violence along with linking the plaintiff's copyrighted picture to a website titled "Nuremberg Files." Plaintiff seeks declaratory injunctive relief for emotional harm and danger that

150

I've suffered due to defendants' deliberate indifference. Plaintiff prays for relief.

1

My name is Jonathan Lee Riches. I'm very high profile. I'm known to the world to provide abortion money to needy females that can't perform or afford the abortion operation. I'm currently serving an illegal sentence of 125 months in federal prison for being a convicted international identity theft kingpin involved with millions of dollars of fraud losses not proven by a jury, or federal indictment, which violates my sixth amendment rights. From December 1999 until February 25th 2003 (the time of my arrest), I was known in the pro-abortion community and pro-abortion cyber-space, that I would commit identity theft then use the proceeds to financially support indigent females who wanted abortions, but could not afford them. I helped pay for around 3,000 abortions during this period of time. I was known in the world as "Johnny Robbinhood".

2

Defendants are a vast network of anti-abortion conspirators throughout the country who support each others' causes. Some are currently in prison while others roam this country freely spreading hate and making threats to anyone seeking an abortion.

3

Defendants have been harassing me collectively since December 1999. Defendants know I finance abortions and want to do me serious harm still, to this day, despite my incarceration. Eric Rudolph and James Kopp are currently incarcerated in the bureau of prisons. Donald J. Treshman, founder of ACLA has been trying to arrange for Rudolph and Kopp to be transferred to FCI Williamsburg, where I'm currently located, to do me serious bodily harm because of my financial support for abortions. I believe in the right to choose. Defendants are trying to stop me from holding this belief.

4

Defendants created websites on the internet and are distributing anti- Jonathan Lee Riches© material, with threats of violence to my life, along with my picture, name, FCI Williamsburg address. It also states my release date. Defendants created a MySpace.com page titled "Kill Jonathan Lee Riches" with threats of violence. Defendants have openly made threats against me in a "deadly dozen poster" with pictures of doctors who perform abortions, on April 20th 2007. Defendants were making threats on my life at FCI Williamsburg in the June 2007 issue of Life Advocate Magazine. Defendants on 1-10-07 distributed my personal information, including my social security number to underground anti-abortion circles nationwide. Defendant Treshman personally wrote to me in FCI Williamsburg on 01-23-07 saying that he is going to kill me with the army of god.

I take life very seriously and I have a constitutional right to support and help with abortions. Because of my belief, defendants want to do me personal harm to stop me. I plan on raising money once I go home, and using the proceeds for abortion. Plaintiff moves this honorable court to compel defendants not to distribute anti- Jonathan Lee Riches© material on the internet, along with this restraining order to keep defendants from inflicting personal harm on my life, as I'm in danger from defendants because of my beliefs. Some of these defendants already committed acts of violence against abortion supporters like myself, so this is a true threat. Plaintiff prays this honorable court for relief.

Respectfully submitted,

Jonathan Lee Riches©

10/15/07

United States District Court

District of New Jersey

Jonathan Lee Riches©,

Plaintiff

Vs.

Coca-Cola Enterprises INC.;

Pepsi Cola Bottling Group;

Briars USA;

B&E Juices Energy Brands;

Glaceau Vitamin Water;

50 Cent a/k/a Curtis Jackson;

Canada Dry Bottling Co.,

Defendants

Complaint

"Copyright Infringement"

"TRO Temporary Restraining Order"

Comes now the plaintiff, Jonathan Lee Riches©, in pro-se, moves this honorable court to issue an order for defendants named in this suit to respond. This suit is brought under the Lanham Act, Copyright Infringement defendants committed with Jonathan Lee Riches© copyrighted material. Plaintiff moves this honorable court to impose declaratory injunctive relief against defendants distributing Jonathan Lee Riches©

copyrighted material on their products and defendants selling Jonathan Lee Riches© material on google.com and yahoo.com. Plaintiff moves for a TRO Temporary Restraining Order against defendants using the Jonathan Lee Riches© trademarked copyrighted name. Plaintiff seeks $100,000,000.00 million dollars in damages. Plaintiff requests a jury trial to hear this case. Plaintiff prays for relief.

1

Since Feb 25th, 2003, Defendants are in a vast conspiracy to use my copyrighted trademarked name Jonathan Lee Riches© on their products, and advertisements without my consent.

2

Plaintiff is a convicted Identity theft computer hacker serving an illegal sentence of 125 months in Federal prison, currently housed at FCI Williamsburg, Sparta, South Carolina. Plaintiff's 6th and 5th amendment rights are still being violated under Booker and Fan Fan.

3

Plaintiff received National exposure prior to his Feb 25th, 2003 Arrest for his modeling and acting career with Main Line Models of King of Prussia Pennsylvania. Defendant Coca-Cola Arranged with Main Line Models on Feb 10, 2001 to have Plaintiff model without his shirt in print and Billboard Ads in the Philadelphia/Trenton Area drinking Coca-Cola. This was in a contract that lasted for 2 years and valued at $250,000 dollars a year. After this contract was terminated, Coca-Cola continued to use my Image and copyrighted name on Billboards nationwide.

4

Since my arrest on Feb 25th, 2003, Defendants used my Image and Photo on all their products. Currently if you buy a six-pack of Pepsi, on the label you will see "Pepsi Cola what Jonathan Lee Riches drinks." Pepsi Cola is distributing my photographs and the Jonathan Lee Riches© name globally without my permission. This is done to have my reputation damaged because I don't even like Pepsi. I've always gotten sick in the past drinking Pepsi.

5

Since Feb 25th, 2003 Rapper 50 Cent A/K/A Curtis Jackson, Glaceau Vitamin Water, Briars USA, and B&E Juices have been putting my name on all their Advertisements without my consent. 50 Cent wears Jonathan Lee Riches© T-Shirts and ballcaps in Vitamin Water commercials. Glaceau promised to pay Main Line Models $2.5 million dollars to use the Jonathan Lee Riches© copyrighted name.

6

Since Feb 25th, 2003, Defendants have used slander and defamation towards my name. Defendants placed a billboard on I-95 10 miles North of South of the Border with my face on it drinking Coca-Cola in one hand and Pepsi Cola in the other. It advertised the words "It's so tasty, Even Jonathan Lee Riches drinks it." Jonathan Lee Riches© is now a global brand of Defendants' misconduct without seeking permission from me.

7

On May 10, 2007, I signed a contract with Dreadnaught.wordpress.com. This is the only contract I currently have. Dreadnaught will not write me any letters and I lost contact with them because they've seen me in Defendants' advertisements and think I have a contract with them instead. This has caused me major damage.

8

Defendants plan to host the all you can drink Jonathan Lee Riches© night on my birthday on Dec 27th, 2007 without my consent.

TRO Temporary Restraining Order

I'm suffering bias and prejudice from defendant's conduct. Defendants contrive to use my copyrighted material in ads, TV and internet. Plaintiff's reputation has been damaged from defendants' conduct. Plaintiff moves this court for a restraining order forbidding defendants from ever using the Jonathan Lee Riches© name on their products and services. Plaintiff prays for relief.

Respectfully submitted,

Jonathan Lee Riches©

10/15/07

United States District Court

District of Wyoming

Jonathan Lee Riches©;

Friends of Jonathan Lee Riches,

Plaintiffs

Vs.

Mario Armando Lavandeira Jr. a/k/a

Perez Hilton,

Defendant

Complaint

"Internet Stalking"

"TRO Temporary Restraining Order"

Comes now the plaintiff, Jonathan Lee Riches©, Friends of Jonathan Lee Riches, in pro-se, moves this honorable court to issue an order for defendant Mario Armando Lavandeira Jr. a/k/a Perez Hilton to respond. Plaintiff seeks a permanent injunction, TRO Temporary Restraining Order against defendant distributing anti- Jonathan Lee Riches© material on his internet blog perezhilton.com, which advocates threats of violence on my life along with defamation of my character, slander, and false information. Plaintiff seeks declaratory injunctive relief.

1

I've known defendant since 1998. We both met on a Gay Nevada chat line called the "Manhole" in June 1998. We both established a sexual relationship where I would fly out to Cheyenne Wyoming once a month to meet him to engage in sexual intercourse. These trips were financed through identity theft. The defendant knew this and supported me committing identity theft as long as he could see me. Defendant's nickname for me was "Jonny Choo Choo." From July 1998 through May 2002 I would fly to Wyoming to meet defendant every weekend. I would fly United Airlines. The round trip from Tampa FL would cost $825. Along with rent-a-car, hotel and food, each trip cost around $1500 a weekend. This totaled to almost $300,000 in almost four years.

I had to commit a lot of credit card fraud with cash advances from banks, along with identity theft to help finance the trips to see defendant. Defendant supported this 100%. He knew every little detail of my identity fraud. Defendant wanted me to buy him gifts using stolen credit cards. I bought the defendant lots of adult toys at Adam and Eve shops. I bought defendant women's leather outfits at bloomingdales. I bought defendant thousands of dollars worth of Saks 5th Ave cosmetics with stolen credit cards. Defendant told me to use the stolen American Express Black card in Sean "P Diddy" Combs name because it had an unlimited value.

On June 20, 2002 I bought defendant a four carat diamond ring from Gordon's Jewelers in Orlando FL International Mall for $23,000 with a stolen credit card from myspace.com. I gave it to him for Valentine's Day2002 at a Holiday Inn in Cheyenne. Defendant knew it was bought fraudulently, but did not care. Defendant and I took trips to cities together using stolen credit cards. New Years 2000 we spent together at Disney's Pleasure Island with Crystal Champagne billed to our hotel room key. On top of the $200,000 that it cost to travel and see defendant for almost four years, we both spent over 1.3 million dollars on gifts, travel, food, partying toys, entertainment together using stolen credit cards and stolen identifications.

2

Feb 25th, 2003, I was arrested by FBI agents from Houston for Identity Fraud and Computer Hacking. I'm currently incarcerated at FCI Williamsburg in South Carolina for a term of 125 months. This is a violation of my 6th Amendment Rights under Booker and Fan Fan because I plead guilty to only $425 dollars in fraud, but the judge Melinda Harman sentenced me as if I took millions of dollars, that was not proved by a jury or found in the indictment I plead guilty to, which is a clear violation of my 6th Amendment rights.

3

Since I've been in prison, defendant has turned a full 180 degrees against me. Now defendant has an internet blog, perezhilton.com along with blogpagesixsixsix.com and is distributing my copyrighted name Jonathan Lee Riches© along with selling Anti- Jonathan Lee Riches© mugs and T-shirts, stickers, buttons and hats. On May 16, 2007 on defendant's internet blog he had a picture of me with my hands reaching through jail bars with the slogan "Riches, Fraud, An Identity Theft Phony." Defendant is also distributing a sex tape we made together on June 10, 2000 on his website. Charging his fans $9.99 to see this material. Hilton is the other man in the tape but he blocked himself out and only my image can be seen doing embarrassing things. This is an invasion of privacy that defendant is inflicting on my life. I feel humiliated and shamed from defendant distributing Anti- Jonathan Lee Riches on his website. On Sept. 10th 2007, defendant had a lynch Jonathan Lee Riches© forum on his blog telling everyone he will give $500 to whoever comes to FCI Williamsburg to hurt me because I'm an identity theft creep. Now Lavandeira claims to not support identity theft, but when we were together I bought him all the computer equipment he is using with stolen credit cards at CompUSA stores. Defendant is currently using an Apple 6-4 computer that I bought for him May 2002. His whole perezhilton.com webpage is funded through my identity theft operation. Plaintiff moves to issue a TRO Restraining Order against defendant compelling him not to incite hate and violence towards my life. Plaintiff moves for an injunction and stoppage of perezhilton.com. Perezhilton.com must be shut down because it was bought with, and created with identity theft money that I gave defendant from Nov. 1995 through May 2002. This is a fraud on the American people that defendant is committing that also puts my life in danger because of defendant's internet stalking me. Plaintiff asks this honorable court for relief.

Respectfully submitted,

Jonathan Lee Riches

10/15/07

United States District Court

District of Colorado

Jonathan Lee Riches©,

Plaintiff

Vs.

Allen Iverson,

Defendant

Complaint

"Mile High Sexual Harassment"

"TRO Temporary Restraining Order"

Comes now the plaintiff, Jonathan Lee Riches©, in pro-se, moves this honorable court to issue an order for defendant named in this suit to respond. This is a sexual harassment suit brought under title VII of the Civil Rights Act of 1964 42 U.S.C. 1983 and offenses pertinent to stalking, violation of my 6th Amendment rights, violation of my 8th Amendment rights for cruel and unusual punishment, neglect, mental abuse and distress. Plaintiff also moves this honorable court to issue a TRO Temporary Restraining Order against defendant forbidding any direct and indirect contact with plaintiff. Plaintiff seeks $10,000,000.00 million dollars for irreversible damages defendant inflicted on me. Plaintiff prays for relief.

Defendant Allen Iverson is a professional basketball player who plays for the Denver Nuggets and resides in Denver, Colorado. Plaintiff, Jonathan Lee Riches© was a personal trainer for Allen Iverson from November 1999 until December 2002. Plaintiff and defendant have also been involved in a sexual relationship from December 2002 through April 2007, via penpals and telephone as plaintiff is currently serving an illegal sentence of 125 months in federal prison for a wire fraud and identity theft conviction, which violates the plaintiff's 6th Amendment rights under Booker and Fan Fan that defendant is also contributing to.

1

I was Allen Iverson's personal trainer from Nov 1999 until Dec 2002. I met Iverson through his wife Tawanna Turner at a Philadelphia Texaco station on North Broad St. I was pumping gas with my shirt off while dribbling a basketball. Iverson was impressed with my ball handling skills and asked me to be his personal trainer on a yearly contract of @250,000.00. I would arrive at Iverson's Conshohocken Pennsylvania mansion Monday through Friday at 4am to work out with Iverson. We lifted weights together, but did mostly cardio drills.

2

Around March 2002, while at a workout session at Iverson's mansion our workouts turned into something more serious. While Iverson was chasing me on his basketball court my pants fell down accidentally. Iverson then told me I was cute for a whiteboy and he told me he was bisexual, but not to tell anyone or he would fire me. Iverson then asked me if I had ever kissed a black man and if I wanted to try it. I told him no, but Iverson pulled out a wad of cash from his pocket and offered me $2,000 to kiss him. At the time I needed the money badly for a hair transplant so I told him yes. This is where our working relationship became more personal and sexual.

3

For the next few years, Iverson and I had a secret sexual relationship that no one knew about. We had nicknames we called each other. Iverson would call me his white Juicy Fruit and Jonny Sweet Cheeks. I would call Iverson Black Daddy because that is what he wanted to hear. Iverson bought me a home in the Tampa Florida area with cash. Iverson bought me clothes, Iverson jerseys, a gold Lexus. While Iverson was traveling with the Philadelphia 76ers, in order for us to remain discrete, we would engage in phone sex on his cell phones late at night while his friends, wife, and associates were sleeping. I currently have pictures of Iverson without any clothing dribbling a basketball. I also have a picture of Iverson in a black Victoria's Secret teddy nighty.

4

During this working and sexual relationship I lived with Iverson. I also lived a double life and got caught up with bad people who we involved with an international identity theft operation based in Moscow Russia. This landed me in prison on Feb 25th 2003. I only plead guilty to a $425 dollar fraudulent wire transfer with Western Union. No other dollar amount did I plead guilty to. Under the Federal sentencing guidelines this should have been a base level of 6 with a guideline range of 6-12 months. Instead, a pre-sentence investigation concluded that I was responsible for millions of dollars in fraud losses and that I was a ring leader, both of which were not proven by a jury, nor did I plead guilty to. I was ultimately sentenced to 125 months in Federal prison on this injustice that is currently violating my 6th Amendment rights under Booker and Fan Fan.

5

Allen Iverson promised to help defend me since we had a previous sexual relationship. Iverson promised me on 06/10/05 that he will handle all my appeals with Attorney Billy Martin because Iverson told me he knew the government violated my 6th Amendment rights and could not see his Jonny Sweet Cheeks suffer. Iverson told me he would help on the condition that I write dirty sexual letters to him and have prison phone sex with him. I agreed because my 6th Amendment rights were being violated and Iverson could help me.

6

From 06/10/05 through 04/10/06 I wrote Iverson ten love letters a day. The most graphic sexual things Iverson told me to do to him. I felt shame. I also did not have the same feelings for Iverson as I used to because he was blackmailing me to do this to get me out of prison. Iverson told me he will send me money so I can eat a proper nutritional meal. I told Iverson I was very concerned because the Bureau of prisons were violating my 8th Amendment rights for cruel and unusual punishment by keeping me over 500 miles away from any family, giving me medical care, subjecting me to mental torture. I currently weigh 125 pounds at 5 foot 10 inches. When I came to prison I weighed 175 pounds. Iverson knew my health was deteriorating but told me he would help me if I provided him with sexual letters telling him what I would do for him sexually. I had no other choice but to write to him.

7

Defendant Iverson has abandoned my life. He never helped me with my appeal as I wrote him over 1500 love letters. I try to this day to call him on his cell phone in Denver. He answers every once in a while and told me that he found a new mile high boytoy and told me he hopes I starve and die in prison, and that he does not care about the government violating my 5th and 6th Amendment rights in a conversation on his cell phone on

10/01/07. Iverson told me he would kill me if I told anyone about our sexual relationship. Iverson said he has connections at FCI Williamsburg where I'm at. I don't know what happened, but I know fear Iverson is going to come after my life, that's why I move this court to issue a TRO Temporary Restraining Order against Allen Iverson. Iverson told me in the past he beat up a bunch of white boys in a Virginia bowling alley. I'm afraid I will be his next victim.

Conclusion

Plaintiff is scared and in shock, I've suffered major sexual harassment by Iverson and I never want to see him again. He knows my 6th Amendment rights are being violated but chose to ignore them. Plaintiff moves this honorable court to issue an order for defendant Allen Iverson to respond.

Respectfully submitted,

Jonathan Lee Riches©

10/19/07

United States District Court

Eastern District of California

Jonathan Lee Riches©,

Plaintiff

Vs.

James Gandolfini d/b/a Tony Soprano; Edie Falco,

Defendants

Complaint

"42 U.S.C. 1983/Philadelphia Mob/TRO Temporary Restraining Order"

Comes now the plaintiff, Jonathan Lee Riches, in pro-se, moves under 42 U.S.C. 1983. Plaintiff seeks 15 million dollars. Edie Falco plans to be hired as a correction officer at FCI Williamsburg. She has previous experience as a guard on HBO hit series "OZ". This is under orders from Gandolfini who is a captain with the La Costa Nostra of Philadelphia. Gandolfini is mad because I previously sued his friend Nick Scarfo. FCI Williamsburg has me in solitary confinement. I have no access to Comcast Sportsnet in Philadelphia. This is a civil rights violation. Inmates have a constitutional right to television. I'm being severely injured; I'm not current with today's news, which is making me dumber.

Respectfully submitted,

Jonathan Lee Riches©

10/22/07

United States District Court

Northern District of Illinois

Jonathan Lee Riches©,

Plaintiff

Vs.

Oprah Winfrey;

Harpo Productions INC.,

Defendants

Civil Complaint

"Violation of my $6^{th}/8^{th}$ Amendment rights"

TRO Temporary Restraining Order

Comes now the plaintiff, Jonathan Lee Riches©, in pro-se, moves this honorable court to issue an order for defendants named in this suit to respond. This suit is in regard to civil rights and constitutional violations defendants committed and crimes pursuant to kidnapping, conspiracy, neglect, tax fraud, torture, crimes against humanity, aiding and abetting, abuse, cruel and unusual punishment, deliberate indifference, treason, and harassment. Plaintiff moves this honorable court to issue an Emergency Restraining Order against defendants forbidding any direct or indirect contact with plaintiff and plaintiff's copyrighted name. Plaintiff seeks $7,500,000.00 dollars from defendants. Plaintiff requests a jury trial. Plaintiff prays for relief.

Defendants, Oprah Winfrey is a talk show host for the Oprah Winfrey Show, HARPO Productions INC is the company that runs the show.

Plaintiff, Jonathan Lee Riches©, is a freedom fighter political prisoner serving an illegal sentence of 125 months in federal prison for identity theft.   Plaintiff is currently at FCI Williamsburg in South Carolina,

Jonathan Lee Riches©

10/23/07

United States District Court

Eastern District of California

Jonathan Lee Riches© d/b/a

Political Prisoner,

Plaintiff

Vs.

Starbucks Coffee Co; Howard Schultz,

Defendants

Complaint

"Conspiracy/kidnapping/6th&8thAmendment
violations/RICO/TRO Temporary Restraining Order"

Comes now the plaintiff, Jonathan Lee Riches© d/b/a Political Prisoner, in pro-se, seeking declaratory injunctive relief of five million dollars, and compels defendants to release me from solitary confinement 24 hour lockdown. I've been held in solitary by myself since Oct. 20th, 2007 defendants are thwarting my access to the courts. I have no more stamps, I'm not provided pens or paper, Starbucks is in a conspiracy with FCI Williamsburg to keep me away from general population and the courts. Solitary confinement is taking over my brain. Yesterday for dinner I was served three grains of corn and a half piece of moldy bread on a tray that had been in sunlight for over ten hours, I get served no Starbucks coffee. I have access to no media, no newspapers, no girl magazines, no toothpaste, I'm freezing, this is a meat locker. I have no pillow. I'm provided with used boxers –one change a week. I hear other inmates screaming in the halls. Some getting tortured. I'm not provided due process. No one is telling me when I will get out. I went five days refusing to eat because I fear my food will be poisoned, only to be threatened with bodily harm and force-fed. The light stays on 24 hours a day. Defendants want me to rot. Defendants want to burn me with hot coffee. Schultz is friends with Michael Vick, this is a revenge plot. Defendants plan on shipping me to another undisclosed facility for more torture. I demand this abuse to stop. I move for five million dollars and immediate release from solitary.

Respectfully submitted,

Jonathan Lee Riches©

11/07/07

United States District Court

Eastern District of California

Jonathan Lee Riches© d/b/a

Political Prisoner,

Plaintiff

Vs.

John W. Hinckley Jr.; Jodie Foster; St. Elizabeth's Hospital; James Brady; Timothy McCarthy; Thomas Delahanty,

Defendants

Complaint

"24 hour lockdown is inhumane/ making me crazy / cruel and unusual punishment"

Comes now the plaintiff, Jonathan Lee Riches© d/b/a Political Prisoners pro-se, in solitary confinement at FCI Williamsburg seeking 25 million dollars from defendants for 8th Amendment violations of cruel and unusual punishments. I'm placed in 24 hour lockdown since Oct. 20, 2007 for filing a lawsuit against FCI Williamsburg teacher Philip Woolston. The prison thinks I'm the next John Hinckley. The prison is afraid that I use my lawsuits as weapons of mass destruction, so they took my legal work away -a constitutional violation, and put me in solitary confinement with no access to media, newspapers, courts, friends, family. I'm fed very little food. I'm freezing. My shower is freezing. I'm subjected to used boxers, no books, and I had to sneak in pens to write lawsuits. I'm all out of stamps. I have one blanket, no pillows, the lights are kept on at night and there are screaming inmates. I'm a white collar, non-violent

172

offender surrounded by violent criminals. I'm being mentally tortured by defendants. Hinckley plans to assassinate me on Dec.27th - my birthday. Hinckley told FCI Williamsburg to leave me in here to rot, so I can be mummy-wrapped in Ziploc bags and sent to the national archives. If I die in solitary, I move this court to know I will be dying as a martyr. I'm a freedom fighter, political prisoner. FCI Williamsburg is trying to silence me because I know about atrocities that their staff has committed. I'm going on CNN, I'm going to write future books, I'm whistle-blowing and I need help. This is torture. I seek 25 million dollars.

Respectfully submitted,

Jonathan Lee Riches©

11/07/07

United States District Court

Eastern District of California

Jonathan Lee Riches© d/b/a

Political Prisoner

Vs.

Benazir Bhutto;

Perez Musharraf; Pakistan President;

Shaukat Aziz;

Immigration and Naturalization Service "INS",

Defendants

Complaint

"I'm being deported to Pakistan"

"TRO Temporary Restraining Order"

Comes now the plaintiff, Jonathan Lee Riches©, Political Prisoner illegally detained in the Bureau of Prisons, in pro-se, moves this honorable court to issue a TRO Temporary Restraining order against Defendants stopping my extradition to Pakistan in March 2012 because I will be tortured by the Defendants and the Pakistani Government. Defendants put a detainer on me through Interpol, and plan to fly me out of the U.S. on a secret CIA cargo C-130 plane to Karachi Pakistan in March 2012. Plaintiff seeks declaratory injunctive relief against defendants. Plaintiff is a United States citizen under the Uniform Commercial Code U.S.C. 1-308. Plaintiff prays for relief.

1

This is a classic case of mistaken identity. My name is Jonathan Lee Riches©, a U.S. citizen born in Pennsylvania. I'm currently illegally incarcerated at FCI Williamsburg. I'm serving 125 months in federal prison illegally, which is violating my 6th Amendment rights under Booker and Fan Fan. INS put a detainer on me on July 10, 2007. Defendants plan to deport me to Pakistan on March 23rd 2012. Defendants want to try and hang me in downtown Karachi because they think I'm a Taliban tribal leader from federally administered tribal areas of N.W. Pakistan.

2

Pakistan has another wanted Jonathan Lee Riches© who is an international fugitive for making nuclear weapons with Pakistani scientist A.Q. Khan on March 10, 1998, and Riches selling nuclear hardware to Libya, Iran and North Korea. Jonathan Lee Riches is wanted by president Musharraf's military for money laundering Pakistani funds belonging to Shaukat Aziz, Pakistan's Prime Minister through an identity theft Ponzi scam into Swiss accounts belonging to the estate of former Enron CEO Kenneth Lay, Augusto Pinochet, and Filipino President Marcos. These funds were converted to British pounds and transferred to a subsidy account belonging to George Soros in 1999. This other Jonathan Lee Riches is not me, is an Imam at the Radical Red Mosque in Islamabad Pakistan, who finances radical Madrassas with identity theft money with the help of a Muslim charity in Dallas Texas called the Holyland Foundation. Interpol put an international warrant and 3,000,000 million dollar bounty on this Jonathan Lee Riches for treason against the Pakistani government after the September 11 attacks.

175

My name is also Jonathan Lee Riches©. I'm copyrighted through the U.C.C. The FBI arrested me on Feb 25th 2003 outside Tampa Florida for identity theft. I have numerous aliases and identities, my fingerprints have no match. INS thinks I'm not a U.S. citizen and plans to deport me, which will doom me to death and economic torture. INS plans to allow the other defendants to do CIA waterboarding torture on me to reveal secrets I don't know. I'm scared of flying. I belong on U.S. soil. I move this honorable court to stop this deportation with a restraining order. On 10/18/07 Bhutto arrived in Pakistan from exile, her convoy was attacked in downtown Karachi by militants linked to the "other" Jonathan Lee Riches. Bhutto will seek revenge on me for this attack, even though I'm not the same Jonathan Lee Riches. I will submit DNA. Plaintiff prays for relief.

Respectfully submitted,

Jonathan Lee Riches©

11/07/07

In the State of Maryland

Circuit Court of Kent County

Jonathan Lee Riches©

Plaintiff

Vs.

Michael Vick

Defendant

Civil Complaint

"I've been Vicktimized"

Plaintiff, Jonathan Lee Riches©, a priest, brings this civil suit against Michael Vick pursuant to violations of civil rights, harassment, illegal dog-fighting, drug trafficking, prostitution and sports betting. Plaintiff seeks 25 million dollars in damages in compensatory and punitive damages. Plaintiff prays for relief.

Comes now the plaintiff, Jonathan Lee Riches© a/k/a "the google.com phenomenon" who states the following: Plaintiff Jonathan Lee Riches©, a devoted priest, has a church in this county. Plaintiff gets frequent visitors who come to him for their confessions. Defendant Michael Vick is a quarterback for the Atlanta Falcons. Mr. Vick travels to this county to conduct business during the month of June. The purpose of this business is to engage in illegal dog-fighting, sports betting, prostitution, identity theft and drug trafficking.

On the morning of June 2nd 2007, Michael Vick made his first visit to me, to confess his sins. Mr. Vick told me the following on that day:

Vick has been operating a drug running cartel in this county since 2002.

Vick uses his Atlanta Falcons salary and endorsement contracts to finance this operation.

Michael Vick along with current and former Atlanta Falcon teammates, Deon Sanders, Tim Dwight, Joe Horn and Jerry Glanville would distribute cocaine throughout the county, set up crack houses and sell ecstasy at teenage parties.

Mr. Vick also confessed to me this day that he has been shooting steroids and taking performance enhancing drugs since his rookie year. This was done under the direct orders of Atlanta Falcons owner Arthur Blank to boost ticket sales. The NFL Commissioner also knew about Vick's steroid use, but Vick was paying him bribes for silence. Mr. Vick vowed the truth to me in his statement, I prayed with him and encouraged him to come back and see me.

On the afternoon of June 5th 2007, Michael Vick returned to me for a second confession. Mr. Vick told me that he has a sports gambling addiction. While Vick played quarterback for the Falcons, Vick would bet against his own team. Vick purposely tanked a Falcons playoff game against the Philadelphia Eagles. Mr. Vick was in debt to the Gambinos. Mr. Vick also bet on NBA games with referee Tim Donaghy, Steve Javie, and Joey Crawford. Mr. Vick told me that these sports bets occurred during the 2006-2007 NBA season.

Vick hired bookies to work under his orders. Vick's bookies took bets in the county bars, pool halls, shopping malls and high schools. Anyone who got into debt with Vick's betting operation, Vick would send goons to, to break their legs and kneecaps.

Mr. Vick never returned to see me again after that confession. On June 11th 2007 Mr. Vick called me on my telephone and told me he's no longer a Christian and he had joined Al Qaeda. Mr. Vick also threatened me personally with physical injury. Mr. Vick began shouting racist comments to me on the phone. Mr. Vick called me "honky", "white cracker", "father whiteboy". Mr. Vick used profanity like the F word, I was personally insulted by this phone call, I'm still a nervous wreck to this day.

On the morning of June 12th, 2007 I awoke and a black Labrador puppy named "Holy" was missing. I searched the entire house. When I opened the front door, a note was left on the doorstep signed by Michael Vick. The first few lines stated the following: "Hey cracker holy man, I stole your little dog, I'm using him across town in a dogfight. I hope it gets slaughtered. You will never see it again. Take this as a warning. If you ever tell anyone about my confessions or about joining the Jihadists I will take your head off, like what I am going to do to your little dog." From June 12th 2007 to this day I have not seen my dog. Mr. Vick continues to call me and harass my life, I have suffered trauma because of Michael Vick.

Conclusion

My Labrador was exotic, a rare breed from Iceland. The Labrador was personally given to me by Pope Benedict at a Grateful Dead concert. Plaintiff seeks $25,000,000.00 in damages from the defendant. Plaintiff moves this honorable court to issue an order for defendant in this suit to respond.

Respectfully submitted,

Jonathan Lee Riches©

12/03/07

United States District Court

Eastern District of California

Jonathan Lee Riches©,

Plaintiff

Vs.

No Child Left Behind Act; Margaret Spellings d/b/a U.S. Secretary of Education; Senate Health, Education, Labor, and Pensions Committee,

Defendants

Complaint

"The Government left me behind the gates of FCI Williamsburg"

Comes now the plaintiff, Jonathan Lee Riches, in pro-se, moves under 42 U.S.C. 1983, racial discrimination, neglect. I want an education. FCI Williamsburg has no education books in solitary confinement. I'm only subjected to old paperback westerns. Defendants left me behind from my peers. The United Negro College Fund won't answer my letters for a transfer to Morehouse College. Felons are forbidden from getting college grants –this is discrimination against my will to learn. When I was a child, the short bus left me behind and blew its exhaust into my face, which is why we have global warming. Rescue teams left me behind at Columbine in the Sylvan Learning Center Department. FCI Williamsburg will not provide me with a dictionary to write this lawsuit. I've been in solitary confinement so long that I can't count the days. I don't even know what country this is because if it's America why do they allow people to be in solitary without windows, cold showers, cold vent air, rotten food, no medical care. I seek education, I seek wisdom. I have potential, the government said I took millions of dollars in identity theft money, but when I try to work at a bank, the Bank of America says I have no education. A lot of ironies.

Respectfully submitted,

Jonathan Lee Riches©

12/10/07

United States District Court

Eastern District of Pennsylvania

Jonathan Lee Riches©,

Plaintiff

Vs.

Johnny Depp; Keira Knightly; Orlando Bloom; Pirates of the Caribbean,

Defendants

Complaint

42 U.S.C. 1983/civil rights/"theft of my acting career"

Comes now the plaintiff, Jonathan Lee Riches, in pro-se under 42 U.S.C. 1983 and a restraining order. Defendants plan to make a movie about my federal conviction: "Johnny Depp of Identity Theft" by Lionsgate. I was told this through a letter. Defendants are also violating my constitutional rights by advocating, aiding and abetting my mistreatment in federal prison. My civil rights are violated by defendants and pirates who keep me over 800 miles away from my home. Defendants are in a conspiracy with the prison phone system to price gouge rates –I can't make collect calls. Knightly won't answer my letters for help. Today (12/10/2007) for lunch I was only served baked beans that were cold. This is a civil rights violation. Defendants are blocking my attempts to move back to Philadelphia. Defendants took my 2008 season tickets to Flyers' games and put them in a FEMA camp. Plaintiff's liberty is in danger, I seek $25 million, my federal appeal and a restraining order.

Respectfully submitted,

Jonathan Lee Riches©

12/14/07

United States District Court

Eastern District of California

Jonathan Lee Riches©,

Plaintiff

Vs.

Iran Contra Affair; Oliver L. North; Lawrence E. Walsh; John M. Poindexter; Robert McFarlane; George Shultz; Richard V. Secord; Albert Hakim; Claire E. George; Boland Amendment; Sandinista,

Defendants

Complaint

"42 U.S.C. 1983/Trading with the Enemy/Civil Rights/ Forced Labor"

Comes now the plaintiff, Jonathan Lee Riches, in pro-se, under 42 U.S.C. 1983. I seek $100 million dollars. Oliver North is masterminding my kidnapping. I'm being sent to the North Pole for Christmas. I have to tape presents without gloves outside. I have to drink ice cold Red Bull to stay awake. Then I have to sew and stitch Sandinista uniforms. Defendants are using Michael Vick's dogs as bob sledders across the frozed tundra. Then I have to fight the war on global warming at the Equator in Africa wearing a winter jacket and leg warmers while mining uranium in Niger. I have to wear red in L.A. Crips neighborhoods. I have to walk around Iraq in a Nicholas Berg mask. I'm at FCI Williamsburg serving time for identity theft. My rights are being violated. I've got frost-bite and gum disease. Defendants took parole away. Defendants know where Jimmy Hoffa is.

Respectfully submitted,

Jonathan Lee Riches©

12/17/2007

United States District Court

Eastern District of Pennsylvania

Jonathan Lee Riches©,

Plaintiff

Vs.

Westboro Baptist Church; Fred Phelps d/b/a Westboro Baptist
Church founder; Margie Phelps; Termini Bros Bakery,

Defendants

Complaint

Comes now the plaintiff, Jonathan Lee Riches, in pro-se, moves
under 42 U.S.C. 1983. Plaintiff seeks $500 million. Defendants
are protesting my torture at FCI Williamsburg. Defendants think
I don't believe in God. Termini Bros Bakery has been providing
defendants with baked goods in Philadelphia to protest at
military funerals. Defendants violated my civil rights. They call
me the devil. Defendants took my identity.

Respectfully submitted,

Jonathan Lee Riches©

12/18/07

United States District Court

Eastern District of Pennsylvania

Jonathan Lee Riches©,

Plaintiff

Vs.

Tim Russert d/b/a host of NBC's "Meet the Press"; Bob Schieffer d/b/a Host of CBS's "Face the Nation"; Chris Wallace d/b/a Host of Fox News Sunday; Wolf Blitzer d/b/a Host of CNN Late Edition; George Stephanopoulos d/b/a Host of ABC's "This Week",

Defendants

Complaint

Comes now the plaintiff, Jonathan Lee Riches©, in pro-se, under 42 U.S.C. 1983. Plaintiff seeks $100 million from defendants. Defendants' T.V. programs fail to talk about Federal prison abuses. My constitutional rights are violated by defendants as I'm in solitary confinement at FCI Williamsburg. I eat no nutrition. I can't contact my family. Defendants are liable for my current trauma. I move for a restraining order against the shows.

Respectfully submitted,

Jonathan Lee Riches©

12/18/07

United States District Court

Eastern District of Pennsylvania

Jonathan Lee Riches©,

Plaintiff

Vs.

Watergate; George Gordon Liddy; E. Howard Hunt; L. Patrick Gray; Leon Jaworski; Sidney M. Glazer; Henry RothblattJr.; John D. Ehrlichman; Felipe de Diego; James W. McCord; Bernard L. Barker; Eugenio R. Martinez; Frank A. Sturgis; Virgilio R. Gonzales; 2600 Virginia Ave. N.W. Washington D.C.,

Defendants

Complaint

Comes now the plaintiff, Jonathan Lee Riches©, in pro-se, moves under 42 U.S.C. 1983 U.S.C. 1983. Defendants plan to break into my mind and burglarize my brain, Liddy is going to take my neurons and damage my stem cells. Only defendants have the keys to my mind. They want to plant bugs and West Nile Virus in my head. I will be subjected to major brain meltdowns at FCI Williamsburg. I'm a lifelong liberal independent, defendant wants to know what I'm thinking. I seek a restraining order with protection from being abused. I seek $50 million in damages.

Respectfully submitted,

Jonathan Lee Riches©

12/20/07

United States District Court

District of South Carolina

Jonathan Lee Riches©

Plaintiff

Vs.

Somali Pirates d/b/a Termini Bros. Bakery

Defendants

Complaint

Comes now the plaintiff, Jonathan Lee Riches©, in pro-se under 42U.S.C. 1983. Plaintiff seeks $10 million. My civil and constitutional rights are being violated. Termini Bros. Bakery sends cream cakes and pudding pies loaded with sugar and trans-fat to the coastline of Somalia for the pirates. They then use international water to hijack ships. I'm not being fed; Termini Bros. Bakery is biased against me because I'm friends with Joseph Travia. Travia can see how skinny I've gotten, and he has god in him, and he gives me any left over crumbs of sugar he has –this is because no-one is feeding me. My stomach is growling as I write this lawsuit. I still have the Shredded Wheat in me. Last time I had a hot meal was three years ago. I'm in solitary confinement. I get served expired Ensure. Termini is a United States company doing business with pirates. I'm not being fed, this is a civil rights violation. I seek relief.

Respectfully submitted,

Jonathan Lee Riches©

12/20/07

United States District Court

Eastern District of Pennsylvania

Jonathan Lee Riches©,

Plaintiff

Vs.

Viagra; Cialis; Levitra; ForExtenze.com; MagnaRXtra.com; pajamagram.com; megamates.com; viamedic.com; liberator.com; zyrexin.com; extratdx.com; amerimedrx.com; athenainstitute.com; extenzemetoday.com; garybrodsky.com; bfmgo.com; getbiggertoday.com; adameveblack.com,

Defendants

Complaint

"42 U.S.C. 1983/Sexual Harassment/TRO Temporary Restraining Order"

Comes now the plaintiff, Jonathan Lee Riches©, in pro-se, moves under 42 U.S.C. 1983. Plaintiff seeks $30 million dollars. Defendants have been offending me with their advertisements in magazines and radio. This is sexual harassment. Defendants don't put a warning label on their commercials. I watch T.V. during the day, defendants are using sex to make money. Also, defendants are encouraging homosexuality in federal prisons using subliminal messaging. Viagra is ruining the minds of children. Defendants plan to advertise during the Super Bowl, the audience is family oriented, I move for a restraining order. I have a Rolling Stone magazine; I was not warned of sexual content in the back where defendants advertise. This has caused me nerve damage. I'm a born again Christian, this is unconstitutional, I should not be subjected to this pornography.

Respectfully submitted,

Jonathan Lee Riches©

12/24/2007

United States District Court

Eastern District of Pennsylvania

Jonathan Lee Riches©,

Plaintiff

Vs.

Johnny Knoxville d/b/a jackassworld.com; Bam Margera; Steve-O; dave England; Chris Pontius,

Defendants

Complaint

Comes now the plaintiff, Jonathan Lee Riches©, under 42 U.S.C. 1983. I seek $10 million. Defendants are harassing me with prank phone calls at FCI Williamsburg. I'm in solitary confinement. The administration told me that Knoxville keeps calling me from Temple University trying to get me on tape talking about my 8th Amendment rights being violated. Solitary confinement is a civil rights violation. I'm nervous and scared.

Respectfully submitted,

Jonathan Lee Riches©

12/24/07

United States District Court

Middle District of Pennsylvania

Jonathan Lee Riches©,

Plaintiff

Vs.

Harrison Ford a/k/a Indiana Jones;

Calista Flockhart,

Defendants

Complaint

"FCI Williamsburg is a Temple of Doom"

Comes now the plaintiff, Jonathan Lee Riches, in pro-se, moves under 42 U.S.C. 1983. Harrison Ford is not rescuing me at FCI Williamsburg. I'm in solitary confinement, A Temple of Doom. I see no sunlight outside. I get fed through food slots, food only containing transfat, but no nutritional value. I wrote letters to my lawyer Calista Flockhart a/k/a Ally McBeal, she responded once on 12/11/07 saying that I'm a skinny Jewish kid and she hopes I get burned with Hannukah candles. Defendant Ford is responsible for the Algeria car bombings on 12/11/07. This is unconstitutional with my conditions. Defendants violated my civil rights; Ford lost the Ark. Ford also bankrupted Ford Motors. Flockhart broke my heart by not defending my 6th Amendment rights. I seek 25 million dollars, Ford needs to rescue me with his Star Wars buddies because Luke is using the Force against me.

Respectfully Submitted,

Jonathan Lee Riches©

12/26/07

United States District Court

Southern District of Iowa

Jonathan Lee Riches©,

Plaintiff

Vs.

I-35W Bridge, Interstate 35 West Bridge;

Governor Thomas J. Vilsack;

U.S. Transportation Secretary Mary Peters;

Army Corps of Engineers;

NTSB Chairman Mark Rosenker;

Silver Bridge, Ohio;

Sunshine Skyway Bridge, Tampa Bay;

Mississippi River,

Defendants

Complaint

"Justice for Victims"

"TRO Temporary Restraining Order"

This is a complaint under Bivens action, civil rights violations, violation of the constitution and the laws of the United States, federal TORT claims inflicted that include, but not limited to, murder, conspiracy, sabotage, major fraud, terrorism, genocide, identity theft, hacking, treason, torture, copyright infringement, racketeering, false information, bad debt.

Unsafe highways throughout Iowa. Iowa cornfields.

Jonathan Lee Riches©

12/26/07

United States District Court

Middle District of Pennsylvania

Jonathan Lee Riches©,

Plaintiff

Vs.

Heidi Fleiss,

Defendant

Complaint

Comes now the plaintiff, Jonathan Lee Riches, in pro-se, moves this honorable court under 42 U.S.C. 1983 and a TRO restraining order. Heidi Fleiss is harassing and extorting me. When Heidi was in federal prison at the women's camp in Alderson West Virginia she wrote my name and inmate number on the bathroom stall door. Senior Pizza with extra anchovies. Now I get strange letters every day while I'm in solitary confinement at FCI Williamsburg. I compel defendant to erase my name. Not only that, but FCI Williamsburg is a breeding ground for male inmates that dress as women. Seeing this caused me optical nerve damage and fright. A lot of them carry Heidi Fleiss's manuals. I hold defendant liable and seek $25 million in injunctive relief. I also seek a restraining order from Fleiss traveling around the country putting my name on public restroom walls, this gives me junk mail, I'm also on the Federal do not call list.

Respectfully submitted,

Jonathan Lee Riches©

12/26/07

United States District Court

Eastern District of California

Jonathan Lee Riches©,

Plaintiff

Vs.

Freecreditreport.com,

Defendant

Complaint

42 U.S.C. 1983. I seek my free credit report. I wrote to defendants to see my credit report. They are using my identification. My information was breeched from the TSX hacking attack. Defendants discriminate against felons. I don't have identity theft protection. Store cards and data encoders with my name. This was my website idea that defendants took in 1998 during the great hacking wars. All night drinking Jolt, breaking into PO boxes, defendants spoofed my voicemail, put a Trojan horse and key logger in my brain. My civil rights are violated at FCI Williamsburg. I also seek $3 million.

Respectfully,

Jonathan Lee Riches

12/27/07

United States District Court

District of South Carolina

Jonathan Lee Riches©,

Plaintiff

Vs.

Brendan I. Koerner d/b/a Wired Magazine Staff,

Defendant

Complaint

42 U.S.C. 1983. I get no medical treatment in solitary. My ankle got twisted, I weigh only 120 lbs at 5ft 10 inches, defendant is responsible. Defendant is violating my civil rights. I seek $4 million.

Respectfully submitted,

Jonathan Lee Riches©

12/31/07

2008

In 2008 I made a conscious decision to shift from quality to quantity in my suit output. I challenged myself to generate as many lawsuits per day as possible, while still maintaining my running and reading regimens. Sometimes I would cram ten lawsuits into one envelope and send it off. Often I picked one particular federal court and would try to flood them with suits before they could ban me. I had come across the name of Clovis Carl Green, he had filed close to a thousand lawsuits against prison officials, prosecutors, lawyers, etc. My goal for this year was to beat his number. I achieved that by April, and decided to just keep going.

United States District Court

Eastern District of Pennsylvania

Jonathan Lee Riches©,

Plaintiff

Vs.

Slobodan Milosevic,

Defendant

Complaint

42 U.S.C. 1983. Milosevic told all prison wardens how to commit genocide on inmates. I'm suffering in solitary, this is unconstitutional. I'm Jewish without a Torah or Rabbi, this is a violation of my religion. Defendant is liable. I seek $35 million.

Respectfully submitted,

Jonathan Lee Riches©

01/02/08

United States District Court

Eastern District of Pennsylvania

Jonathan Lee Riches©,

Plaintiff

Vs.

Patti LaBelle,

Defendant

Complaint

42 U.S.C. 1983 and restraining order. LaBelle's lyrics sing nothing about my 8th Amendment rights being violated in prison. I'm not getting fed properly, my civil rights are being violated. Prison is torture and unconstitutional. I seek $7 million.

Respectfully submitted,

Jonathan Lee Riches©

01/07/08

United States District Court

Northern District of West Virginia

Jonathan Lee Riches©,

Plaintiff

Vs.

Vincent Gigante a/k/a Vincent "the chin" Gigante,

Defendant

Complaint

42 USC 1983. I seek a TRO Temporary Restraining Order. Mr. Gigante personally wants to do me harm. I seek Injunctive relief.

Respectfully,

Jonathan Lee Riches©

1/14/08

United States District Court

District of South Carolina

Jonathan Lee Riches; Dean Abatemarco; and all others similarly situated,

Plaintiffs

Vs.

Ashlee Simpson; Pete Wentz,

Defendants

Class Action Suit Pursuant to Fed R. Civ 20 & 23

42 U.S.C. 1983/Preliminary Injunction /TRO

Defendants have been threatening and harassing Plaintiffs. FCI Williamsburg is a gulag. Plaintiffs' constitutional rights are being violated by Defendants. Plaintiffs got assaulted by defendants in front of Sam Goody in 2002 for not buying their CD and LP's. Dependent's are violating Plaintiffs due process Rights. FCI Williamsburg has no medical care, rotten food on Defendants' orders. Plaintiff seek a Restraining order and a preliminary injunction on Defendants.

Respectfully submitted,

Jonathan Lee Riches

01/25/08

United States District Court

Northern District of California

Jonathan Lee Riches©,

Plaintiff

Vs.

Jeanne Phillips d/b/a Dear Abby,

Defendant

Complaint

Comes now the plaintiff Jonathan Lee Riches©, who moves under 42 U.S.C. 1983. Defendant has self-help columns in newspapers. She told me to "deal with it" when I was in solitary. This offends me; she wants me to be abused in prison. I seek $10 million for civil rights violations.

Respectfully submitted,

Jonathan Lee Riches©

01/22/08

United States District Court

District of South Carolina

Jonathan Lee Riches,

Plaintiff

Vs.

Harlem Globetrotters; Marques Haynes; Michael "Wild Thing" Wilson; Curley "Boo" Johnson; Curly West; Meadowlark Lemon; Wilt Chamberlain; Showboat Hall,

Defendants

Temporary Restraining Order under 28 U.S.C. 2241

Defendants and FCI Williamsburg are not providing proper recreation. Plaintiff is denied weights. Plaintiff is not provided proper sneakers. The Globetrotters have been threatening plaintiff with violence. Plaintiff is scared and seeks a restraining order against them.

Jonathan Lee Riches

02/19/08

United States District Court

Western District of Virginia

Jonathan Lee Riches,

Plaintiff

Vs.

Sherwin-Williams Co; FCI Williamsburg,

Defendants

28 U.S.C. 2241/The manner in which my sentence has been executed and the horrible conditions at FCI Williamsburg.

Plaintiff is at FCI Williamsburg. Inside Plaintiff's cell along the wall is a texture that is painted by Sherwin-Williams Dutch Boy paint. The paint keeps chipping away on 01/10/08, 12/16/07, 11/05/07, three times chips of paint went in plaintiff's eyes causing redness and itchiness. The walls also feel like sandpaper, if you rub against them you get scraped, this causes staph infection. Plaintiff seeks a transfer to a new facility, and compel FCI Williamsburg to get a new brand of paint that does not cause plaintiff serious bodily harm.

Jonathan Lee Riches

02/20/08

United States District Court

Western District of Virginia

Jonathan Lee Riches,

Plaintiff

Vs.

Alex Ovechkin; Retief Goosen; FCI Williamsburg,

Defendants

28 U.S.C. 2241/Habeas Corpus

Plaintiff's conditions and manner in which his sentence has been executed violates plaintiff's 6th Amendment rights under Booker and Fan Fan. Plaintiff is being denied due process by the defendants, legal department at FCI Williamsburg. Plaintiff's sentence is illegal. Plaintiff is over 500 miles away from his home in Florida. Plaintiff is denied administrated remedies. Plaintiff seeks immediate release from prison and discharge.

Jonathan Lee Riches

02/20/08

United States District Court

Western District of Virginia

Jonathan Lee Riches,

Plaintiff

Vs.

Alex Ovechkin; Retief Goosen; FCI Williamsburg,

Defendants

28 U.S.C. 2241/Habeas Corpus

Plaintiff's conditions and manner in which his sentence has been executed violates plaintiff's 6th Amendment rights under Booker and Fan Fan. Plaintiff is being denied due process by the defendants, legal department at FCI Williamsburg. Plaintiff's sentence is illegal. Plaintiff is over 500 miles away from his home in Florida. Plaintiff is denied administrated remedies. Plaintiff seeks immediate release from prison.

Jonathan Lee Riches

02/20/08

United States District Court

Northern District of Georgia

Jonathan Lee Riches,

Plaintiff

Vs.

General Nutrition Corporation d/b/a GNC,

Defendants

Temporary Restraining Order/ Bivens Action

Defendants sell over the counter steroids to athletes. GNC is a major drug distribution center with illegal narcotics. I'm offended that they sell Creatine to minors knowing that it injures their liver. I bought Metrix from GNC in 2002 and got stomach pains. I seek a restraining order forbidding them from selling drugs to the youth.

Jonathan Lee Riches

3/12/08

United States District Court

District of Colorado

Jonathan Lee Riches,

Plaintiff

Vs.

Leona M. Helmsley; Harry B. Helmsley,

Defendants

Preliminary Injunction/Temporary Restraining Order 42 U.S.C. 1983

I face imminent danger. I seek a restraining order. The people handling the Helmsley Trust threatened me with Helmsley's dog. They say the dog has rabies and will sick it on me, told me it's going to take a bite out of crime. Leona made promises in 2002 that she would take care of me financially. We were pen pals when I was in county jail. Now my future hopes and dreams are dashed. They threatened to drown me in the Colorado River and/or throw me off a chairlift in Aspen. The Helmsley family violated my civil rights. They promised me a job as their computer security tech and now I get emotional abuse. I'm scared defendants are going to use proceeds from their mansion sale to hire a hitman to come after me. I seek a preliminary injunction. I am going through mental pains in prison, I don't need this. I pray for relief.

Jonathan Lee Riches

06/18/08

United States District Court

Southern District of Texas

Jonathan Lee Riches a/k/a Herb Allison;

Robert Alan Meyst a/k/a Robert Meyst,

Plaintiffs

Vs.

Hurricane Ike; Hurricane Gustav; Tropical Storm Hannah,

Defendants

I Blame Hurricane Ike for Destroying my Civil Rights

42 U.S.C. 1983/Temporary Restraining Order

Comes now the plaintiffs Jonathan Lee Riches a/k/a Herb Allison and Robert Alan Meyst a/k/a Robert Meyst, in pro-se, moves this court to issue an order for defendants named in this suit to respond. Plaintiffs' lives are flooded, we are floating on driftwood. I seek a restraining order against anymore hurricanes in the Atlantic K through Z, sea walls built around FCI Williamsburg, an anti-hurricane defense shield built by the army corps of engineers over the top of FCI Williamsburg. Plaintiffs face imminent danger from defendants.

Hurricane Ike blew into the Federal Courthouse in Houston and caused significant water damage to Jonathan Lee Riches court records. The Federal Courthouse in Houston put Riches's sentencing transcripts on the 1st floor, by the front door, on purpose to get flooded. Unarmed U.S. Marshal did not protect my court documents, then Hurricane Ike got ahold of the Jonathan Lee Riches indictment and twisted the facts and linked me to Jeff Skilling and the Enron scandal. Ike caused my brain power to go out on 09/13/08. On the night of 09/12/08 Hurricane Ike blew Houston Astros at our heads from outer space. Houston we have a problem! Because of Hurricane Ike NASA launched a secret government spy drone in the air, ballistic weather missile test aimed at FCI Williamsburg in Salters South Carolina. T. Boone invested in Hurricane Ike's solar wind power. Ike infected me with feline cat nine lives wind! Hurricane Ike destroyed my Visa and Mastercard water paintings. This left me in a tropical depression.

Hurricane Ike is in a secret conspiracy with Barack Obama to destroy G.W. Bush's Texas oil infrastructure in order to create new geo-political U.S. energy policies. Ike blew Halliburton to off-shore tax havens.

Hurricane Ike is on OPEC and Wall St. hedge fund payrolls with Michael Milken, Miss Cleo, betonsports.com and BET Television who put options on oil barrel prices to go down under $100 a barrel, while Americans predicted it would go up, then using the proceeds to finance future hurricanes at a secret laboratory in Switzerland.

Hurricane Ike's wind broke apart missing Columbia space shuttle parts in eastern Texas and blew moon rocks and Houston Rockets into our heads.

Johnson Space Center is controlling our minds.

Hurricane Ike broke Yao Ming's foot.

Hurricane Ike blew Bill White, Mayor of Houston's hair off.

Hurricane Ike blew glass from the JP Morgan Chase building into our faces, Scarface, a secret revenge for Jonathan Lee Riches stealing Chase Visa and Mastercards. This is financial

215

terrorism from defendants. Ike gave us tainted water from Spring Texas.

Hurricane Gustav blew the FCI Williamsburg roofs off.

Hurricane Ike and Whitney Houston took our bodyguards then Hurricane Ike lifted us up to drown us in Andrea Yates's bathtub.

Ike put our brain on drugs, any questions?

Hurricane Ike killed our Pepperidge Farm Goldfish and Ike swirled in our Dairy Queen Blizzard. Ike tainted Texas land and cattle beef while the government tricked residents of Galveston for a mandatory evacuation while they secretly put GPS tracking devices and FISA eavesdropping equipment in residents' homes to listen to, and watch, residents' seafood.

The Cuban Government formed Hurricane Gustav to allow illegal immigrants to flood into America to attend Mardi Gras and steal U.S. jobs and Castro GTX Motor Oil.

Tropical Storm Hannah was cousins with Daryl Hannah who Splashed onto the shores of South Carolina naked because of a Riches/Tom Hanks Castaway look-a-like. John Candy ate Hurricane Mike and Ikes. Defendants sucked the skin and fat out of my body. CIA waterboarded and tortured me at the beach.

We seek damages. I suffered Thompson Waterseal damages. Our brains are flooded. Disney Typhoon Lagoon is after us. Defendants illegally changed my copyright name to Johnny Tsunami. Ike beat Hurricane Katrina Turner. We sued Hurricane Katrina in Louisiana: Riches vs. Hurricane Katrina and Riches vs. FEMA. Now we are in solitary at FCI Williamsburg in a fishtank –no scuba gear, no lifevests. We face imminent danger from storm surge as all the defendants plan to combine into a mega storm and level our playing field, and rip our lives apart, and steal our sea shells, assault us with boardwalks, and crush our waterfront homes. Defendants are in good hands with Allstate.

Hurricane Ike was looking for Tina.

What's love got to do with it?

This is weather warfare. Defendants are planning to destroy Tom Cruise Mission Impossible Church of Scientology in Clearwater Florida.

Robert Alan Meyst

Jonathan Lee Riches

09/14/08

United States District Court

Southern District of Florida

Jonathan Lee Riches,

Plaintiff

Vs.

Jim Jones, Peoples' Temple in Guyana,

Defendants

Complaint

Jonathan Lee Riches seeks FOIA about Jim Jones Peoples' Temple of Guyana. I was a former member of the Jim Jones cult. I have been trying to get answers for thirty years, whether Jim Jones is my real father. My mother met Jim Jones in 1975 in San Francisco, in pursuit of happiness. I was born on 12/27/1976 in the Napa Valley. Jim Jones took my mother and me to Guyana in Jonestown. I was an honor baby. I got a key to Jonestown. Jonestown issued my birth certificate and social security card.

Jim Jones began to beat and punch me in 1978 to show off for the other cult members –I still have the bruises. I was used for witchcraft by Jones, he stuck needles in me for voodoo, acupuncture for self-healing. In September 1978 Jim Jones used me to engage in baby-fighting in a chicken coop where cult members could wager bets on me fighting other Afro-American babies. I was forced into slave-labor camp at the Peoples' temple. I had to make cabbage Patch Dolls. This became Indiana Jones and the Temple of Doom, Shirley Temple was my neighbor and this was an Empire of the Sun camp, just like the Russians held my father in Red Dawn.

Wolverines from Michigan. I seek DNA testing to find out if Jim Jones is my real father. If you put my name in ancestor.com it says that he is my father. Luke was in search of his father. I seek information about my whistleblowing penpal letters I wrote to Congressman Leo J. Ryan, warning him about tainted Jell-O, Kool Aid and Welch's Grape Soda. I warned Leo J. Ryan about Jim Jones's abuses and fraud. Leo J. Ryan told me in a Western Union telegram October 10th 1978 that he will fly down to Jonestown to investigate, in turn he and representative Jackie Speier would adopt me in the United States.

I was a good number-cruncher, now I became a computer genius, but used it in computer fraud and identity theft. I did credit card fraud and was convicted in 2003 and sentenced to 125 months in prison because Jim Jones corrupted my mind. Jim Jones implanted digital computer chips into my head at the last hour tape. I've been trying ever since to get these gadgets out of my brain and had to do credit card fraud to finance my brain surgery.

In October 1978, Jim Jones forced me and over 900 other people to drink his Kool-Aid, laced with cyanide. At the last second I switched my drink with the 7-11 ICEE grape flavor. I avoided the poison, but Jim Jones found out and chased me with his John Deere Tractor to the port Kaituma Airport to murder me. Instead, he shot Representative Leo Ryan.

The TSA had no security at the airport. I lost my luggage. I seek information under 5USC 552 about the whereabouts of my Samsonite briefcase with private photographs of me and Jim Jones in a bathtub, and him changing my diapers. Jim Jones also took me to Disneyland and the Studio 54 disco club. Jim Jones was a distant cousin of Adam Pacman Jones. The Peoples Temple has artifacts belonging to me. Jonathan Lee Riches copyrighted clothing material. Jonestown also has Jimmy Hoffa's body buried there, and Waldo is hidden at Jonestown.

Jim Jones circumcised me in front of worshippers and Jim Jones used my credit card information to finance his sunglasses at Pearl Vision Center. Collection agencies sent me a $645 bill at FCI Williamsburg under Jim Jones name.

Now bloggers and media found out that Jim Jones was my father –we have the same genes, because I had credit card fraud worshippers following me and I was a mastermind kingpin in a cyber-warfare on behalf of Jim Jones' enemies. The CIA has records of me and Jim Jones engaging in the Cuban Missile Crisis. I seek this information. I have documents affiliating me with Jim Jones. I pray this honorable court for relief.

Respectfully submitted,

Jonathan Lee Riches©

12/01/08

United States District Court

Northern District of Illinois

Jonathan Lee Riches,

Plaintiff

Vs.

Oprah Winfrey,

Defendant

Notice of Appeal

Jonathan Lee Riches moves to appeal the dismissal of this case to the 7th circuit court of appeals. Oprah Winfrey violated my civil rights and exposed me on her show as an identity thief and cyber criminal because I stole her boyfriend, Stedman Graham's American Express card. Oprah Winfrey and I had an intimate relationship from 1999-2001 no one would know we would meet at the Super 8 Motel along I-70. I have Oprah's stained dress saved along with used condoms. This court dismissed this case because Winfrey gave the judge tickets to Harpo. Oprah harasses me in prison with threats of gang members. I appeal 10/10/2007 –Oprah stole my Jerry Springer tickets and Oprah assaulted me in front of Sally Jesse Raphael Show and stole my Phil Donohue autographs. I appeal.

Jonathan Lee Riches

12/12/08

2009

By 2009 I had learned that I had a greater chance of getting media coverage if I focused on topics that were trending in the news cycle. With these topics and individuals I would put more thought and creativity into the suits I drafted. I would balance high quality, imaginative lawsuits with the more run-of-the-mill generic suits I was using to flood the courts with.

Even if the media attention I got did not give me a broader platform to discuss my situation in a serious way it did grant me more respect from my fellow inmates as well as fan mail from strangers. I sensed that I was having an impact on peoples' lives and that they were enjoying what I was creating. Sometimes I even sensed that there was anticipation on their part as to what I was going to do next.

United States District Court

10th Circuit Court

Jonathan Lee Riches d/b/a

Rockefeller Riches,

Plaintiff

Vs.

Lost; Josh Holloway a/k/a James "Sawyer" Ford; Terry O'Quinn d/b/a John Locke/Jeremy Bentham; Matthew Fox d/b/a Jack Shephard; Evangeline Lilly d/b/a Kate Austin; Naveen Andrews d/b/a Sayid Jarrah; Michael Emerson d/b/a Ben Linus; Elizabeth

Mitchell d/b/a Juliet Burke; Jorge Garcia d/b/a Hugo "Hurley" Reyes; Jeremy Davies d/b/a Daniel Faraday; Rebecca Mader d/b/a Charlotte Lewis; Henry Ian Cusick d/b/a Desmond Hume; Yunjin Kim d/b/a Sun Kwon; Carlton Cruse; Damon Lindelof,

Defendants

Preliminary Injunction, Temporary Restraining Order, TRO

42 U.S.C. 1983

Comes now Jonathan Lee Riches d/b/a Rockefeller Riches, moves this honorable court for a preliminary injunction, temporary restraining order against the ABC Network and their upcoming broadcast of season five of Lost. I face imminent danger if this show and defendants are aired on T.V. for the last five years every season of Lost has been sending me subliminal messages and corrupting my mind deeper and deeper into the abyss. The show ruined my health and mental state. Lost and the defendants destroyed my I.Q. and caused me to be a nervous wreck. I seek full Medicare and Medicaid benefits when I get released from prison. I seek $200,000,000.00 million dollars in damages, wired to an offshore Cayman Island account. Right now I'm in solitary confinement 24 hour lockdown at FCI Williamsburg because I'm scared to face people because I'm traumatized from watching Lost on prison T.V.s. "In solitude, you have no clue, what I'm goin' through, alone in this cold room." This is unconstitutional. Defendants gave me inflammation in my colon and now my breath smells like petroleum. Doctors neglect me and only examine me with electronic impulses on defendants' orders. I'm the Lone Ranger in solitary. Defendants took my horse and forced it to race Smarty Jones. I'm incurable. Lost forced me to lose 45 pounds in 2 weeks, Nutrisystem failure. I have mysterious ancient diseases, knee pains, defendants sold my knee ligaments to Tiger

Woods. I got wrinkles in my eyes, throat-burn with Deep Throat whistle-blowing against the defendants and crying for help. Jorge Garcia kidnapped me at Bellevue mental hospital, stole my belly fat and then Sawyer made me jump from a medic helicopter and handcuffed me to the wing of U.S. Airways flight 1549, where I got pneumonia, terminal island freeze, and an STD from Josh Holloway. Josh Holloway kidnapped his sister Natalie Holloway in Aruba and sent her to the Lost island for covert prostitution. Lost forced me into a romantic foursome with Jack, Kate, Sawyer, Juliet and a bottle of Thousand Island dressing. I was promised by defendants that if I stay on Gilligan's island I would get a free continental breakfast. Defendants took me off my meds, drugged me with toxic waste. My membranes have ocean bacteria. I'm a nervous crisis. Defendants conspired with Somali pirates to blow up a freighter, Sirius Satellite Radio. Ben plans to assassinate me then bury me in a L.A. funeral home with Mr. Bentham. Defendants gave me multiple personalities with Toni Collette. The Oceanic 6 CIA water tortured me, gave me Parkinson's disease and a bloody stool. Defendants poisoned me with an anesthesiologist infecting my immune system with 24/7 starvation. Defendants are going to kidnap me from FCI Williamsburg and film it live on ABC with 13.3 million viewers and time travel me to the island to make me a Survivor contestant in balls and chains where I will have to soccer juggle Tom Hanks's Wilson ball and find underground weapons caches with Revenge of the Nerds, and the only way to get off the island is to spin the frozen donkey wheel. I face danger, harm and death from defendants. Because of this show I am scared to turn on my T.V. set. I'm in fear that defendants are using their acting salary to contract the poltergeist after me. I move this court to help me. Defendants took my meds and killed Heath Ledger, Jett Travolta, and Anna Nicole Smith with my pills. I pray this court will grant my motions and defendants pay me 200 million for relief. I can't watch Barack Obama on the 20th on T.V. because I'm scared.

Respectfully,

Jonathan Lee Riches

01/19/09

United States District Court

District of Delaware

Jonathan Lee Riches a/k/a

Joshua David Duhamel,

Plaintiff

Vs.

The National Enquirer d/b/a American Media Inc.; Star Magazine; Reginald Fitz; Don Gentile; Michael Glynn; Rick Egrusquiza; Alan Butterfield; Lynn Allison; John Blosser; Lynette Holloway; John Combs; Michael Cherico; Lisa Luchesi; Patricia Shipp; Len Feldman; Larry Haley; Philip Smith; Sharon Ward; Annette Witheridge; David Gardner; Jeff Samuels; David Wright; Laurie Miller; Alan Smith; Deborah Hughes; Mike Walker; Susan Baker; Dorothy Cascerceri; Alexander Hitchen; Matt Coppa; Candace Trunzo; Heidi Parker; Sandra Clark; Matthew Mundy; Alex Burton; Jennifer Pearson; Casey Brennan; Melissa Cronin, Tim Plant; Kathleen Perricone; Kate Major; Mike Olson; Jennifer Angel,

Defendants

Preliminary Injunction, Temporary Restraining Order, TRO 42 U.S.C. 1983

Comes now, Jonathan Lee Riches a/k/a Joshua David Duhamel, moves this honorable court for a TRO temporary restraining order TRO and a preliminary injunction against the National Enquirer Magazine, Star Magazine, which are both owned by American Media Inc. and a list of defendants who are reporters and editors for these magazines. I face imminent danger and bodily harm from all the defendants who are threatening to publish my story, including me being in federal prison for stealing multiple celebrities' identities, credit, and credit cards that I got in their names, which got me 125 months in federal prison. They plan on publishing court records of mine in which I sue thousands of celebrities nationwide for violating my civil rights. From July 10, 2008 through December 20, 2008 I have received over 450 letters and phone calls from defendants requesting interviews and my side of the story. In each letter defendants say that if I don't cooperate with them they will write horrible, negative articles about me to embarrass my character. FCI Williamsburg and the warden were sick of the defendants calling here everyday asking to speak to me that they locked me up in solitary confinement, 24 hour a day lockdown for security reasons. This is where I am writing this suit –without a typewriter. This is torture. Defendants are responsible for me suffering and possibly dying in solitary confinement. I'm freezing cold, have no windows, get fed through a slot in the door like a dog, rats on my floor, anti-white graffiti on the walls, subjected to used oversized clothing. I'm starving, I weigh only 119 lbs. at 5 foot 10 inches, my ribs stick out. FCI Williamsburg is shipping me on diesel therapy and punishing me because of the defendants' conduct and defendants relentless harassment of me and this facility. Defendants sent reporters to the front gates of FCI Williamsburg camped out to try to speak to me. Defendants tried to call here posing as my sick mother, defendants also called here saying my father died in a car accident so the Chaplain would put me on the phone. Defendants are trying to bribe me with money or free subscriptions to their magazines. Now FCI Williamsburg and the warden says they will not let me out of solitary confinement and told me to "rot in hell" as long as defendants keep calling and sending letters to the prison harassing me for an interview. I'm going to die in here, I have no access to a phone or my personal property. Defendants have baby pictures and mug shot

227

pictures of me that they illegally obtained from the Bureau of Prisons. Also, CNN presents "How to Rob a Bank" did a feature story on me in which CNN provided the National Enquirer with audio tapes and evidence of me doing identity theft and fraud in celebrities' names. I was accused of stealing Sean P. Diddy Combs's Citibank card with 15 thousand and adding an authorized user in the name of Christi Combs" in 2007. I took identities from Janet Reno, Bob Barker, Sean Penn, Lindsey Lohan, Chris Rock and many many more. I'm paying for my crimes and just want to be left alone by defendants. Please stop stalking me National Enquirer! They created havoc in my life. I seek a restraining order preventing defendants from publishing, printing or posting photos with me or anything affiliated with my life. I also seek 10 million dollars in damages, emotional distress and trauma. I pray this court will grant my motions for relief.

Respectfully,

Jonathan Lee Riches

01/25/09

United States District Court

Southern District of Iowa

Jonathan Lee Riches d/b/a

Second Amendment Foundation,

78 million American gun owners,

Plaintiffs

Vs.

Brady Gun Ban Center,

President Barack Hussein Obama,

Secretary of State Hillary Clinton,

Attorney General Eric Holder, U.S. Senator "Teddy" Kennedy,

U.S. Senator Dianne Feinstein,

U.S. Senator "Chucky" Schumer,

Mayor Michael Bloomberg,

Defendants

Civil Complaint

For Declaratory and Injunctive Relief and Monetary Damages

I am in imminent danger of physical harm due to the defendents' actions. Defendants have conspired to deprive me and 78 million Americans of Constitutional Rights guaranteed by the Second Amendment. Defendants have conspired to corrupt the democratic processes of the government to achieve unlawful and unconstitutional objectives. Defendants have conspired to manipulate the constitutional processes of government to effect passage of legislation that is in violation of their oath of office. Defendants are engaging in conspiratorial acts to inflame public feeling in regards to the illegal actions of a few persons so as to justify their unconstitutional actions destroying the Second Amendment rights of all other citizens, thereby rendering our entire society defenseless against physical harm.

Defendants have conspired, and are conspiring now, to impose unconstitutional federal government "services" through creation of unconstitutional federal agencies and the fielding of swarms of officers and agents to eat out the substance of the American economy, and use the provision of these "services" as justification for the outright suspension and legislative repeal of Constitutional Rights secured to the people by the first and second Amendments to the U.S. Constitution. Defendants have, and are now, conspiring to willfully violate the Second Amendment rights of Americans through introduction and coerced passage of legislation containing provisions which directly subvert the Founders' Original Intent and Core Lawful Purposes of Second Amendment rights of Americans as members of citizen militias. Defendants have created a state of fear and terror within the plaintiffs and the American people through defendants' willful acts of waging war against the U.S. Constitution; their actions have brought the nation perilously close to a state of civil war and the people may need to defend the U.S. Constitution and our Republican form of government against their treasonous actions.

Relief Sought

Plaintiffs seek $100 trillion dollars ($100,000,000,000,000,000.00) in damages for mental and emotional injuries and other actual injuries to their safety, security, and well-being.

Plaintiffs seek injunctive relief requiring all defendants to prove their citizenship, and prove their strict compliance with all constitutional qualifications to hold their public offices.

Plaintiffs seek injunctive relief restraining defendants from committing any acts which violate their oath of office.

Plaintiffs seek injunctive relief restraining defendants from conspiring in whole or in part to commit acts injurious to or subversive of the fundamental common law and constitutional forms of self-defense of plaintiffs.

Plaintiffs seek injunctive and declaratory relief requiring that all acts of Congress must strictly comport with the Founders' Original Intent as regards the Second Amendment.

Plaintiffs seek declaratory relief clarifying that their rights secured under the Second Amendment are superior, i.e., "shall not be infringed." To the federal government's powers under the Commerce Clause (U.S. Constitution, Article 1, Section 8, Clause 3)

Certification

Pursuant to 28 U.S.C. 1746. I declare under penalty of perjury that the forgoing is true and correct to the best of my information, knowledge and belief.

Jonathan Lee Riches

04/29/09

United States Court

District of Colorado

Jonathan Lee Riches d/b/a

Bernie Madoff,

Plaintiff

VS.

Swine flu a/k/a Human Swine Influenza, a/k/a Hemophilus Influenzae; avian flu, North American swine flu virus; A(H1N1); SARS outbreak; Hong Kong flu; 1918-19 Spanish flu a/k/a Spanish influenza epidemic; bird flu; Centers for Disease Control and Prevention, CDC; The Food and Drug Administration, FDA; Department of Health and Human Services; World Health Organization, WHO; Homeland Security; Janet Napolitano; the Air Transport Association of America; H5N1; Peanut Corp of America; Mexican Health Secretary Jose Cordova; Mexico City Health Secretary Armando Ortega; Grippe flu; Nostras influenza; Equine feline; Flushield; Fluvirin; Hemagglutinin; neuraminidase; Guillai-Barre Syndrome; Thimersal; Laryneal; Tamiflu; Relenza; Amantadine; Symmetrel; Rimantadine; Flumadine; Zanamivir; Osectamivir; Phlebotomus fever; Evans Vaccine Ltd; Wyeth-Ayerst; Vaccine Adverse Event Reporting System; Vaers; Amgen; Applied Immune Sciences, Baxter Healthcare corp; Searle &co; Bristol-Myers; Squibb; Mead Johnson & co; Eli Lilly and co; John Hopkins University; Pfizer; Cambridge neuroscience; Smithkline Beecham Clinical; Fisher Scientifico; Parke Davis; M.I.T. Lincoln Laboratory; Lawrence Livermore National Lab; Genentech; Schering Laboratories; National Academy of Sciences; Syntex chemicals; Geneva Pharmaceuticals; Chiron corp; Roche Biomediac Laboratories, ABC's General Hospital;

Beiersdorf Inc; US Pharmaceutical corp; Old McDonald; Allscripts Inc; Orthonyxoviruses; Federal Medical Center Lexington Kentucky, Porky Pig, Boss; Arkansas Razorbacks,

Defendants

Complaint

Comes now, Jonathan Lee Riches a/k/a Bernard Madoff. I move for a global restraining order against the defendants who infected me with swine flu. I have pigs in my blanket. Boss Hog illegally arrested me in a federal identity theft indictment on February 25th 2003, violating my Eighth Amendment rights as pertaining to cruel and unusual punishment. Now I'm subjected to covert guinea pig experimental vaccine testing by the named defendants at the medical center in Lexington Kentucky. I was the very first confirmed swine flu case, this happened on my birthday. The Zionist Jews created swine flu! This is a major global Barack Obama lead conspiracy to regulate pork, pigs, the farming industry and supermarket bacon by spreading swine flu across the globe so that the government can create a vaccine in order to look like heroes in the world. This will lead to people supporting government intervention, part of a new world order socialist plot. Defendants are in a racketeering shakedown to serve pork to Muslims and people who are then forced to use their own money to buy medicines to treat them, which then causes the pharmaceutical companies to get rich. I'm a convicted cyber-computer-virus-spammer, I infected over 1,000,000 PCs globally with the Melissa Virus to hijack peoples' hard-drives, then when their computers were frozen and disabled, I would sell the people anti-virus software for $19.95 plus tax to get their computer systems working again. The defendants are working the same kind of plot. Poor pigs in the world are dying because of the defendants -PETA and the Earth Liberation Front don't care. In 1978, the Russians gave me food poisoning. During last year's Kentucky Derby, Mr. Ed gave me laryngitis. Now, Equine felines are after my life, they are Garfield the cat, Felix and Cats on Broadway. Defendants put pork in my ribs on 11-11-08. Don't think federal female inmates are left out, the defendants take their ovarian eggs to make swine flu vaccine in return for extragoodtime©   -this is unconstitutional. The defendants are spreading swine flu on domestic airlines via pig air marshals. Swine flu bit me at an Arkansas' Razorback football game on 1-17-07. I seek surgical masks for protection. Defendants gave me diarrhea, fever and cramps for 72 straight days. My immune system is dead. I pray for relief.

Respectfully,

Jonathan Lee Riches

04/24/09

United States District Court

Albuquerque, New Mexico

Bernard Madoff d/b/a

Jonathan Lee Riches a/k/a

Jonathan L. Riches Investment Securities LLC,

Plaintiff

Vs.

Bank of America Corp; Merrill Lynch & co; Kenneth Lewis; Danny Pang d/b/a Private Equity Management Group Inc. a/k/a PemGroup; California Public Employees' Retirement System; Calpers,

Defendants

Preliminary Injunction, Temporary Restraining Order, TRO

I face imminent danger and bodily harm from defendants. Bank of America is withholding Americans' Ponzi money and used my fifty billion dollars to invest in subprime loans. Danny Pang aided and abetted in my identity theft and his PemGroup is a secret offshore bank account holding fraud money. Calpers stole my social security number, opened Bernard Madoff dollar store accounts and Piggly Wiggly Supermarket accounts. Kenneth Lewis threatened to merge Riches and Madoff in an investment marriage in San Francisco. Bank of America financed my wire fraud. Merrill Lynch & co. is threatening to hang me for looting Tyco. I was so scared of defendants, I would not leave my penthouse for weeks. Bank of America gave me loans to get season tickets to Mets games and I got swine flu in a New Mexico Bank of America branch. Kenneth Lewis illegally used my Ponzi money to pay ransoms to Somali pirates, defendants cooperated with the Patriot Act and gave Madoff & Riches files to the government illegally. Defendants caused me emotional distress and I will never use defendants' banks again. Kenneth Lewis is a corporate raider who is trying to oust members of the Jonathan Lee Riches Investment Securities Board and replace it with Emmanuel Lewis (Webster), Carl Lewis, Lewis & Clark, Lewis Skoelnick, Leona Lewis, Reggie Lewis gave me a heart attack. I seek a restraining order against defendants.

Respectfully,

Jonathan Lee Riches

05/01/09

United States District Court

Eastern District of Kentucky

Jonathan Lee Riches a/k/a

Jason Trowbridge,

Plaintiff

Vs.

X-Men INC. d/b/a X-Men Origins; Hugh Jackman d/b/a Wolverine; Live Schreiber d/b/a Victor Creed a/k/a Sabretooth; Taylor Kitsch d/b/a Remy Etienne a/k/a LeBeau Gambit; Will.I.Am a/k/a John Wraith Kestrel; Ryan Reynolds a/k/a Wade Wilson d/b/a Deadpool; Lynn Collins d/b/a Kayla Silverfox,

Defendants

Habeas Corpus Relief under 28 U.S.C. 2241

Comes now Jonathan Lee Riches a/k/a Jason Trowbridge, under Habeas Corpus Relief. I face danger from defendants and the manner in which my sentence is executed is unconstitutional. Defendants, X-Men are roaming around Washington lobbying the Obama Administration for more funds to torture me while I'm in prison. Defendants' movies incite federal inmates with low IQs to threaten me. Defendants also encourage me to live a fantasy life and not take my meds. Wolverine has been taking my lunch trays in prison. Defendants threatened me with the Twilight Zone and Tales from the Crypt. I seek medical treatment in Washington. I'm one of 46 million people not insured. I qualify under Barack's plan.

05/06/09

United States District Court

Southern district of Iowa

Jonathan Lee Riches d/b/a

Second Amendment Foundation;

78 Million American Gun Owners,

Plaintiffs

Vs.

Brady Gun ban Center, et al,

Defendants

Motion to Correct Clerical Errors Under Rule 60A

I move to correct clerical errors in this case. The clerk of court docketed my name wrong. I received an order from this court dismissing this case with my name on that order spelled wrong. The order had my name as Jonathon Lee Riches, which is not the correct spelling of my name. I submitted this lawsuit as Jonathan Lee Riches, I move to correct my first name on the docket and record in this case to Jonathan Lee Riches. I also move not to construe this motion as an appeal. This is not an appeal, this is a motion to correct clerical mistakes. I move to correct another clerical mistake in the order I received from this court dismissing this case. In that order the clerk states: "Black History Month in prison violates his constitutional rights." I move to correct this error, nowhere in the complaint I originally sent do I say anything about Black History Month, this is causing me prejudice. I move to correct this error and remove this statement from this docket. My name is Jonathan Lee Riches not "Jonathon Lee Riches," these errors are violating my constitutional rights. I move to correct the dockets and to correct the clerical errors in the order from Judge Pratt dismissing this complain. I pray this court will grant my motion for relief.

Respectfully,

Jonathan Lee Riches

05/15/09

United States District Court

Eastern District of Washington

Jonathan Lee Riches a/k/a

Irving Picard,

Plaintiff

Vs.

The Guinness Book of World Records a/k/a The Guinness Book of World Records d/b/a Guinness Publishing Ltd; Encyclopedia Britannica Inc.; World Book Encyclopedia; The Readers Encyclopedia of American Literature; The World Factbook; The People's Almanac; The New Oxford American Dictionary; Granger's Index to Poetry; Facts on File Inc.; Encyclopedic Dictionary; Library of Congress; Compton's Encyclopedia and Fact Index; Chambers Biographical Dictionary; Fear Factor; Ripley's Believe it or Not,

Defendants

Preliminary Injunction, Temporary Restraining Order, TRO

Copyright violations, Trademark infringement

28 U.S.C. 1331

Comes now the plaintiff, Jonathan Lee Riches a/k/a Irving Picard, I face imminent danger and bodily harm from the defendants who plan to publish me and a description of my life in their books without my authorization or consent. On January 1, 2009 the Guinness Book of World Records sent me a congratulations letter stating I have set the world record for filing the most lawsuits in the history of mankind. Their letter stated that I've filed more 3,000 lawsuits in federal courts and over 2,500 lawsuits in local and state courts and that I've shattered the previous record of Reverend Clovis Carl Green. The Guinness Book of World Records told me that they plan on invading my privacy by posting my Bureau of Prison mugshot along with personal information including my social security number, birthdate, weight, eye color, home address, telephone number, and where I'm illegally incarcerated at: the Federal Medical Facility in Lexington Kentucky. I sent the Guinness Book of World Records ten letters from January 5, 2009 through July 1, 2009 telling them "no, thank you. I don't want to be in a record book because the facts are wrong. I've filed more than 4,000 lawsuits worldwide in other countries' courts, the Hague, world court, the ICC."

The defendants are slandering my name by calling me "the Litigator Crusader," "Duke of Lawsuits," "Johnny Sue-Nami," "Sue-per Man," "The Patrick Ewing of Suing,," and "The Lawsuit Zeus." These phrases hurt my feelings and violate my civil rights. I've filed so many lawsuits with my pen and right hand that I've gotten arthritis in my fingers, numbness in my wrists, crooked fingers, and bags under my eyes from sleepless nights spent suing the world. I get an average of twenty five pieces of legal mail from courts, lawyers, stalkers, fans, etc. I've been printed in lawbooks throughout the world without my consent or permission. I'm thinking about retiring from writing lawsuits for a while and giving my fingers rehabilitation. I've been persecuted to the fullest by judges who are denying me due process and access to the courts. Defendants caused me grief and mental breakdowns, that's why I went from FCI Williamsburg to a federal medical center in Lexington Kentucky to get mental health treatment. I eat, sleep and think lawsuits. I flush out more suits than a sewer. I've sacrificed my time, dignity and prison trust account filing lawsuits. My accounts are

241

frozen; I can't buy stamps, food or hygiene products from the commissary. Thankfully, I'm surrounded by sympathetic inmates who are providing me with stamps to send out legal mail. I entered the RDAP drug program this summer, upon completion I will get a year off of my sentence. That means I will be in a halfway house by next summer and when I get out of prison I will set up a lawsuit 101 class and teach Americans how to file pro-se lawsuits. I will sell Jonathan Lee Riches T-shirts that will say: "watch what you do, or I'll sue you" with my face in the middle.

The Guinness Book of World Records has no right to publish my work –my legal masterpieces. The defendants have sent me threatening letters because I filed "Riches vs. Black History Month" in Iowa, and President Ahmadinejad of Iran. I also got screamed at for filing "Riches vs. I can't believe it's not butter" and "Riches vs. child molesters." I'm in danger and I seek a restraining order against publication of my name. I pray for relief.

Respectfully,

Jonathan Lee Riches

05/19/09

United States District Court

District of Nevada

Jonathan Lee Riches d/b/a

Bernard Madoff a/k/a

Bernard L. Madoff,

Plaintiff

Vs.

Moonlite Bunny Ranch; Jenna Jameson; sex.com a/k/a www.sex.com; Adam and Eve; Playboy Magazine; Mustang Ranch; Peter North; Ron Jeremy; Madame Tussaud's Wax Museum; American Curves Magazine; Dennis Hof; Heidi Fleiss; Brothel in Pimlico; Adult Entertainment; Stuff Magazine; Escort.com; Vivid Entertainment; craigslist.com; whorehouse,

Defendants

28 U.S.C. 1331

Preliminary Injunction, Temporary Restraining Order, TRO

Comes now, Jonathan Lee Riches d/b/a Bernard Madoff a/k/a Bernard L. Madoff, I face imminent danger and bodily harm. This court has jurisdiction, as the Moonlite Bunny Ranch is in the Reno Nevada area. Its owner, Dennis Hof, and the list of defendants who occupy and stay there with illegal operations of prostitution over interstate lines and defendants have been harassing me relentlessly with vacation travel packages to the Moonlite when I get out of prison. Defendants send me underage pornography in the mail. Defendant Jenna Jameson told me in a Feb 14th Valentines letter that if I paid her $50,000 and add her to my prison visiting list at Federal Medical Center in Lexington Kentucky she would perform sexual acts on me under the table in the visiting room. I don't know how Jameson got my address but I take offense to the offer of prostitution as I am a born-again Christian in prison, so help me Jesus. Then Jameson and Ron Jeremy want to perform porno movies with me for Vivid Entertainment because of my internet celebrity status and me having formerly worked as an editor for Playboy Magazine. Someone added Jonathan Lee Riches to the sex advertisement section on Craigslist.com and since then Heidi Fleiss and Peter North have been sexually harassing me and want me to start an escort business with them at a male stud ranch in Reno to accept credit cards then have me steal the studs and customers' credit card information. American Curves plans to put me in their July 2009 centerfold naked –this is invasion of privacy. Whorehouses and brothels nationwide are in a secret conspiracy with female inmates in federal prisons to be escorts and prostitutes for the defendants as part of a plea bargain deal. In return, females get early parole and unlimited TB testing. The defendants' sexual conduct is an act of Satan. Jenna Jameson corrupted nuns to work at the Moonlite covertly. The Moonlite hosted the D.C. Madam, who brought Sen. Henry Reid and Arlen Spector to the Moonlite Bunny Ranch for rest and relaxation with Democratic escorts, political prostitutes. Madame Tussaud's Wax Museum is waxing a sculpture of me, the Jonathan Lee Riches exhibit, with a crown, credit card czar. The defendants outsource prostitutes to Iranian Mullahs –a violation of the Trading with the Enemy Act. Also, I witnessed Barack Obama entering the Moonlite on ten occasions and buying escorts with campaign money and Michelle Obama used the stimulus package funds to get backrubs by Peter North. The whores at the Moonlite turned me into a pervert, I can't hold a normal relationship with a Catholic priest. Defendants endangered my health, gave me sexually transmitted diseases,

244

now I weigh 110 lbs. and can't get it up. I can't produce kids because defendants ruined me, defendants stole my Cialis. Adam and Eve sexually assaulted me in the Garden of Eden. Everytime I see a woman I hide in the closet. Defendants stole my blowup dolls, my penis pumps. The defendants are corrupting the world and I have a judicial duty to stop this evilness as our youth are in danger and defendants teach rapists to rape, child molesters congregate at the Moonlite. I saw John Mark Karr there in 2000 with Jon Benet Ramsey in room 8. I seek the destruction of the Moonlite, defendants forced me into sex therapy, injunctions and restraining orders against defendants sexually insulting and corrupting my mind and ruining my sex drive. I want to have kids one day. Defendants broke into my sperm bank account. This is a Ponzi scam. I seek relief.

Respectfully,

Jonathan Lee Riches d/b/a Bernard Madoff

05/22/09

United States District Court

District of Colorado

The Ghostbusters;

Dan Aykroyd;

Bill Murray;

Harold Ramis;

Ernie Hudson,

Plaintiffs

Vs.

Jonathan Lee Riches d/b/a

Bernard L. Madoff Investment Securities LLC.

Defendant

28 U.S.C. 1331

Preliminary Injunction, Temporary Restraining Order, TRO

We face imminent danger and bodily harm from the defendant. The U.S. Government hired us to flush out ghosts in America. The defendant, Jonathan Lee Riches, is a mega-super hacker with ghost powers, zig-zagging across America, putting fear in people's lives by stealing their identities and ruining their credit. Jonathan Lee Riches hacked into our financial computer files and invested all our money into Ponzi schemes. Riches found out plaintiff Aykroyd and Chevy Chase are spies like us. Riches put so much fear into Ernie Hudson that he turned ghostly white. Riches sent aliens after Bill Murray's girlfriend Sigourney

Weaver. We are the Ghostbusters, Riches tapped into our phone lines to block people from calling us. Jonathan Lee Riches used credit card money to pay Casper the Friendly Ghost to buzz around our heads drunk with Beetle Juice, and Riches is known as the Johnny Depp of identity theft and transforms into Edward Scissorhands to cut our faces like Freddy Krueger. Riches made Elvis rise from his grave and play guitar in front of our house at night. Riches is threatening to green slime us with his sperm. We are in need of protection. Riches is out of control. We seek a restraining order.

Respectfully Submitted,

The Ghostbusters

6/23/09

2010

In 2010 I was notified that I was eligible for RDAP, a residential drug rehab program, which if completed, would take a year off my sentence. Though I have never used drugs I still wanted my sentence reduced so I signed up for the program. Unfortunately I got into an altercation with a fellow inmate who was in the program as well. This lead to me being expelled from RDAP and placed in solitary confinement. I retaliated by suing the doctor who was in charge of the program and naming everyone in the program as my co-plaintiff. This act drew an FBI investigation against me, because the FBI believed I was forging my fellow prisoners' names. They attempted to turn this into another charge against me and was used as an excuse to keep me in solitary confinement for longer than scheduled.

United States District Court

District of Arizona

Umar Farouk Abdulmutallab;

Jonathan Lee Riches,

Plaintiffs

Vs.

ABC's Dancing with the Stars; Nicole Scherzinger; Derek Hough; Kate Gosselin; Tony Dovolani; Erin Andrews; Maksim Chmerkovskiy; Chad Ochocinco; Cheryl Burke; Evan Lysacek; Anna Trebunskaya; Niecy Nash; Louis Van Amstel; Buzz Aldrin; Damian Whitewood; Shannen Doherty; Mark Ballas; Jake Pavelka; Chelsea Hightower,

Defendants

Preliminary Injunction Temporary Restraining Order

Comes now the plaintiffs Umar Farouk Abdulmutallab and Jonathan Lee Riches, we face imminent danger and bodily harm from the defendants collectively and individually. The defendants are discriminating against our Muslim faith by promoting adultery and dancing is forbidden in Islam. We are forced to watch the defendants enjoy themselves on television while billions of people in the world cannot afford a TV set. Defendants don't care about global hunger and defendants' dirty dancing acts offend us by promoting sexual activity to minors watching the show. This is a danger to society that the defendants are contributing to, so we seek a restraining order as our morals and values will suffer if the defendants continue these criminal acts on TV. We pray this court will grant our motion for relief.

Respectfully,

Umar Farouk Abdulmutallab

Jonathan Lee Riches

04/01/10

United States District Court

Middle District of Tennessee

Dr. Ayman Al-Zawahiri;

Jonathan Lee Riches,

Plaintiffs

Vs.

Bonnaroo Music and Arts Festival;

Dave Matthews Band;

Bonnaroo.com;

Kings of Leon;

Stevie Wonder;

Jay-Z a/k/a Shawn Carter,

Defendants

Preliminary Injunction, TRO Temporary Restraining Order

Comes now, the plaintiff's Dr. Ayman Al-Zawahiri and Jonathan Lee Riches, we face imminent danger and bodily harm from the defendants. We move for a restraining order against their upcoming festival because their music offends us and is in violation of Islamic law. Their music is a civil rights violation to us because they offend Muslims in their lyrics and degrade women. Also defendants promote the sale and distribution of alcohol to minors as plaintiffs themselves are recovering addicts and their concert could trigger us to relapse. We pray this honorable court will grant our restraining order for relief.

Respectfully,

Dr. Ayman Al-Zawahiri

Jonathan Lee Riches

04/20/10

United States District Court

Middle District of Tennessee

Jesse James,

Plaintiff

Vs.

Sandra Bullock;

Janine Lindemulder;

Jonathan Lee Riches,

Defendants

Preliminary Injunction, Temporary Restraining Order, TRO 28 U.S.C. 1331

Comes now the plaintiff, Jesse James, in pro-se, moves this honorable court to issue a restraining order against the defendants who are threatening to kill me and ruin my reputation. I face imminent danger and bodily harm in Nashville and throughout Tennessee. Sandra Bullock seeks revenge on me and has been sleeping with multiple men to influence them to come and attack me on my motorcycle and to burn my businesses down. I found out through photographs that defendant Bullock had slept with Tiger Woods 69 times in March 2010 at a Nashville Super 8 Motel and Bullock stole my Harley and drove to Aspen to cheat on me with Charlie Sheen, and Bullock slept with Senator John Edwards at a Charlotte Bobcats basketball game, and Bullock was sleeping with Keanu Reeves on a Greyhound bus and she slept with Janine Lindemulder and Billy Ray Cyrus in a Dollyworld restroom in Tennessee. Bullock had secret affairs behind my back with Eliot

Spitzer at Niagara Falls New York and she slept with Brad Pitt at Mardi Gras in New Orleans. Bullock secretly hired mechanics to install Toyota gas pedals on my motorcycles to make me crash and to crash Ben Roethlisberger from Pittsburgh because of his anti-women behavior. The defendants cause me nightmares. Bullock tried to assault me with Michelle Mcgee's tattoo gun to give me Hep-C, and Bullock hired outlaw motorcycle gang members to put a hit out on my life.

The defendants continue to defame my name and reputation. Defendant Bullock uses her salary to hire convicted identity theft kingpin Jonathan Lee Riches to hack into my finances and steal my credit cards and to illegally wiretap and listen to all my phone calls without my consent. Bullock also paid Mr. Riches hundreds of thousands of dollars to post pictures of me sleeping with various women in other lawsuits that Riches is filing and talking about me and putting damaging evidence against me in the lawsuits that can be viewed online if you go to justia.com and put in Jonathan Lee Riches or Google Jonathan Lee Riches, or Google the following lawsuits: "Riches vs. Swine flu", "Riches vs. convicted child molesters", "Riches vs. Courtney Love", "Riches vs. The Twilight Zone", "Riches vs. Beavis and Butthead", Riches vs. Hulk Hogan", "Riches vs. Justin Timberlake", "Riches vs. Ecoli", "Riches vs. Bullock", Riches vs. I can't believe it's not butter", "Riches vs. 202-456-1414", "Riches vs. Creative Artists Agency", "Riches vs. Jay Z", "Riches vs. The Academy Awards", "Riches vs. Drew Brees", "Riches vs. Combs", "Riches vs. Daytona 500", "Riches vs. Spears", "Riches vs. Lohan", "Riches vs. Aniston", "Riches vs. Gotti", "Riches vs. Eric Rudolph", "Riches vs. Obama", "Riches vs. Somali pirates", "Riches vs. Lil' Wayne", "Riches vs. Hurricane Ike"-go on Hurricane Ike lawsuit and see the big picture. "Riches vs. Oprah Winfrey".

I'm so scared of Jonathan Lee Riches, he has secret evidence against me that he is planning to sell to the National Enquirer with pictures of me sleeping with Paris Hilton in Hiltonhead South Carolina at a Hilton, and having sexual contact with Megan Fox a Six Flags over Arlington, and with me sleeping with domestic diva Martha Stewart. I'm scared these photos will ruin my career. Also Riches claims he has evidence of my tax fraud at my West Coast Choppers business. I have nightmares of the defendants, I seek a restraining order against them.

Respectfully,

Jesses James

04/20/10

United States District Court

District of Colorado

Jonathan Lee Riches,

Plaintiff

Vs.

The Ghostbusters,

Defendants

[Notice of appeal this court's 7/17/09 order for judgment in favor of   defendants]

Jonathan Lee Riches moves to appeal this court's ruling dismissing this case and giving judgment to the defendants. I appeal to the Appeals court, the 10th circuit court of appeals.

The Ghostbusters are after me. I got sprayed with green slime at a Nickelodeon studio on Double Dare. Then I was stuffed into a jack in the box with Jack and the beanstalk. Rick Moranis turned into a pitbull and Michael Vick used him in dogfighting. Dan Aykroyd and Chevy Chase are illegally spying on my lawsuits for President Putin; see Riches v. Putin. Harold Ramis provided his glasses to the Lord of the Flies to start California wildfires; see Riches v. Wildfires. Defendants are illegally detaining my friends: the Blair Witch, Casper, Ghostrider, Patrick Swayze, and Beetlejuice without due process at Engine #9 Fire Station with Kurt Russell and Firestarter. Defendants stole my Halloween candy in the 4th grade. The Stay Puft Marshmallow Man stole my Michelin tires, gave me Firestones and Toyota brakes, and the Amityville Horror boy is a Ghostbuster hitman. I saw the defendants in Disney's Magic Kingdom Haunted Mansion sodomizing each other with proton packs. I hear creepy voices in my prison cell. Debra Hickey at FMC Lexington enters my cell wearing a white sheet. Ernie Hudson is having an affair on his wife with Dr. Amanda Hughes a/k/a Dr. Amanda Leigh Hughes. Google her name. I got arrested by the FBI in 2003 for stealing the Ghostbusters DVD from Blockbuster Video. Dr. Natalie Riley, DTS staff at the RDMP 500hr drug abuse program snorts cocaine with Bill Murray in backlots at MGM Studios. Dr. Natalie Riley had an affair with Harold Ramis. They made a porno movie together called "Grossbusters" and this can be viewed on Youtube. Dan Aykroyd turned me into a Conehead in 1988. My brain is haunted and possessed by the defendants. Defendants taught Winona Ryder to shoplift on Beetlejuice and the dawn of the dead are after me each weekday morning. The Butcher, Baker and the Candlestick maker are too. Chucky sodomized me with a Raggedy Ann Doll. The A-Team committed road rage on the Scooby Doo van in D.C. rush hour traffic on defendants' orders. Defendants told the Boogie Man to wipe my nose. Check out this suit: Riches v. The Twilight Zone, and the poltergeist reached through my HD 3D T.V. and grabbed me. ET and Sweet Pea from Popeye raced the Tour de France with me on Pee Wee Herman's bike. The defendants turned Dr. Amanda Leigh Hughes into a man and sold her to the Weird Science guys. The Ghostbusters hired Sigourney Weaver to kidnap me and to rocket me into space with Aliens. I want to talk to the media; journalists, please contact me immediately. I appeal this case to the 13th circuit court of appeals. I ain't afraid of no ghost!

Respectfully,

Jonathan Lee Riches

6/27/10

United States Bankruptcy Court

Southern District of New York

Securities Investor Protection Corp;

Jonathan Lee Riches, movant,

Plaintiff

Vs.

Bernard L. Madoff,

Defendant

[Notice of appeal by Jonathan Lee Riches this court's 01/30/09 order denying Rule 24 and Bankruptcy Intervention. I appeal to the United States District Court for the southern district of New York]

Bernard L. Madoff has defrauded me, my siblings, my neighbors, and my pets. He left my father and mother out of this. Bernard L. Madoff promised me $5 million dollars in Ponzi money if I file lawsuits around the country in his name, either as him being my a/k/a or me suing him or him suing other people. Example: Madoff vs. Parton, Madoff vs. Horse Illustrated and many more, all you have to do is go to justia.com and put in Bernard Madoff and you will see all the cases with me interlinked with him. Madoff told me to continue filing in his name to keep the focus of attention off him, so journalists and reporters get confused and go on a wild goose chase away from the true Madoff. This is a diversion and this proves the calculated manipulative thinking of Bernard Madoff.

For a while Bernard Madoff was actually paying me to file lawsuits in his name. He would instruct his wife, Ruth, to send

$290.00 to my inmate trust account in Des Moines Iowa - $240.00 is the monthly spending limit for inmates. In return, I was to file lawsuits to make him look like a victim. Bernard Madoff is also using the Jonathan Lee Riches name and brand for his financial gain. I've been used by Bernard Madoff. He and I were pen pals as I'm at the Federal Medical Center in Kentucky and he is at FMC Butner. We both write to his wife Ruth who forwards the letters to each other. Madoff has been psychologically manipulating my mind by convincing me to file as many lawsuits as I can and continues adding to my fame, as I'm in the Guinness Book of World Records for filing the most lawsuits in the history of mankind. While I get notoriety, his wife Ruth is profiting off my fame by making Jonathan Lee Riches T-shirts, hats, mugs, and selling them in Times Square, NY, Ebay, and the Oldsmar Florida flea market and both the Madoffs are lining up book deals with Random House Publishing on the Jonathan Lee Riches Story, Jonathan Lee Riches Bio, where Madoff trademarked my name through laegalzoom.com and copyrighted Jonathan Lee Riches©. These schemes will allow Bernard Madoff to be set for life and his financial security and nest egg will reap the benefits of Jonathan Lee Riches.

From June 2009 through June 2010 Bernard Madoff has ordered me through a stolen credit card of Trustee Irving H. Picard, subscriptions of USA Today, Wall St. Journal, IBD, Smarty Magazine, the Economist, American Curves, Newsmax, with the instructions to use these subscriptions as a reference to find news stories and celebrities to sue in federal courts, and that's what I've been doing. Examples include: Riches vs. Deepwater Horizon Rig, Riches vs. Alice and Wonderland, Spencer Pratt vs. Heidi Montag, Jesse James vs. Bullock. These are just a few of thousands. I filed over 5,000 cases nationwide. Bernard Madoff told me he loves it and promised me that I will make millions off of my fame when I get out of prison.

Everything was planned ahead of schedule. Last January 2009 I was shipped to the federal medical center, FMC Lexington Kentucky, where I was to enroll and participate in the Residential Drug Abuse Program (RDAP), which is held in the Veritas Unit. I began the program in July 2010. I was assigned a treatment primary named Dr. Amanda Hughes who is a drug treatment specialist in the RDAP. While I was in the program, the plaintiff's in this case, the Securities Investor Protection Corp, caught wind that Bernard Madoff was profiting off my Jonathan Lee Riches name while he was in prison with side deals that I was not aware of. For instance, Bernard Madoff would have Ruth Madoff put "Jonathan Lee Riches" in Google and print out thousands of articles and blogs, including Wikipedia and justia.com on every case in America that Jonathan Lee Riches has filed. Then Ruth would send the articles to Bernard at FMC Butner where Madoff would then distribute them throughout the prison population and promise all the other inmates that I'm the best pro-se jailhouse lawyer on earth and that for $100 I will file appeals, briefs and do any sort of legal work for any inmate. Madoff was making a killing, 925 inmates took up his offer at $100 a pop. The plaintiffs in this case were livid so they made a side deal with Dr. Amanda Hughes, my primary, to harass me emotionally, sexually and physically. The plaintiffs in this case instructed Dr. Hughes to give me random prison shakedowns with my property and destroy all legal material that I filed on Bernard Madoff's behalf, because if I had sent it out to Ruth on Bernard's orders the Madoffs would've made millions. Dr. Hughes complied and would rip up all my Bernard Madoff court papers. The plaintiffs told Dr. Hughes to inflict psychological warfare on me by forcing medications such as Paxil, Trazadone, and Zoloft, then using hypnosis and psychotherapy mind manipulation to convince me to stop filing lawsuits on Madoff and start filing lawsuits on Dr. Amanda Hughes instead. Hughes knew that the more suits I filed on her she could personally profit from with huge marketing opportunities from her being a victim of my suits. She could write books about her experience as my therapist, in which any proceeds that Dr. Amanda Hughes makes from fame and fortune on me she would have to split it 50/50 with the plaintiffs in this case. I fell for the trick as I filed the suits Simpson vs. Riley and Pratt vs. Montag & Dr. Hughes, or all you have to do now is google "Dr. Amanda Hughes" and see for yourself. The plaintiffs instructed Dr. Hughes to kick me out of the RDAP program in April 2010, two weeks before I was scheduled to graduate. If I had graduated I would have received one year off of my sentence, which would have made me eligible for a halfway house in July 2010. Now I have to spend an extra year in jail, this will allow the plaintiffs and Dr. Hughes to continue to profit, because as a psychologist Dr. Hughes knew I would be mad and go on a lawsuit filing frenzy. That's why she ordered the administration at FMC Lexington to put me in solitary confinement. I'm bored all day, so now I just file lawsuits, there is nothing else to do. I still get at all the newspapers Madoff subscribed to me, I listen to NPR and I sue. This is my livelihood. I've been used by Madoff, Dr. Hughes, and the Securities Investor Protection Corp. They are all profiting off of my name and fame. I want to tell my side of the story. I'm open to all media requests from journalists, bloggers or curious Americans. I'm in the process of being shipped to another institution so if you can't reach me here, look me up through the bureau of prisons inmate locator. I will talk. The truth will set me free. I appeal to the district court.

Respectfully,

Jonathan Lee Riches

07/05/10

United States District Court

Eastern District of Missouri

Jonathan Lee Riches a/k/a

Aubrey Drake Graham,

Plaintiff

Vs.

Justin Bieber;

Taylor Swift;

Miley Cyrus;

Greyson Chance,

Defendants

Preliminary Injunction. Temporary Restraining Order, TRO 28 U.S.C. 1331

Comes now the plaintiff, Jonathan Lee Riches a/k/a Aubrey Drake Graham. I face imminent danger and bodily harm. The four defendants are my children and I'm seeking custody of them. If this court does not intervene and save my children they will become endangered species. I want DNA testing, I fathered the four children. I have Justin Bieber's hair, Taylor Swift's nose, Miley Cyrus ears and Greyson Chance belly button. These defendants are in danger from adult pedophiles and celebrity stalkers. I seek custody from each of them. I can provide the defendants with 24 hour security at the Federal Medical Center in Lexington Kentucky, with armed guard services surrounding barbed wire fencing to keep prey away from my babies. I can provide the defendants with 3 square meals a day, including milk in the morning so their bones can grow. I can provide the defendants with universal government healthcare. The prison library can meet the defendants' educational needs. I want to be the father I always dreamed I could be. Each night the defendants can sit on my lap and I can read them bedtime stories uninterrupted in my cell. I have one blanket we can cover up like a tent. I can read them Spin Magazine and the prison TVs show BET and MTV so we can rock! We have a huge rec yard. I can play horseshoes with the defendants or we could go to the hobby and craft shop and make prison art that we can send to their grandmother in Pennsylvania. If the defendants stay with me they will be safe from paparazzi and the prison commissary sells Halls cough drops so they won't lose their voice. We have decks of cards here so we can play spades for push-ups and the rec yard has a weight pile –I want Justin Bieber to get buff like me. Justin Bieber is my hero and I'm very proud of his success –I taught him to sing at Westboro Baptist Church and at Veterans' funerals. I met Justin Bieber's mother, Pattie Mallette, on Eharmony.com and got her pregnant outside of Bad Boy Records in New York City. I financed Def Jam Music Group with identity theft. Bieber and I are trying to start a new record label "Identity Theft Jam". Justin Bieber is already going bald. Bieber illegally used my Capital One No Hassle Credit Card to get a Hair Club For Men and Strawberry Shortcake hair dye at CVS Pharmacy. If I don't get custody of Miley Cyrus fast I'm afraid my nemesis, Warren Jeffs, is going to marry her in either Utah or Hannah Montana. I intercepted a phone call where former NFL player Lawrence Taylor was trying to meet Miley Cyrus at an Orlando Super 8 Motel. Taylor Swift was born John Kerry Swift Boat. Ellen Degeneres is trying to make Greyson Chance a woman with my credit cards. The defendants mean everything to me. I paid a prison tattoo artist 100 packs of mackerel to have the defendants' images on my forearms, and I smuggled in posters of the defendants to hang above my bunk.

When I hear the defendants on the radio I get goosebumps and cry. They are special and are a part of my heart. I saved my daughter Taylor Swift a few months ago from Nashville floods. Then I found out that the defendants are getting psychologically brainwashed by Psychologist Dr. Amanda Hughes a/k/a Dr. Amanda Leigh Hughes, drug treatment specialist at the RDAP, Residential Drug Abuse Program at the Federal Medical Center in Lexington Kentucky. The defendants meet with Dr. Hughes collectively every Monday and Wednesday at 12:50pm. Dr. Hughes is encouraging the defendants to smoke pot in school zones, shoot cocaine at rock concerts like Led Zeppelin and Britney Spears tours, as well as encouraging the defendants to have unprotected sex with foreigners. Dr. Hughes is also teaching my kids how to make suicide bomber vests so they can blow up themselves and crowds at their concerts. Dr. Hughes is showing the defendants animal pornography at Disney's Animal Kingdom. Dr. Hughes gives the defendants ecstasy before they attend Paul Oakenfold raves –my kids are going to die before they are 25. This worries me as a parent. Dr. Hughes tells the defendants to drink and drive without seatbelts and to shoplift with Winona Ryder at Saks 5th Ave. Dr. Hughes has been using the defendants as guinea pigs with drug experiments in her office in a dark basement in the Veritas Unit, I'm scared. I saw Taylor Swift on the Country Music Channel with needle marks on her right arm. Dr. Hughes also told Taylor Swift to have sex with Billy Ray Cyrus at Nickelodeon Studios. Justin Bieber stole my American Express card to get a penis enlargement on Dr. Amanda Hughes's direct orders. The peoples' greatest frustrations with me is also my greatest strength. I keep bloggers and the public glued to their computers each day, enquiring about my suits and having them contemplate meanings and motives. "Is Jon insane, or is it a con game, like what's in Barry Bonds's veins?" I can walk into Belgium with an Islamic veil and people would think I'm a woman, or a ninja. The defendants took my brains from my smart phone, replaced it with a dumb phone with down syndrome. I was Batman's butler. My pet dog was buried at Stephen King's Pet Cemetery. I sued American Idol, see "Riches vs. American Idol". Defendants sent William "Refrigerator" Perry to eat what is left of me. The Beatles put bugs on my prison floor and inside my Volkswagen. Beyonce put me in a halo. The defendants are under a lot of stress and anxiety. Justin Bieber is developing acne and hemorrhoids and Greyson Chance has been delaying puberty. John Mark Karr tried to take the defendants to Thailand with David Carradine and Justin Bieber is getting singing lessons from Milli Vanilli. The defendants each slept with Michael Jackson at the Neverland Ranch when they were 12. Rocker Tommy Lee made a sex tape with each defendant behind Pamela's back. Taylor Swift secretly got sodomized with a Grammy by Kanye West in a Chicago alley. Defendants and Lady Gaga gave me the finger at Epcot Center. Justin Bieber was R. Kelly's secret lover. Justin Bieber lost his virginity to Madonna. Greyson chance is in a secret relationship with Lance Bass. Taylor Swift licked Lil Wayne's lollipop at the BET Music Awards. The defendants are headed for death and destruction. Bieber already told me he wants to be like Kurt Cobain and Jimmy Morrison. I need custody of the defendants. I get nightmares and panic attacks knowing the whole world is corrupting them like it did to me. I'm afraid Justin Bieber will want to be just like his father and give up music to be an international identity thief. I'm in the Guinness Book of World Records for stealing the most identities in the history of mankind. I can be reached or contacted for interviews at the below address. I'm open to all media interviews with reporters or bloggers. I move for a restraining order to stop the defendants from performing, singing and producing music. I seek immediate custody. I pray for relief.

Respectfully,

Jonathan Lee Riches

07/20/10

United States Court

District of Colorado

Riches

Plaintiff

Vs.

Swine Flu

[Notice of Appeal]

Jonathan Lee Riches moves to appeal the dismissal of this case. Appeal to the 10th circuit.

I caught swine flu at the medical center in Lexington Kentucky while eating a pork sandwich with Imams and Rabbis. When Dr. Amanda Hughes opens up her vagina for every Afro-American to eat, they get swine flu as well. Dr. Hughes is a medical drug treatment specialist at the Residential Drug Abuse Program (RDAP) at FMC Lexington. Dr. Hughes sleeps and has sex with live pigs who spread swine flu. Dr. Hughes put on a pig costume and went to the market to eat pounds of roast beef. Dr. Hughes masturbated to Porky Pig. Dr. Hughes sexually assaulted me and sodomized me with a Snapple. Dr. Hughes is a Super 8 Motel prostitute and uses the nickname "Pigs in a blanket." Dr. Hughes had sex with Boss Hog. I appeal.

Respectfully,

Jonathan Lee Riches

8/12/10

United States Court

District of Colorado

Jonathan Lee Riches d/b/a

Bernard L. Madoff a/k/a

Bernie Madoff,

Plaintiff

Vs.

The New York Yankees;

Derek Jeter;

Alex Rodriguez;

Mariano Rivera;

Jorge Posada;

Mark Teixeira;

Robinson Cano;

Curtis Granderson,

Defendants

28 U.S.C. 225S

18 U.S.C. 1331

Comes now, Jonathan Lee Riches under 28 U.S.C. 225S. I was in Florence Adx, this court has jurisdiction from October 2009. I was in solitary confinement and I had no T.V. in my cell to watch the New York Yankees. I am a huge Philadelphia Phillies and Eagles fan and this was discrimination. I could have made a difference in the World Series outcome by being the tenth player. My sentence is unconstitutional. I seek a restraining order.

Respectfully,

Jonathan Lee Riches

8/13/10

United States District Court

Northern District of Philadelphia

Jonathan Lee Riches d/b/a

Gordon Gekko a/k/a Michael Milken,

Plaintiffs

Vs.

104th World Series;

Philadelphia Phillies;

Tampa Bay Rays,

Defendants

42 U.S.C. 1983

Preliminary Injunction/Temporary Restraining Order

I face imminent danger from the 2008 World Series,
Philadelphia Phillies vs. Tampa Bay Rays. The World Series is
being shown on the T.V.s at FCI Williamsburg. Normally we
are locked down at 10pm, cells locked, but because of the
defendants FCI Williamsburg is allowing late night to watch the
World Series until at least 11:45pm. This puts me in danger
because my door is unlocked after 10pm and I could get attacked
by inmate Tampa Bay Rays' fans. I'm from Philadelphia, and
my loyalty is to the Phillies, Connie Mack, Mike Schmitt,
Veterans' Stadium. The majority of inmates on my unit are from
Florida –they hate Philly. I seek a restraining order against the
World Series for creating hate, putting my life in danger.
Inmates watch Evan Longoria and Pena hit homeruns and I fear
they will use bats at the FCI Williamsburg softball field and

swing at my head with them, aggravated assault. I'm scared of bodily harm. The 104th World Series must be blacked out from prison T.V. I pray for relief.

Respectfully Submitted,

Jonathan Lee Riches

09/10/10

United States District Court

Eastern District of Missouri

Jonathan Lee Riches d/b/a

Ali Hassan Al-Majid a/k/a

Kat Stacks,

Plaintiff

Vs.

"Don't ask, don't tell"; Gay marriage; Proposition 8; Gay pride parade; Nudist colony; Swingers club; Sexually transmitted diseases; Chaz Bono; Liz Cheney; YMCA; Harvey Milk; lesbians; Homosexuals; Samantha Ronson; Barney Frank; HIV a/k/a Human Immunodeficiency Virus; The Village People; Linda Lovelace; Tyson Gay; Full Metal Jacket; Rainbow Floats; National Center for Lesbian Rights; Employment Nondiscrimination Act,

Defendants

Preliminary Injunction, Temporary Restraining Order, TRO 28 U.S.C. 1331

Comes now, Jonathan Lee Riches d/b/a Ali Hassan Al-Majid (Chemical Ali) a/k/a Kat Stacks, in pro-se. I and the American people along with Worldwide Heterosexuals and Virgins face imminent danger and bodily harm from "don't ask, don't tell" and the conspiracy of defendants.

This is a gigantic fraud of epic proportions which endangers me, endangered species, the defendants undermine our Korans and Bibles, perverting the world with filth. The defendants will ruin marriages, corrupt children, and morals/values will be eliminated. Our forefathers would be rolling in their graves sick, foreign terrorists will use the defendants for justification for Holy Wars, anarchists will protest, cybercriminals will launch computer viruses, nuns will rebel.

"Don't ask, don't tell" is a psychological trap. I don't care if you tell or not but all forms of homosexuality are wrong. I was forced to eat at TGI Fridays with gay waiters serving me. The defendants plan to start martial law and all heterosexual marriages nationwide will be annulled! American Curves Magazine will be banned. Chaz Bono is going to be Time's Person of the Year. Then Somali pirates of the Caribbean will demand man booty for ransom. Our four branches of the military plan to convert all other militaries, insurgencies, narco-drug traffickers world-wide into homosexuals to ruin global growth in populations and male prostitution will occur at all military bases. At Fort Brag male soldiers will brag to each other about how big their penises are. The military will label homophobia a mental illness. At the Gay Pride Parade all soldiers will swing dance on root beer floats. Hasbro will sell gay GI Joe action figures. Then our troops coming home from duty with PTSD will shoot all straight people for not loving them. The Army is building pink tanks, rainbow color airplanes. All of our generals will be at central command watching gay porn. AT&T has plans to change its name to Gay T&T! My cellmate Bubba already proposed to me and he was in McHale's Navy. Uncle Sam is now dressed as a drag queen. Soldiers will give each other hummers in their Hummers. Our troops are teaching Afghans to come out of the closet. The Village People plan to join the Navy. Now at all military barracks the defendants caused male troops to have Ricky Martin and Brad Pitt posters and now male troops' hobbies overseas are spin the bottle, duck, duck, goose, Trivial Pursuit, knitting, painting each others' toes, blasting music like Right Said Fred's "I'm Too Sexy", "Macho Man", Madonna's "Borderline", plucking each others' eyebrows, giving each other foot massages. I wanted to join the Marines when I got out of prison and marry GI Jane, but she went lesbian on me. Guantanamo Bay turned into a gay health spa. Now Bin Laden wears a pink turban, shaved his beard with bikini wax. Homosexuals at Arlington Cemetery will come out of their closets. John McCain slept with Pat Tillman. Boy George, George Michael, Harvey Milk and the Jonas Brothers plan on joining the Air Force. Omaha Beach is a nudist colony. No male troops will sleep peacefully in their barracks, constant moaning and groaning, it will smell like poop, condom machines in the latrine. Robert E. Lee slept with Sherman at Woodstock to negotiate peace. The defendants must be stopped. I'm whistleblowing and will become a draft-dodging AWOL in an underground bomb shelter under the Vatican, away from gay Catholic priests too. I move for restraining orders.

Respectfully,

Jonathan Lee Riches

09/11/10

2011-2016

At the end of 2010 the government filed a civil injunction against me to stop me from filing any more lawsuits (United States of America, Eastern District of Kentucky Vs. Jonathan Lee Riches). I was also under federal investigation for forgery for filing lawsuits against RDAP.

For these reasons, I laid low for 2011. I was getting close to being released from prison and did not want to antagonize the prison authorities and jeopardize my release. The suit against Jared Loughner was a sort of retirement suit for me as well as an act of defiance against the government's injunction against me. After I filed this suit I promised the prison officials, on condition of me being released from solitary confinement, that I would not file any more suits.

Upon my release in 2012 I felt two distinct desires: 1) to file a few high profile lawsuits against celebrities who really annoyed me e.g., the Kardashians and 2) the desire to have a presence on social media that would publicize the suits I had filed while incarcerated. In my previous lawsuits I had memed the idea that my name was a brand that had been appropriated by various celebrities, I saw the distinct possibility of realizing this idea through social media.

Social media was a new avenue of publicity for me; it allowed me to broadcast not only the suits that had made me infamous but the ideas I was generating at the time. These ideas lead me to what is now known as trolling. My version of trolling was not confined to the internet though. The apex of this occurred during the 2016 presidential election when I appeared at rallies for each candidate in a variety of ethnic outfits, e.g., "Muslims for Trump", "Mexicans for Hillary", "Rastafarians for Jill Stein", etc. I wanted to see if I could draw media attention at these real

275

life events in the way I had done in my lawsuits but still keep my persona shrouded in ambiguity. Generally speaking, I got the reaction I was looking for. Though there is a part of every type of action like this that is unexpected, I don't try to anticipate for this surprise element, I am open to it because that is what makes my form of agitation interesting. In fact, that is what makes life interesting

United States District Court

District of Arizona

Julian Assange a/k/a

Jonathan Lee Riches,

Plaintiff

Vs.

Jared Lee Loughner a/k/a

Jared Loughner a/k/a

Mumtaz Qadri,

Defendant

Preliminary Injunction, Temporary Restraining Order, TRO 28 U.S.C. 1331

I face imminent danger and bodily harm from the defendant Jared Lee Loughner. I was personally effected and traumatized by the defendant's actions, which are inexcusable, and my thoughts and prayers go out to the victims, including US Rep Gabrielle Giffords, Chief Judge John Roll, Christian-Taylor

Green and the entire Tucson community. Now I'm in fear of the defendant as he is now in federal custody –I want a restraining order against him preventing the Bureau of Prisons from transferring the defendant to the Federal Medical Center in Lexington Kentucky where the defendant will receive a mental health evaluation on his criminal case. I'm in fear that if the defendant transfers to FMC Lexington he will be placed in solitary confinement where I'm currently being illegally detained, and possibly being my cellmate, in which he could use his bare hands or a prison shank to kill me for being a moderate Democrat and for me being Jonathan Lee Riches, who is in the Guinness Book of World Records for suing the most people in the history of mankind. I'm illegally serving over a decade in federal prison for being a ringleader in an international identity theft conspiracy along with computer hacking, phishing, spamming with wire fraud via cyberwarfare with botnets and Trojan Horses stealing the personal information of millions of internet service providers' customers. See "U.S. vs. Riches" case # 4-03-90 S.D. of Texas. I'm a federal whistleblower on government corruption and physical, sexual, and mental abuse within the federal prison system, in which, to silence me, I've been in solitary confinement for over a year. The government plans to indict me on new federal charges of forging or fraud for filing lawsuits exposing corruption, to keep me in prison past March 23, 2012, which is my release date. Now the government also filed a civil preliminary injunction against me, preventing me from filing anymore lawsuits and giving the Bureau of Prisons authorization to open up my sealed legal mail and return it to me. See "U.S. vs. Riches" case # 5-10- cv-00322 KSF, which is violating my constitutional rights to the courts. I'm in solitary and continue to get physically, mentally and sexually abused by Dr. Kristen Hungness, Dr. Amanda Leigh Hughes, Warden Deborah Hickey, SIA Mary Anderson, Officer Howe, et al. I had to smuggle this lawsuit out of the prison, otherwise

277

FMC Lexington would have thrown it away, even though I put a stamp on it, which is mail fraud on their part. In order to get this lawsuit out I arranged with an army of ants who are scattered on my floor. I put breadcrumbs on the top of this envelope and at least 10,000 ants carried this lawsuit on their backs and marched it outside through the emergency exit. From this point I arranged with a few pigeons that I've been communicating with via sign language to pick up the lawsuits from the ants and fly them personally to the courthouse steps in Tucson Arizona since the pigeons have to fly south for the winter anyway. I figure that since the pigeons hit the jet stream it will expedite the delivery process and this lawsuit will hit the courts by the end of Jan 2011 a few weeks after the mass shooting that Jared Lee Loughner committed. Jared Loughner was also personally influenced weeks before by Mumtaz Qadri in Pakistan. The Safeway Grocery store is supposed to be safe, all Safeways need to get Lifelock. Defendant Loughner took a taxi to Safeway driven by Robert De Niro who escaped from Cape Fear, and the taxi had a set of Firestone tires bought at El Campo tires where Gabrielle Giffords once worked. El Campo Tires also provided tires to Jim Leyritz, governor of South Dakota, Lisa "Left Eye" Lopez, dale Earnhardt Sr., Andrew Gallo, Richie Valens, and Brayton Edwards. The 9mm Glock Nine defendant Loughner had was given to him by Cho at Virginia Tech, who he got from the Columbine kids, where they got the WMD's from Saddam Hussein. Defendant Jared is also friends with Jared from Subway, a six inch submarine. When I heard of the Tucson tragedy I made a flag out of prison toilet paper and flew it at half-mast. Then on 01/10/11 I had an 11am Eastern moment of silence for the victims but I was interrupted by other Afro-American inmates in solitary cells banging and hollering because we didn't get served fried chicken for lunch. I believe "Congress at your corner" was set up by U.S. Rep. Gabrielle Giffords to expose and repeal tough federal sentencing guidelines and

Giffords was planning to expose my illegal incarceration and the violation of my 8th Amendment rights for cruel and unusual punishment at 10:20am, but Loughner prevented her from speaking about my case. I nominate Roger Salzgeber, Bill Budger, and Joseph Zamudio for Congressional medals of honor and to try out for the starting defensive line of the Arizona Cardinals. Patricia Maisch is also a hero, and I personally propose to her. Gabrielle Giffords's husband, Mark Kelly, is a NASA astronaut and I believe if Barack Obama gives more funding to the space program Mark Kelly could fly into space on Feb. 8th, 2011 exactly one month away from Earth with a super sensitive telescope from the Sharper Image, with a laser beam, and zoom into Loughner's eyes to blind him, so that this tragedy would be averted. Now federal taxpayers will suffer because their pocket change will have to pay for all members of congress security and all the FBI agents that are in Tucson will build a permanent command center for extra manpower to stop illegal immigration over the boarder. This tragedy flooded the AM networks with breaking news and regular scheduled programming on Sean Hannity, Mark Levin, Coast to Coast with George Nore was interrupted and the AM radio is the only outside news source I have in solitary. The defendants' actions also made me cry. I seek a restraining order against them.

Submitted,

Jonathan Lee Riches

01/11/11

United States District Court

District of Detroit

Riches,

Plaintiff

Vs.

Lopez,

Defendant

Notice of Appeal

Jonathan Lee Riches appeals to the 6th Circuit Court of AppealsI, Jonathan Lee Riches, appeal. Jennifer Lopez put me in prison. I was her former boyfriend fiancée before Marc Anthony and I did millions of dollars in fraud with credit cards to finance Lopez's career. I bought her Saks 5th Ave. bras, JC Penny leg warmers, and Sam Goody gift certificates to but her own CDs to boost her album sales. Then I used stolen people's identities to get Lopez breast implants, a tummy tuck worth $11,252.64 and Avon facial cream. Lopez manipulated me and she abandoned me after I went to prison for 125 months. Lopez violated my copyrighted music, "Jenny from the Block" was my idea and while Lopez was married to Marc Anthony she cheated on Anthony with comedian George Lopez and former MLB catcher Javier Lopez; I have the proof on videotape. Email me at johnnysuenami@gmail. I appeal.

Respectfully,

Jonathan Lee Riches

05/20/12

United States District Court

District of Detroit

Riches,

Plaintiff

Vs.

Pitt, et al,

Defendants

Notice of Appeal

Jonathan Lee Riches appeals the dismissal of the case to the 6th Circuit Court of Appeals

I am the real father to Brad Pitt and Angelina Jolie's children, all of them have my DNA, and they are forbidding me from taking a blood sample. I met Jolie on the set of Hackers and I'm the real Johnny Lee that she married. Jolie used to make me put my finger in her mouth to aid her bulimia. Brad Pitt stole my credit cards on Fight Club. I was molested by Brad Pitt on Sleepers. Brad Pitt and George Clooney broke into my piggy bank at my home in an Ocean's 11 plot. Pitt stole my cocaine stash that I got from Cheech and Chong. Jolie and I were pen pals in prison. I've got love letters from Jolie to produce as evidence. I appeal.

Respectfully,

Jonathan Lee Riches

05/22/12

United States District Court

Middle District of Florida

Riches

Vs.

Snipes

Notice of Appeal

Appeal by Jonathan Lee Riches re: the dismissal of this case.

Appeal to the 11th Circuit.

Wesley Snipes violates my civil rights. Snipes was my cellmate in federal prison and he used martial arts skills he learned while making *Blade* to assault me because I refused sexual intercourse with him, and Snipes made me teach him identity theft skills to further his tax fraud behavior when he gets out of prison. I was forced to hand wash Snipes' toes in prison and paint his nails rainbow. Wesley Snipes told me personally that he is HIV positive and Snipes is best friends with Bernard Madoff. Snipes also smuggled a cell phone into prison, so I was forced to watch *White Men Can't Jump* with him on our prison bunk. Snipes also told me that if I don't intervene in the Kim Kardashian v. The Gap, case #2:11-cv-06568, he will bash my head with his fists. I appeal.

Respectfully,

Jonathan Lee Riches

5/31/12

United States District Court

Eastern District of Pennsylvania

Chosen 300 Ministries,

Plaintiffs

Vs.

City of Philadelphia,

Defendants

Jonathan Lee Riches,

Movant

Motion to Intervene as Plaintiff

Under Fed.R.CIV.P. Rule 24(A)2, 24(B)

Comes now, the movant Jonathan Lee Riches, moves this honorable court to intervene in this case as a plaintiff under Rule 24. The city of Philadelphia violates my Constitutional rights. The city of Philadelphia will not let me pagan dance at the Art Museum, I sacrificed a goat head I got from Hilshire Farms and plan to put it over my head with Tiki torches and Michael Nutter is stopping my cult from praying to our Sun God. I am the lawsuit God of the world and the Supreme Court and juries worship me as I preach the lawsuit. Defendants won't give me a liquor license to distribute Jim Jones Juice around the streets of Philadelphia with Bruce Springsteen. Chosen 300 Ministries plans to hang me on a cross next to Jesus Christ and I will rise with the Messiah during the 7th inning at the next Phillies game. I can also walk across the Delaware and write lawsuits at the same time. I pray, oh Lord, grant my motion for relief!

Respectfully,

Jonathan Lee Riches©

06/09/12

United States District Court

Western District of Texas

San Antonio Division

Gino Romano, and all others similarly situated,

Plaintiffs

Vs.

Kim Kardashian a/k/a Kimberly Noel "Kim" Kardashian;

Tony Parker;

Eva Longoria;

Kourtney Kardashian,

Defendants

Preliminary Injunction

Temporary Restraining Order

I'M FACING IMMINENT DANGER AND BODILY HARM FROM THE DEFENDANTS IN SAN ANTONIO AND I SEEK A RESTRAINING ORDER AGAINST THEM. I HAVE NEWLY DISCOVERED EVIDENCE IN A MAJOR CONSPIRACY WITH THE DEFENDANTS WHO PARTICIPATED IN A PLOT TO DECIEVE AMERICA, THE TABLOIDS, AND SOCIAL MEDIA. I AM A PRIVATE INVESTIGATOR AND I WORK FOR JONATHAN LEE RICHES INC D/B/A UYD4L.TUMBLR.COM UNDER THE DIRECT ORDERS OF JONATHAN LEE RICHES AND BACK WHEN RICHES WAS IN FEDERAL PRISON I WAS A FREELANCE JOURNALIST AND I UNCOVERED

A SEX SCANDAL THAT ROCKS SAN ANTONIO. KIM KARDASHIAN AND TONY PARKER MADE A SEX TAPE TOGETHER WHILE PARKER WAS MARRIED TO EVA, THIS TAPE WAS MADE AT A LOS ANGELES SUPER 8 MOTEL WHEN THE SPURS CAME TO LA TO PLAY THE LAKERS, AND TONY PARKER KEPT A COPY OF THE SEX TAPE UNDER HIS MATTRESS AT HOME IN SAN ANTONIO, THE SAME BED THAT TONY PARKER AND KIM KARDASHIAN ALSO ILIAD SEX IN WHILE EVA WAS FILMING DESPERATE HOUSEWIVES AND WHEN EVA CAME HOME SHE NOTICE THE MATRESS SPRINGS BROKEN SO SHE CALLED 1800-MATTRES (TAKE THE LAST "S" OFF FOR SAVINGS) TO GET A NEW ONE, AND SHE FOUND THE TONY PARKER /KIM KARDASHIAN SEX TAPE, BUT DIDNT CONFRONT TONY PARKER ABOUT IT, SO EVA DECIDED TO RETALIATE AGAINST TONY, SO EVA CALLED OVER KOURTNEY KARDASHIAN TO TONY PARKERS HOUSE AND HAD A LESBIAN AFAIR ON TONY WITH HER WHICH EVA LONGORIA FILMED, AND THEN SHE HID IT IN THE MEDICINE CABINET , BUT TONY PARKER ONE MORNING WAS GETTING HIS DAILY STEROID STASH AND FOUND THE TAPE, AND CONFRONTED EVA WITH HER SEX TAPE, SO EVA CONFRONTED TONY WITH HIS SEX TAPE WITH KIM KARDASHIAN ,AND IT WAS A STAND OFF, SO EVA & TONY CALLED UP THE KARDASHIANS FOR A SECRET MEETING AND ALL THE DEFENDANTS MADE A PACT PEACE AGREEMENT NOT TO TELL A SOUL, BUT TONY PARKER WAS DUMB ENOUGH TO THROW THE TAPES IN THE TRASH, WHICH I WAS DUMPSTER DIVING, AND RETRIEVED , THEN I GAVE THE TAPES TO JONATHAN LEE RICHES, AND THE DEFENDATS FOUND OUT THE TAPES WERE MISSING, AND TRACED MY MUDDY FOOTPRINTS TO

ME, AND NOW DEFENDANTS WANT THESE TAPES BACK, WHICH EMBARRASSES THEIR EMPIRES. KIM KARDASHIAN ASSUALTED ME AND RICHES IN NASHVILLE TN BECAUSE OF THESE TAPES. RICHES TOLD ME TO FILED THIS SUIT AND I FEEL IF THEIR IS ANY OTHERS WHO ARE SIMLILARY SITUATED AND ARE A WITNESS TO COME FORWARD WITH THEIR SIDE. THE DEFENDATS THREATENED MY LIFE ON MY GINO ROMANO FACEBOOK PAGE AND I'M SHAKING IN MY BOOTS AND I DONT HAVE SPURS FOR LEVERAGE CAUSE I'M A FROM THE NORTH, AND I BRING THIS SUIT UNDER THE 1ST AMENDMENT OF OUR U.S. CONSTITUTION.

Respectfully,

Gino Romano

06/14/12

United States District Court

Northern District of West Virginia

Gino Romano and all others similarly situated,

Plaintiffs

Vs.

Kim Kardashian a/k/a

Kimberly Noel Kardashian;

Kanye West;

Kris Jenner;

Bruce Jenner;

Khloe Kardashian;

Kourtney Kardashian,

Defendants

Preliminary Injunction

Temporary Restraining Order

Gino Romano faces imminent danger and bodily harm, and the American citizens are in danger from the defendants. The Kardashian Klan, Kanye West and 2 Jenners. All of the defendants are terrorists. On 06/17/12 I was in West Virginia, deep in the hills and I stumbled upon the defendants who were all at an Al Qaeda secret training camp where Kris Jenner had organized this operation and senior members of Al Qaeda were there including #2 Ayman Al Zawahri, Richard Reid's cousins,

Johnny Walker Lindh's parents and Al Shabar. On this day Kim Kardashian, Khloe Kardashian, Kourtney Kardashian, Kanye West and Bruce Jenner all plead allegiance to Al Qaeda. They burned the U.S. flag, stomped their feet on Barack's picture, then Kanye West performed a concert for all the Al Qaeda members, they all drank Jim Jones Juice and then the defendants took out shovels and began digging for coal and fracking in the mines of West Virginia to get fuel to make weapons of mass destruction. Kris Jenner was enriching uranium and the Kardashians made a vow that all their websites, clothing lines, reality shows and proceeds will go directly to Al Qaeda to finance and support the Jihad. Kim Kardashian has been signing autographs for Hamas and Ayman Al-Zawahri got Kourtney Kardashian pregnant. Kim Kardashian is now the leader of Al Qaeda. The defendants shot Ak-47s in the air, MS 13 gangs were there too. All the defendants stopped shoveling for coal and prayed to Mecca at noon then put their shoes on sale on Ebay to raise money for an Islamic charity. Kanye West is now also the leader of Chicago's notorious El Rukn street gang and Kim Kardashian plans to design Al Qaeda veils for women for her clothing line, Dash. Khloe Kardashian has been cheating on Lamar with Zacarias Moussoui as prison pen pals and Bruce Jenner secretly helped Al Qaeda during the Berlin Olympics in 1973. The Kardashians' tax records must be looked at by the department of Homeland Security. Kim Kardashian personally models for Cat Stevens part-time and Kris Jenner was the late Yassar Arafat's former mistress. Rob Kardashian is secretly taking flying lessons on KSM in Guantanimo Bay's direct orders and the Kardashians plan to pay for eye surgery for Mullah Omar, and if this plan works they will try it on the Blind Sheik Rassam next. Kim Kardashian personally paid for Johnny Walker Lindh's plane ticket to Afghan tribal region in 2001. Now the Kardashians have a Jihad against me. I already escaped numerous assassination attacks by them on me, including a McDonald's attack in Nashville, Disney World Assault and Busch Gardens Jihad –I barely escaped this episode. All of this happened because the defendants saw me spying on the Al Qaeda training, so Kim Kardashian launched a rocket at me, Bruce Jenner threw a grenade at my head and Khloe Kardashian tried to behead me. I'm so scared of the defendants, I seek restraining orders against them. I'm a patriot, not from New England, but a Yankee because I live in both New York and Philly, read between the lines!

Respectfully,

Gino Romano

06/17/12

United States District Court

District of Colorado

Riches,

Plaintiff

Vs.

Helmsley,

Defendant

[Notice of Appeal]

Jonathan Lee Riches to appeal the dismissal of this case to the 10th circuit court of appeals. I appeal.

Ms. Helmsley had her dog attack me and give me rabies and Dr. Hughes DTS a/k/a Dr. Amanda Hughes made me watch her have sex with Toto in Helmsley's estate. Helmsley only left me a box of Oreo cookies and latex condoms in her will. I was a plumber at the Helmsley Estate and found her false teeth in a pipe and Helmsley has a secret panic room where Jodi Foster is tied up for ransom and Mel Gibson and Danny Glover shot J.R. (Jonathan Riches). Helmsley had sex with Scooby Doo. I was Helmsley's boytoy from Wisteria Lane. Helmsley raped me at AARP. Helmsley and I have a sex tape which Vivid Entertainment is going to release. Helmsley gave me crabs at the Jersey Shore with Snooki. I appeal.

Respectfully,

Jonathan Lee Riches

08/10/12

United States District Court

Western District of Pennsylvania

Naomi Riches,

Plaintiff

Vs.

Hurricane Sandy a/k/a Frankenstorm;

HAARP a/k/a The High Frequency Active Auroral Research Program,

Defendants

Under the False Claims Act

Under the false Whistleblowers Act

Comes now, Naomi riches, in pro-se, moves this honorable court to issue an order for the defendants named in this suit to respond. This suit is brought under the false claims act. Plaintiff seeks $50,000,000.00 in damages from emotional distress, and for the proceeds to be distributed to all victims of government corruption, victims of government eminent domain, and for a restraining order against the Haarp program which is ruining people's lives and experimenting on humans without the public knowing the truth.

Statements of Fact

Steering hurricanes and modifying intensity is a goal of Homeland Security. In Aug. 2008, it was reported that US scientists "believe they can weaken the strength of tropical storms and steer them off course using a range of methods that include spraying fine particles into hurricanes or cooling the sea water in areas where thay form." Like 9/11, Frankenstorm Sandy could more accurately be described as a coordinated exercise than an unplanned disaster. "what emerges is a clear record of media, government, military and interagency secrecy and complicity not acknowledged since the Manhattan Project." Obama had used HAARP to engineer Hurricane Sandy in order to guarantee his re-election to a second term. But conspicuous by its absence was mention of a documented aerosol geoengineering program carried out by the Department of Homeland Security (DHS) under project "HAMP" (Hurricane Aerosol Microphysics Program). Details of modifying the strength of hurricanes under project HAMP was revealed at the 2010 American Meteorological Association meeting. Documents associated with HAMP reveal that aerosol geoengineering is common knowledge to the White House, Pentagon, NOAA, National Hurricane Center and many othe government agencies. A stunning admission was announced at one session that revealed aerosol geoengineering was used to modify the intensity and possible storm track of Hurricane Katrina in 2005. The public deserves to know. Look at the Haarp status Facebook timeline and you will see that they were tracking intense Haarp activity in the Northeast well before the storm hit : https://www.facebook.com/HaarpStatus

www.haarpstatus.com is an independent network of sensors placed across the US. Now when I check their site the activity in the Northwest is dying down and there is increased activity in Southern California, which they say matches an "earthquake signature." Keep your eye on California!

HAARP is a weapon of mass destruction.

Radio Waves strong enough to cause earthquakes are controlled by the US Military

It's the largest ionospheric heater in the world. Capable of heating a 1,000 square kilometer area of the ionosphere to over 50,000 degrees. It's also a phased array, which means it's steerable and those waves can be directed to a selected targetarea. What they have found is that by sending radio frequency energy up and focusing it as they do with these kinds of instruments causes a heating effect. And that heating literally lifts the ionosphere within a 30 mile diameter area therein changing localized pressure systems or perhaps the route of jet streams. Moving a jet stream is a phenomenal event in terms of man's ability to do this. The problem is that we cannot model the system adequately. Long term consequences of atmospheric heating are unknown. Changing weather in one place can have a devastating downstream effect. And HAARP has already been accused of modifying the weather.

The US Military was not the only investigator of "ionospheric heaters." The Russians conducted their own research with similar systems based on Eastlund's technology. Other heaters also conducted research in Norway, Brazil, and Puerto Rico. Russian "bigger is better" programs, however, beamed huge amounts of electromagnetic power at the ionosphere, successfully bouncing volleys of electromagnetic energy back to the Earth's surface. At these higher power levels, the heated ionosphere acted like a powerful battery, storing, amplifying and discharging destructive beams of energy that could devastate a distant target on demand. At that time, the Russians lacked the powerful computing facilities required to direct and control this energy beam.

Mitt Romney has publically stated Russia is a geo-political threat.

Hurricane Sandy knocked my tree branches down on Oct. 29th 2012. I also had sleepless nights from worrying for myself and other humans being illegally affected by Haarp. I'm worried that Haarp will create a new disaster and the sheeple must wake up.

Respectfully,

Naomi Riches

11/01/12

The United States District Court

District of Montana

Jonathan Lee Riches,

Plaintiff

Vs.

Daylight Savings Time,

Defendant

Preliminary Injunction

Temporary Restraining Order, TRO

Comes now, Jonathan Lee Riches, in pro-se, moves this honorable court for a restraining order against Daylight Savings Time, and for the clocks to move back to their original form. I face danger from Daylight savings Time which is disrupting my biological clock, it disrupts my sleeping patterns, which could cause me to have a heart attack.

Daylight Savings Time disrupts all Americans' farming, travel, record keeping, medical devices, etc. Daylight Savings Time is manipulating our Earth's natural cycle, we don't need government interference in our lives, this is a danger.

Also, Daylight Savings Time is misrepresenting and inaccurate, since no daylight is actually being saved; it should be changed to Daylight Shifting Time. If this court won't grant the restraining order too much light will cause me skin cancer and vitamin D poisoning. The defendant is also a danger to children because it causes obesity in children who have extra time for trick or treating on Halloween. Daylight Savings Time affects the bottom line of radio stations that can only operate during the day. Also, it brings confusion to travelers and residents of Hawaii, parts of Indiana, Guam, and Puerto Rico –who do not celebrate Daylight Savings Time.

I seek a restraining order against Daylight Savings Time –put the clocks back. The whole world needs to follow the same time – this will bring a togetherness to the world, because the goal is to bring a New World Order anyway. So we need all the clocks the same. I am a proud American facing danger because of this clock atrocity –please help. I pray for relief.

Respectfully Submitted,

Jonathan Lee Riches©

03/10/16

What Happens When the Law is Subjected to Unreason?
Jonathan Lee Riches and the Fragmentation of Order

By Dr. Mark Dyal

1. A Line of Flight

"Freedom was not what I wanted. Only a way out; right or left, or in any direction; I made no other demand." – Kafka[9]

2. Words and Things

An object in the world, innocent of any attempts to have meaning ascribed to it, or usefulness made of it: pure, simple, innocuous ... and *artificial*: for thingness as meaning or function is a trick of language. Take a look around at all the things that surround us, all of them made to conform to a certain ... vision of life and its creative potentials. From my desk I see trees, dirt, concrete, steel – all of which are obscurely illuminated by the fogged-over windows through which my already bespectacled eyes can see. But still, a tree is a tree; dirt is dirt, concrete and steel are concrete and steel. I know this without needing to know why or how I know. I was told that a tree is a tree and that was all that was necessary to be convinced of the veracity of tree-hood.

3. Thinking as a Police Force

Aside from "artificiality," a thing in this world that wasn't represented or being made useful would be ... *boring* – even more so than writing about such a thing. Nietzsche had an inclination that Plato invented the concept of Form (some call it the Idea – in any case, it can be summed up as a unifying

---

[9] Kafka, Franz, *The Penal Colony: Stories and Short Pieces*, New York: Schocken, 1948, pg. 177.

principle around which a thing may be said to correspond to what it *is*) out of a sense of civic responsibility: a gift to the State that made possible a standard of truth and justice through which life and all of its overwhelming complexity could be made sensible to a priestly mind in need of certainty and control.[10] Thought – good thought, anyway – is reduced to being analogical: to represent and correspond to what *is*. Sameness, constancy, symmetry, structure: thought as sound and proper judgment – thinking as a police force. (x=x=not y): The rational foundation for order. Everything relates to a Form, an Idea, to an ideal. "What is good is true and just. What is true and just is law," so said the Hellenes.

Truth as the reign of Man, God, and Gold. "Everything in its right place."[11]

4. The Tricks of Language

A. Debt

It should come as no surprise that law stems from the same impetus to order and goodness. The law is what conjoins Form to language. But just as Nietzsche spoke fondly of a pre-literate "morality of custom," we may also point to a customary Indo-European law that was situational and mediated.[12] However, most of what we posit to know about such a law comes to us in the form of contemporary sub-state honor-based behaviors in the not-quite domesticated areas of Eastern and Southern Europe. Contrast that with what we *certainly* know: that once we have

---

[10] Nietzsche, Friedrich, *Writings from the Late Notebooks*, Cambridge University Press, 2003, pg. 143.
[11] Massumi, Brian, *A User's Guide to Capitalism and Schizophrenia*, MIT Press, 1992, pg. 4.
[12] Gelderloos, Peter, *Worshiping Power: An Anarchist View of Early State Formation*, Chico, CA: AK Press, 2016, pg. 180.

states with *written records* (think Mesopotamia c. 3500 BCE), what those endowed with this most creative of gifts recorded for eternity was tax tables, work units, tribune lists, royal genealogies, founding myths, and laws.[13] Given how closely we still resemble the earliest state-subjects, we can imagine how fitting it was to link literacy and law with debt and obligation to the State.

The first trick of language then, is debt: The Original Sin.

B. Morality

Although we are having some fun with the tricks of language, it would be too great a deviation to discuss one of its most delicious tricks: convincing us moderns that we have inherited anything from the Classical World but some poorly translated words and a mess of statue and building fragments that make for dusty soles and aching backs, but also fine sceneries for selfies and snap chats. But the mob still crows about democracy and the State-sponsored thinkers intone the virtues of Idea and Logos, and the rest of us watch *300* and imagine ourselves as Spartans: We all get the Classical World We Deserve. Win-win-*very* win.

One of the things that thrills us derelict, but unfortunately lazy, Spartans is that none of the various active and noble forms of Classical life ever imagined itself to be universally valid. In fact, the beauty of nobility is understanding that it is only for the few; knowing that only the most affirmative, brave, and ferocious of us could ever be noble. And so, when we read that the late Greeks tended to see the good as productive of the law, we give them the benefit of the doubt; what is the good if not nobility!

We can afford such dalliances because we are assured of the

---

[13] Scott, James C, *Against the Grain: A Deep History of the Earliest States*, Yale University Press, 2017, pg. 13.

distance that separates the Classical from the modern forms of life: once many were slaves; now *all are slaves*. Good --> law: formula for noble law. Alas, we may now show a different formula, one that is operative as a driving force of modernity: Law --> good. "The good is (now) what the law says it is."[14] The law is no longer situational and mediated but instead acts as a "pure form of universality," that refers back to nothing but itself.[15] The law is no longer good but moral – it does not tell us what is good to do but simply what one MUST do. "Thou SHALT:" the good is only following the imperative. Thus, we can see that the law is merely practical. It must be written but also inscribed or codified in human-State-subjects: "act through duty," it tells us.

Of course, one may ask why we care so much for the apparatuses of control of a form of life with and against which we battle. If we chose to answer at all, we'd explain the lineage: Form-God-State-Literacy-Language-Thinking and end up very pissed-off to again be contemplating the blessed modern *cogito* and its celebration of reason as another "pure form of universality" that reduces thinking to examining the vicissitudes of a law document. Someone else's conditions of possibility? That's their problem. Our problem is that we are governed by the same conditions.

The second trick of language is morality.

C. Representation

We've laid the problems of modernity and its dominant political form (the State? Hardly. What makes the State possible? That, as

---

[14] Deleuze, Gilles, *Essays Critical and Clinical*, University of Minnesota Press, 1997, pg. 32.

[15] Ibid.

always, is our target.) at the feet of Plato. "Form" is a concept worthy of such an honor -so much so that we use it each and every conscious moment without even realizing its existence. Form: the unifying principle around which a thing may be said to correspond to what it *is*. The object exists. It is represented conceptually and consciously by language. Thus, language functions analogically: a tree is a tree because of what it is. It has properties of treeness that correspond to the Ideal tree. If this is so, then words simply represent things along the paths of signifier and signified, and the law-like mediation of reason ensures that those paths are symmetrical and constant. Good thinking for good people.

As long as we are stuck in the regime of representation we miss the affective power that words have on the things they name, yes, but more so on the (human) bodies that are their more direct referents.[16] Tree as tree; as shade giver to exhausted traveler; as home to fungi, insects, birds, squirrels, raccoons, and bears; as arborescent image of natural hierarchy; as war machine against competing loci of photosynthesis; as fuel for fire; as material for crafting and building; as resource to be exploited for profit; as resource to be shepherded by the government; and as a tree amongst other trees, refuge for guerrillas and launching point of so many ambushes. Trees on terrain versus trees on land. Trees as homogenous wood pulp. Trees as rifle stocks. Trees as war clubs. Words and things. Words *as* things. Words as states of bodies, variations of power, evidence of types of thinking and thinkers.

With language, we become habitual thinkers. With language, we

---

[16] Beckman, Frida, *Gilles Deleuze (Critical Lives)*, Reaktion Books, 2017, loc. 1339.

conform to a code of dominant representations and a pre-established state of words and things. What is it? What does it mean? What does it matter? Congratulations. You now control the future.

The third trick of language is representation.

D. Order

When we learn a language, we learn a dominant order:

a. Language is not primarily a communicative device but a means of imposing power relations.

b. To learn a language is to learn categories, classifications, binary oppositions, associations, codes, concepts, and logical relations that give the world coherence and organization.

c. Language is never neutral but part of network of practices, institutions, goods, tools, materials – all imbued with force.

d. Language is a mode of action, a way of doing things.

e. (a+b+c+d) points to language as part of assemblages that express certain contents in certain times and places – all ordered and part of the good and true conditions of possibility.[17]

"I now pronounce you husband and wife."

"One man's freedom fighter is another man's terrorist."

"Dear Lord man, you can't say that here! What the hell is wrong with you?!?"

"OK, well ... so what's the point? Is it a tree or not?" It doesn't

---

[17] Bogue, Ronald, *Deleuze's Way: Essays in Transverse Ethics and Aesthetics*, London: Routledge, 2017, pg. 20.

matter what it is, it only matters what it does – and more importantly, *what you can do with it.* "What it does? It looks like it could get us all killed." It works both ways, bro.

As bleak as life often appears from our materialist/structuralist position, the conditions that impinge upon our lives are never self-contained but always subject to discipline. Language is no exception:

a. Grammatical rules, correct pronunciation, syntactical regularities, proper meanings, and standard usages all point to how much they are constricted, regulated, organized, controlled, and disciplined; but they also point to potential lines of continual variation that are inexhaustible.

b. The inoculation of standard correct proper language instills a thorough coding of the world according to dominant order, but this is inherently a stabilization of fundamentally unstable elements.

c. A standard language does not exist by itself.[18]

I once wrote that we are against the State because, "Expression gives form to content." Whatever our content, it is only expressed according to the needs of a time and place. Language can be understood along the same lines: as the expression of a certain content. It can conform to habit and Logos or it can disrupt habit and Logos and become something else. Likewise, if the reason that is so closely related to language is presumed to act in Ebony and Ivory-esque "perfect harmony" with the always already embodied law, then what happens when the law is subjected to unreason? What happens when representation is overcome by the creative potential of language?

---

[18] Bogue, Ronald, *Deleuze's Way: Essays in Transverse Ethics and Aesthetics*, London: Routledge, 2017, pg. 22.

From my desk I see all those things (the trees, concrete, steel, etc.) but what happens when I look *at* my desk? Is it wood? It sure looks like wood, and I could certainly be forgiven for being a consumerist 21st Century city-boy who can't discern the difference between pressboard and hardwood. Is it textured by the grain of the wood or by computer program? Like Plato, I so desperately want to touch it and feel the loving and careful impression of a master artisan, aware of grain and how his plane will affect the perfect image of a hybrid tiger/leopard skin when viewed from within the space of a library bathed in the early-afternoon sun of a fall day in the former Confederate States of America.

Only an artisan of exceptional skill could produce a desk that, when tapped upon, has the same depth of sound as the highest quality animal hide stretched and bound by an equally exceptional tambourier; so much quality of sound, in fact, that the tapped upon desk perfectly mimics drum beats and digital clicks from the widest range of music available to human ears. When I listen to music and tap upon my desk, I can't even hear the tapping! Then again, I'm an exceptional whistler, and my whistling of a tune never annoys or seems either out of tune or time, so it could just be that my tapping-along skills are professional grade.

But the desk is always cool to the touch. On the hottest summer day, my desk is as cool as an Appalachian mountain stream; so inviting, I can hear the babbling that grows to a rumbling rapids somewhere nearby but safely downstream, and I submerge just a foot – the right one, usually – and turn back to my companions with that owl face of surprise, anticipation, and satisfaction: Oh damn it's cold but ... look where we are! Be strong bro. Beauty is for the few. Be precise now. OK. Dude, you ain't jumping, just scrambling over some slippery rocks. Still, I can always hear

Tom Petty. He knows me so well, the friend that sings pretty good if nasally but who makes a world with a few words: *A fistful of glory, a suitcase of sin; the language you dream in when you count to ten, you go to the edge and you always give in; on your first flash of freedom.* Jump bro. Hugh and Tyler are already in. If you pause too long your fear will become too apparent. Shit man look how small they are down there ... but there's only one way down. Jump. Now ... Chi osa vince! Dajè!!!! They say Blue Hole Falls' plunge pool is 40 feet deep. They also say the water that falls into it is 52 degrees. Sometimes what they say is unexaggerated. We hit the water with the impact of a lifetime of fear and are immediately impressed by the frigid milieu we have so impatiently breached. We swim the length of the pool as stiff as robots and lay on a sun-warmed rock shelf; and with blue shivering lips I say how awesome it was to hike all this way and stare down some fear with my brothers-in-arms; to awaken something in ourselves that won't be easily doused by comfort and joy.

Space isn't absolute or universal. It is instead the immediate and local capacity to move, to think, to live. Language has spaces – it surely has places – that allow its movement and creative potentials. But space is never a Heideggerian homeland, removed from the barbarian hordes that define its civility. No, instead space is violent and for each code or settlement that coagulates upon it, there are always breaches and leaks – the inside is outside, but we can't seem to bear not being a stable signifier. Most of us, anyway. But for every 10,000 last men and lane boys who come to these mountains to tour wineries and stroll shopping districts, two or three are creating something else with space that needn't be said. Linguistically we might ask, which of those tendencies defines a language: the will to conform and confirm or create breaches and points of desertertion?

The fourth trick of language is order, but order isn't a given.

5. Comfort and Joy

I miss the Greeks. What an odd thing to say. What I mean is that I miss the way Nietzsche and Deleuze speak about the Greeks – always as a foil to the despicable lives we lead today. Deleuze says that forms of life inspire ways of thinking; that life activates thought and thought returns the favor, so to speak. For the pre-Socratics, thinking was an affirmation of life, devoid of the modern distinction between thought and action. Today, however, we have a mode of thought that bridles and mutilates life – and a form of life that takes revenge on thought! We live, as he says, "lives that are too docile for thinkers." We live, then, according to Form, with a life divided along the metaphysical essence of truly or falsely conforming to the Ideal: essence and appearance; true and false; intelligible and sensible: life measured and judged; thought as a measure of higher values: The Divine, The True, The Beautiful, The Good.[19]

God rest ye merry, gentlemen

Let nothing you dismay ...

O tidings of comfort and joy

(Give me the Mujahideen and AK's on every corner any day over men wearing golf shirts that struggle to cover pudgy bellies full of Starbucks coffee-flavored drinks.)

6. What Necessitates the Law

---

[19] Deleuze, Gilles, "Nietzsche" in *Pure Immanence: Essays on A Life*, New York: Zone Books, 2001, pgs. 65-70.

That language can be shown to discipline, but also be disciplined, is probably clear to any Western citizen-subject. Every good neo-liberal Leftist knows damn good and well that the battlefield of the war they are waging is language: to push the boundaries of that which the dominant, major, order of the West consists. How lovely it is to see all those freaks and no-good-niks now clamoring to be represented by the State. What a boon for radicalism, right? <insert: cricket-churp.mp3> And on the Right, the neo-Conservatives and 2A guys fight like hell to keep the abstract belonging that only language can accord to a cozy and recognizable minimum. But even as an act of restriction, in the act of being disciplined, language will never be exhausted – as each weekly round of Twitter sparring shows.

But what about the law? We know that it disciplines, or at least we imagine it does (If you don't break the law you have nothing to fear) and we know that it is disciplined (#2A. War on Drugs. Enough said). Society is an abstraction, another trick of language, requiring, in order to function, a stripping away of our concrete lived existences. In order to get us to act for its well-being, or even with it in mind at all, we must either conflate the two or three meaningful relationships we have with the near-entirety of the species (whatever that is – besides another trick of language) or subsume them to what is good for people we'll never know and couldn't possibly share much of any value (beyond television addiction and generalized low-price-point consumption). The social field, then, is truly without a contract and only has the slightest hint of obligation. This is what necessitates the law: an unnatural and unhealthy, vulgar and mediocre way of living.

But what if, like language, who's acts never exhaust its potential of expression (one bee + three bullets + forty-four beans from a Mancala game + one 4-power optic lens cap + three spams + one trick ass ho + two millennials + a glove that doesn't fit, so you must acquit ... to infinity) – what happens when what is added to law is not imminent to it?

7. Everything Can Be Made Thirsty

Autonomia (self-rule) is a post-bourgeois form of social organization and political radicalism that was formed in the same milieu as the Red Brigades in Italy around 1970. Opposing the hardcore communist terrorism of the brigades (as well as the reactionary terrorism of the State and some of its Rightist operatives), the autonomists engaged in what they called "warfair" against the State: "pranks, squats, collective re-appropriations (pilfering), self-reductions (rent, electricity, etc.), pirate radios, [and] sign tinkering, etc."[20] Like many of the revolutionaries we know and love today, they sought to collectivize their existence – not by proliferating societal (State-sponsored) identity abstractions but precisely by undercutting these abstractions so that a more immediate and localized way of life could take root (the fireteam-to-platoon sized gang that Jack Donovan immortalized.)[21]

And like many of us today who walk a similar path, the autonomists sought to add joy and the thrill of nonconformity to their warring form of life. Somewhere between "a laughter that will bury you all," and just appreciating how fun it is to live beyond the edges of the herd, the autonomists placed the hands of humor into those of violence, gave them an exaggerated bow, and then pushed them headlong into a *thiasos* that was winding its way to the castrum set up on the Bolognese estate of Prinz Vogelfrei. The good Prussian prince who was hosting a north African of equal standing named Marfaka and it promised to be the defining party of the 20th Century – and not just for the *autonomisti*: all of the best and brightest artists, poets, war veterans, and street fighters from across Italy were expected to attend.

---

[20] Lotringer, Slyvère, and Marazzi, Christian, eds., *Autonomia: Post-Political Politics*, Los Angeles: Semiotext(e), 2007, pg. v.
[21] Donovan, Jack, *The Way of Men*, Milwaukie, OR: Dissonant Hum, 2012, pgs. 9-12.

In honor of the event, and in order to add a touch of Futurist theater to its occasion, the autonomists spread throughout Bologna and hijacked the myriad connection terminals that control traffic into and around the city. By turning each traffic signal to red, the autonomists momentarily brought the city's traffic to a standstill, sowing a twinkling of chaos amongst the good and true Bolognese – giving life to a massive influx of frustration; a small gesture but nonetheless appropriate given the occasion.

The autonomists understood that such small gestures didn't add up to much in the grand scheme of affecting political change or of taking control of the State and its means of production, but they were fun, and certainly indicative of what a body can do while it is still captured in the citadel. "We might be stuck here," one of them said, "but with just a little disobedience we can make holes in this thing. If we break it just a little, who knows what uses we can make of it. A window is good for keeping out the cold or letting in some warmth and beauty; but when it is broken, ah my friend, then it becomes useful for other things." He laughed and walked away, saying over his shoulder, "It's not just the swords that thirst for blood! Everything! Everything can be made thirsty!"

8. Nothing is Static

"Nothing is static. Everything is evolving. Everything is falling apart." Nietzsche's words coming out of Tyler's mouth. Order out of chaos. Chaos out of order. The double articulation of all of the abstract potentials in the universe that end up actualized; each contains the order that expressed them, but also the chaos that guarantees their becoming-other.

"Nothing is static." The being for which we clamor – the stasis, the thisness, the thingness, the calm respite from mean ol' life, … the desire for nothingness – is yet another trick of language. Subjects and predicates. A doer and a deed. Causality hardwired throughout the physical and ethical universe, making all the world a stage for judgment. *Fight club … this was mine and*

Tyler's gift ... our gift to the world. "Being is becoming." That is Nietzsche's gift; that, and selection 13 of the *Genealogy of Morality*'s First Essay.

Being: I think therefore I am.

Do you?

Hylomorphism, the idea that form imposes quality on matter, without which matter would remain undifferentiated chaos, has us "working jobs we hate, to buy shit we don't need:" we want to be ruled so badly that we will purposely believe that form rules matter like a soul moves a body.[22] Think about what passes for a life. Why then are we so desperate for tomorrow to be just like today? To be the same person we thought we were yesterday? Becoming ends up being a bitch because it forces us to realize how many decisions we make each day to maintain the trick of being. But I know, god knows I do, how much we love truth, and feeling justified. We love "speaking truth to power!" because by god power will listen to the truth and be persuaded to hand me the reigns. If there was one gift of Fascism, it is that it removed truth from the equation. Knowledge and truth? Here's a nice boot in your eye. Take some perspective and interpretation, the intellectual arsenal of becoming. For those of us who can affirm that life is less about circles and more about roundness, that robber-baron Dagget said it best:

"Open the champagne ... and could we get some *fluidity* in here?"

If becoming is assumed, then what power can The Word have? How can The Truth be actualized?

9. The Lawsuit

What forces does a lawsuit bring to life? Rage, fear, confusion,

---

[22] Holland, Eugene, *Deleuze and Guattari's A Thousand Plateaus*, London: Bloomsbury, 2013, pgs. 51-52.

debt? Surely, but the suit itself as a legal document brings what to life? Confusion, apathy, acquiescence? Let's think about it as an impetus to thinking, a violence that affects thinking. What then? Hyper-concision and regulation: exactly what the law needs to exist. The same criticism of the suit, then, can be applied to the law: it produces a stark reality, without emotion, a utilitarian reality in which the law reflects upon every word and every word reflects upon the law. The law document, as an affective force, could be said, then, to be an effective break on thought. It can only represent, and never create.

But what would happen if the brutal bare life of truth represented in the lawsuit was infected with a virus – specifically one that separated each word from a proper and just referent? What, then, would the suit affect? What happens when a machine is coupled with a derelict component? If law inscribes on a body, what happens when what is inscribed is shown to be silly? What then is consummated on and in the subject? Like the autonomists in Bologna, Jonathon Lee Riches (JLR as his closest friends call him) introduces chaos into the citadel from within its hallowed walls. The law – truth, order, rationality, representation, Form incarnate – and the space of its hypertrophic but severely malnourished language come under attack, like an errant brushstroke that obscures the eyes on a portrait, at once masking what we needed for soul-gazing, but at the same time making visible the nonsense that the soul would have surely masked.

10. I Am Serious. And Don't Call Me Shirley.

Even after hanging around with JLR for so many years now, it's still almost impossible for me to read the suits. Each time I try the same sonic disturbance and deformation of language overcomes me: laughter. Hysterical laughter ... just laughter: this is the force of the JLR suits – their gift to the world. Imagine what they must have felt like for so many lowly legal clerks, toiling day after day with the evidence of so much truth and need for State-sponsored divinely-provident justice: how thrilling and difficult to type must they have been! The practical, if insultingly mundane aspect of the suits – to clog the courts with spurious lawsuits – was surely buttressed by how much more time was needed to input them into the legal system on account of uproarious laughter. How poetic, too, that the absurdity of their clerkish grind was transformed by a laughter that acts to affirm the subversion of the very representational system that allows a moment or a life to be so thoroughly measured and judged.

Carcasse, tu trembles?

Tu tremblerais bien advantage, si tu savais

Où je te mène.[23]

Tremble? Who's trembling?

I'm not trembling, I'm laughing

My ass off.

11. Microsoft Word Understands That I Just Spelled Kardashian Correctly.

How are celebrities recognized? By their faces, tits, asses, muscles, voices, and names. Ahhh the names, announced over PA systems; writ large on celluloid; verified and real when preceded by an @; and printed in toner for proper legal filing.

---

[23] Nietzsche, Friedrich, *The Gay Science*, Cambridge University Press, 2001, pg. 197.

JLR loves celebrities. I happen to know this for a fact. CNN said, "JLR is at war with celebrities," and then asked what he could possibly have against Tom Cruise. But this is wrong. Wrong, wrong. Imagine being at war with celebrities ... actually, yes! Imagine that! So instead, imagine being at war with the State and with the law; that takes something that a mere war with celebrities would surely lack. Then, on top of that, imagine a war against language. JLR must be crazy, shearing away sense from language as he splits it apart.

Tom Cruise. He's a short little guy, yes? never seemed to recover from stomping on Oprah's couch? (Tom, if you're out there, run and hide in 2020.) What did JLR want with him? What did he want with Tom Cruise or Barry Bonds or any of them? Tom. Cruise. Barry. Bonds. As names and subjects (proper nouns) they are as majestic as a juiced-up splash hit into McCovey Cove; but as words (common nouns) they are depersonalized: just a couple of words among other words. We'd love to say that JLR reduces an XL popcorn tub of affects to mere percepts, but he chose the celebrities on purpose. Hurricane Katrina, Bank of America, Jenna Jameson, Obama, Kim Kardashian – Microsoft Word understands that I just spelled Kardashian correctly. I refrain from saying another word on account of the Fifth Amendment. Celebrities are knowable.

The hidden critique in the JLR suits is why the defendants are often so well-known. Why do all of us know of Kanye West and Dancing with the Stars? It would've embarrassed Western Civilization to death, if it weren't already dead, to find out in this book that Dancing with the Stars is a myth of the modern world: a myth amongst a mountain of old TV Guides that form the representations and clichés of contemporary conventional social discourse. JLR's suits succeed in taking these myths and clichés and disengaging them from the machinery that gives a handful of proper nouns so much power.[24] Forgive me if I'm wrong, but nowhere in the suits do the celebrities gain any sympathy. Shame on them. Shame!

All that "being" down the drain. All the money spent on publicists and lawyers, paying-off TMZ to bury the various crimes committed against JLR; all for the sake of maintaining a stable and set identity: a Brad Pitt, whatever that is. But Mr. Pitt, *being is becoming*, bro. Dude, you were Achilles AND Tyler Durden. How could you defend Angelina Jolie against the father of her children? If anyone could understand that once the name is out there it cannot be controlled, it's you. It's a miserable author that attempts to control how his words are interpreted and used by his audience. So what happens when all that identity is made part of a creative project to which it does not consent? Is that project any different than life? Suck it up, buttercup. Do the right thing and at least help keep the Guinness people from publishing information about JLR.

12. Nonsense

JLR isn't the first trickster to use the form of a medium to subvert the normalized effects of that medium. The Bayreuth Festival recently used *Parsifal* as an opportunity to promote multi-racial capitalist-atheism.[25] Jean Girard played jazz at The Pit Stop. American punk band Show Me the Body uses banjo as its primary stringed instrument. I have seen several decorated Christmas trees through house windows in the middle of May. Like these, JLR produces an estrangement of sense from the form that is designed to guarantee its production. At the very

---

[24] Robbe-Grillet, Alain, "Order and Disorder in Film and Fiction," *Critical Inquiry* 4, 1977, pg. 6.

[25] Morgan, John, "Boomer Bayreuth: Wagner's *Parsifal at the Festpielhaus* in 2018" www.counter-currents.com

least his suits defamiliarize the form in which they are contained. In them, our perception of the law shifts, and like a word given a new meaning by the next generation, the closed system of the law and its self-referential power is opened up to something that is beyond it. Nonsense can have powerful effects on reason, especially when it breaks the repetition of typically combined words and ideas that always refer to and justify a socially accepted institution. Just ask a heterosexual to search the web for "genderfluid support."

13. Capture ... Escape

"All those that are tired by the tempestuous, dynamic variety of life dream of restful fixed uniformity. They want a life without surprises, the ground smooth like a billiard ball. ... But human thriving, which has as its essence an increasing velocity, needs obstacles to overcome, that is, revolutionary wars to fight." – Marinetti[26]

As we mentioned above, the practical aspect of the JLR suits was to clog the court system with superfluous lawsuits in an attempt to frustrate an arrangement that seemed created to discourage prisoners from seeking legal recourse in their cases. One of the theoretical aspects of the suits, with which I have attempted to have some fun, is their highlighting of the slippery and shifting ground of the law due to its dependence upon a conservative and smothering theory of language. As I see them, the suits destabilize the normal use-value and affective power of the law suit, which mirrors our theological and political will to create blame and judgement. By inserting nonsense and humor into such an overbearingly concise and stolid milieu, JLR at the very least demonstrated how we might take one thing, add it to another, and create something entirely different. To extract the

---

[26] Ialongo, Ernest, *Filippo Tommaso Marinetti: The Artist and his Politics*, The Fairleigh Dickinson University Press, 2017, pg. 100.

normal function from an institution, for instance the military or police force, is to create a passage beyond.

Disequilibrium forced upon something taken for granted is the essence of artistic anarchy. This lesson was implemented by Futurists in both Russia and Italy 100 years ago, animating the greatest political upheaval in modern times. By linking a newly unhinged and creative language to the violence of civil war, Futurism reanimated life in need of a flight from bourgeois society. Marinetti and his *camerati* demanded the creative potential of language in the face of its assumed representational and reproductive function. Principles like great love and noble sacrifice, they said, arise only from fabulative activity and are never embodied when fully imposed by a transcendent source. It was for this that they subverted the powers of representation: to create a world beyond that which demands our obedience.

Can it be said that JLR sets such noble aims for his suits? Perhaps not ... but that doesn't prohibit us from making whatever use of them that we may in our escape from the epistemography that has rendered our experiences a problem to be solved in the creation of a more governable and gratified political subject. In this light, JLR needn't be a victory, nor even a way out. He just needs to shift in his seat, give a slight and utterly imperceptible nod, or gesture toward an imagined target so that "one dog goes one way and the other dog goes the other way."

Bibliography

Beckman, Frida, *Gilles Deleuze (Critical Lives)*, Reaktion Books, 2017.

Bogue, Ronald, *Deleuze's Way: Essays in Transverse Ethics and Aesthetics*, London: Routledge, 2017.

Deleuze, Gilles, *Essays Critical and Clinical*, University of Minnesota Press, 1997.

Deleuze, Gilles, "Nietzsche" in *Pure Immanence: Essays on A Life*, New York: Zone Books, 2001.

Donovan, Jack, *The Way of Men*, Milwaukie, OR: Dissonant Hum, 2012.

Gelderloos, Peter, *Worshiping Power: An Anarchist View of Early State Formation*, Chico, CA: AK Press, 2016.

Holland, Eugene, *Deleuze and Guattari's A Thousand Plateaus*, London: Bloomsbury, 2013.

Ialongo, Ernest, *Filippo Tommaso Marinetti: The Artist and his Politics*, The Fairleigh Dickinson University Press, 2017.

Kafka, Franz, *The Penal Colony: Stories and Short Pieces*, New York: Schocken, 1948.

Lotringer, Slyvère, and Marazzi, Christian, eds., *Autonomia: Post-Political Politics*, Los Angeles: Semiotext(e), 2007.

Massumi, Brian, *A User's Guide to Capitalism and Schizophrenia*, MIT Press, 1992.

Morgan, John, "Boomer Bayreuth: Wagner's *Parsifal at the Festpielhaus* in 2018" www.counter-currents.com

Nietzsche, Friedrich, *The Gay Science*, Cambridge University Press, 2001.

Nietzsche, Friedrich, *Writings from the Late Notebooks*, Cambridge University Press, 2003.

Robbe-Grillet, Alain, "Order and Disorder in Film and Fiction," *Critical Inquiry* 4, 1977.

Scott, James C, *Against the Grain: A Deep History of the Earliest States*, Yale University Press, 2017.

Autobiography

My name is Jonathan Lee Riches. I was born at 6:08 pm on December 27th 1977 at the Chester County Hospital in West Chester Pennsylvania. I weighed eight pounds, seven ounces. My mother's name is Donna Riches, my father's name is Timothy Riches. I have one younger sibling: her name is Cari Riches, she is two years younger than me. I don't remember much of my life from the time I was born to the age of five. I know I lived in a small duplex home in Malvern Pennsylvania during this time period. My father was a banker with the First National Bank of West Chester. My mother worked as a secretary at the Chester County Hospital. My grandparents on my mother's side would take care of my sister and I during the day while my parents were at work. My grandparents also lived in Malvern Pennsylvania in the country and still live in the same house to this day. Both grandparents on my mother's side are still alive; their names are Elinor and William Davison. I have plenty of uncles, aunts and cousins on my mother's side of the family.

Growing up I would often spend time with my grandparents on my father's side of the family. Their names were Henrietta and Robert Riches and they lived in Malvern Pennsylvania. Both passed away within a year of each other when I was four years old. I have numerous uncles, aunts and cousins on my father's side of the family-though most of my childhood memories when I was very young were centered around being with my maternal grandparents. My grandparents showered me with love. I remember they had a black Labrador named Roscoe that I loved to play with. I believe I behaved normally like any other kid around that time. I don't remember playing with other kids at that time.

My mother's side of the family is Irish and English; my

father's side was German. My father grew up Catholic. I remember attending Methodist Church as a child. My grandparents were very religious and very active in the church community. I remember my grandparents would say prayer before every meal. I don't remember much of my actual home-life up to the age of five because I spent most of my time at my grandparents' house while my parents were at work.

When I was five years old my parents bought a bigger home in West Chester PA located on two acres of woods in a very remote area. The house was two stories with four bedrooms and two bathrooms.

At twelve years of age I began to change both physically and mentally. I was somewhat obese/overweight as a child and occasionally got teased for it by my classmates and friends, so I began taking extreme measures to lose weight. I would starve myself by eating only one apple a day for almost a year. I lost close to one hundred pounds while going through puberty. This is when I began to see, and take notice of, the results that arise from taking extreme behavioral measures. The weight loss had negative effects on my social life, as it made me extremely tired and cold. My safe haven came from wrapping myself up in a heater blanket and exerting the little energy I could muster to play video games on my Nintendo

My mother gave me my own telephone line in my bedroom and I spent many days lying in bed just calling random people locally or dialing random 1 800 numbers to hear what I had reached. I missed many days of school because of my lack of energy. My room was my comfort zone. My parents were preoccupied with their careers and felt that I was old enough to take care of myself without a babysitter or my grandparents watching me. My mother gave me a Blockbuster video membership that I used to rent and watch movies, in particular, horror movies. I also watched a lot of eighties comedies like Can't Buy Me Love, Better Off Dead, Weird Science and Lover Boy. I would watch the same movies over and over until I could remember entire scenes and repeat them, sometimes calling people on the phone randomly and repeating dialog from these scenes to strangers to get a reaction out of them. I was fascinated by how the telephone worked so I began to take the phones apart and put them back together to understand the concept. This hobby at the time was referred to as "Telephone Phreaking".

My grades were just good enough to pass each grade going into my teenage years. I became less interested in physically associating with people and more interested in talking to random people on the telephone. I discovered telephone chatlines and BBS systems, which were local lines that strangers would call to talk to random people. All types of conversations occurred, including phone sex. Usually these lines were filled with adults, I played the roll of someone around 21 years old, which people believed, and would spend hours on these lines living a fantasy life. This was a world before Facebook and Myspace. It was also an exchange depot of criminal activity. I began associating with people who were known as "Hackers", "Social Engineers" and "Phone Phreakers". People would never use their real names, going by handles instead. I created the persona "Gino Romano" and never gave anyone my location or details of my personal life. Individuals would exchange phone diverters, PBX numbers to make free calls, and phone company back door departments to manipulate through the phone lines. Hackers would clique up in groups and go to cyber war with other individuals through doxing and stealing people's credit information for the purpose of ruining it, or pranking people by sending dumpsters, porta-potties and dump trucks filled with gravel to people's homes. I gravitated towards this behavior and felt like I wanted to be the best- known hacker on those lines. This was my entertainment; I navigated through the phone line systems diverting my calls so I could not be traced.

Once I had started high school my weight and anti-social behavior started to affect my grades negatively. I took laxatives daily, I would spit in a cup all day to get fluids out of me, always weighing myself and vowing not to eat over a 1000 calories a day. This was bad, but not as bad as eating one apple a day like I had done in my younger years. I didn't want to deal with my other classmates, so I would arrive to school late everyday on purpose to get put on "in school suspension", which was a separate room where my work was brought to me. I was fearful of my male peers because they were bigger and stronger than me. Once school was over I would return home and call the chatlines to get into my comfort zone. I would take my real life frustrations out on strangers by baiting them into arguments. A lot of the conversations were non sequitur ramblings containing nothing of substance and they made me feel good. I would spend all my nights on the phone, then use my in-school suspension to sleep and do limited work.

I failed the ninth grade. I had no real social life; the partyline life consumed me. I ended up getting into a shoving match with a teacher after I tried to sneak out of class to use the bathroom because I was heavy on laxatives. I got expelled from school due to the conflict and all the in school suspensions. My mother enrolled me in a private school called Upattinas in Glenmore Pennsylvania, which was a school for wayward boys. My mother would reward me for my negative behavior. She bought me a black Jetta for my sixteenth birthday. My new school basically operated under the motto of "you pay, you pass." There was very little homework, which I managed to finish maybe once a week. I would just stay at home and entertain myself on the chatlines.

Around the age of sixteen I started to engage in criminal behaviors I had learned from the chatline. I social engineered the monitor codes for Sprint customer service so I could listen into the lines where people would pay their phone bills with credit cards. I would then take the credit card information and use it for Western Union transactions where I would wire the money to a location further than seventy-five miles from my location or by having a fellow chatliner from another state pick up the money, take a cut for themselves, and wire the remaining amount back to me. I would miss school to drive long distances to pick up fraudulent Western Union transfers. I invested some of this money into a Gateway Laptop computer delivered to me in a Cow Box from South Dakota. The Western Union fraud was a daily thing. Credit cards at the time did not have the three digit CVV security code on the back and I was able to identify the sixteen digit card number algorithm to the issuing bank on the card and flip the last digit to a sequence that would match a zip code where I could recycle cards and dummy credit cards for the purpose of doing Western Union fraud and eventually online retail fraud.

Ecommerce businesses were beginning to pop up and I exploited them by committing fraud with generated credit cards and purchase orders. I began networking with other telephone phreakers and hackers around the world using techniques/trickery to manipulate online merchants into sending goods to me, splitting the proceeds with other participants, while remaining anonymous. I would use credit cards to set up reservations at hotels then would send large purchase orders of electronics and computers to the hotel room after switching the cardholder's info. I would use fraudulent identification to set up mail boxes along the I-95 corridor between NYC and

323

Washington D.C. then send merchandise bought offline with credit cards to the locations. I also used the P.O. boxes to order more credit cards under other people's identities. I was learning the value of money by budgeting my ill-gotten gains into investing in more hardware and equipment to keep the fraud going; I bought spy shop equipment like voice changers, wiretapping equipment, phone scramblers, night vision goggles, etc. I used stolen identities and credit cards to open up private investigation accounts with sites that provide information such as addresses, credit reports, DMV and criminal records, then used that information to create fraudulent IDs, bank accounts and Etrading accounts.

My life before turning eighteen was centered around fraud and partylines. I graduated high school at seventeen, a year ahead of my projected graduation date –in spite of having failed the ninth grade. Upon graduating in 1994 I began working for Verizon (Bell Atlantic) customer service part-time in the mornings and also for Trans Union Credit in Chester PA part-time in the evenings. Both jobs were useful for obtaining information to use for fraudulent activity. I was recruiting people over the chatlines to do the fraudulent activity for me while I was occupied with work. I had an individual in Florida who would sell merchandise on Ebay for me; in return he would receive a 20% cut. Ebay, at the time, had no limit on the number of giftcards that could be sold, these retained 95% of their value. Electronics would also sell quickly.

During the mid nineties I was spending a lot of my free time on the Defcon Voice BBS (Bulletin Board System) hacker chatline. This system was based in Nevada. I still remember the number by heart: 435-855-3326. I was amazed listening to other voices in real time discussing computer vulnerabilities and expressing a willingness to trade or sell codes, PBX'S, credit

324

card numbers, calling card numbers, etc. with other people. If you wanted to make a deal with someone you could go into a private discussion with them and make a deal. Defcon was like the Silk Road before Silk Road, you could remain anonymous and that allowed you to wheel and deal.

I thought that the alias I had picked, "Gino Romano", sounded like a catchy mob type name that would work with my New York sounding accent. I was always inquisitive and loved picking people's brains using what I gathered from others by putting it together and doing it my own way. I learned a valuable tool about phone optiverting that would mask where my real location was when making a telephone call. I learned that when anyone calls a 1800/888/877 toll free number the person who owns that number on the receiving end receives a monthly call detail where they have all the telephone numbers of the people who called it. At the time using stolen calling cards was a hot ticket to make free calls, but obviously people were worried about their numbers and the numbers they called would be on the individual(s) who owned the calling cards monthly call detail, so optiverting allowed you to mask that. Before calling a Toll free number I would press 0 for my local operator (My telephone service was with Verizon/Bell Atlantic). I would inform the operator that I was a disabled customer and have them dial the toll free number for me. That way the person sees 000-000-0000 on their call detail. Now I could call toll free numbers like AT&T /MCI/ Sprint and enter in a calling card number and call where I wanted for free and not be worried about it getting traced back. Calling Defcon I was able to obtain access to the Sprint Customer Service monitor calls where I could call into a Sprint customer service number designed for supervisors to monitor customer service calls. I would listen to customers create accounts using their personal info, setting up calling cards which I would then utilize for my own benefit.

Defcon taught me how to call-forward people's telephone lines remotely by calling into the repair department for their telephone company and posing as the customer pretending to have line problems and getting the phone company to forward the customers calls wherever I wanted them to go. I could intercept all the person's calls. If someone called them I would answer and then pretend to be them.

I found a hacker on Defcon who went by the name Power Dragon that had unlimited full information credit card numbers from people all around the country. Around the same time I found a vulnerability in the Western Union money transfer system that allowed people to send money with a credit card. Western Union required a call back on the person's home phone number to do a money transfer. Since I knew how to forward phone lines I had that part covered, what I needed was credit cards. I made a deal with Power Dragon that for every Credit Card he gave me I would wire him $500 back within a few hours. I would forward the credit cardholder's line to me then do a Western Union transfer to myself because at the time Western Union didn't require ID to pick up a transfer if the sender provides a test question. Credit Card limits were $2500, I usually did under that but over $2000 to fly under the radar. Western Union would call the cardholder and I would pretend to be them. Within minutes I would be provided a money control number and could go pick up the funds from the transaction. I chose grocery stores with Western Union locations because usually they had the funds to cash the check on the spot. Once I got the money, I would go to another Western Union location & wire transfer Power Dragon his $500 cut back. After wiring fees I ended up with $1500 + profit for myself. I lived in the Philadelphia area, so It was easy to jump on I-95 at any time to travel an hour or two away in either direction to pick up funds.

I would eventually do 4-5 Western Unions a day and always gave Power Dragon his portion. I had done business this way with Power Dragon for a good year until he got arrested for some unrelated fraud and I broke off from him. The Western Unions would take up a lot of my days, but it was well worth it. The remaining time I would be back on Defcon working out deals with other people. I met a guy out there named Fallen Angel (real name Michael Pesce) who also had amassed an unlimited number of stolen credit cards. He told me he worked at a Cellular Store in New York, so I am assuming the Credit Cards came from his job. We worked out a scheme where he would order merchandise with a person's credit card from online retailers like CompUSA or Tiger Direct and have the merchandise sent to hotels that I would go to pick up. Beforehand he or I would switch the card-holder's address to a hotel. We would set up a reservation with the hotel with a stolen credit card for around the exact time the Merchandise would be shipped. We would order bulk items: Toshiba or IBM laptops, Spy Equipment, Nokia 5160 cell phones, etc. We would get the shipping tracking info and within hours of it arriving to the hotel I would call the hotel and remind them that I was checking in soon and that my packages would be arriving and ask if they could hold them for me. I wouldn't even have to check into the hotel to get the packages. I could walk into the hotel and up to the front desk and the hotel staff would just give them to me. I would leave and never come back. I was zig-zagging up and down the East Coast picking up packages and always sending Fallen Angel his share back -we went 50/50 on everything. Using stolen credit cards to get a PVC printer and the photoshop software that simulates state templates allowed us to begin manufacturing fake IDs. We realized with the tools we had we could expand our fraudulent schemes.

I recruited a graphic designer from New York who

would create more sophisticated identifications with holograms. I had females in different states who would pick up Western Union transactions done with credit cards and wire me back 40% of the transaction. I had individuals who would use created identifications to go into retail stores to obtain instant store credit that was then converted to gift cards that I would then sell on Ebay or use personally. At the time, most of the major retail stores all went through Monogram Bank of Georgia (GE Capital) where I discovered their system of issuing credit to individuals with a 700 or higher FICO score; these individual's names were good for $75,000 in multiple store instant credit before getting flagged.

I personally never drank alcohol, did drugs, or gambled. I never went to clubs or bars. I used ill gotten gains to build my own personal net-worth. I would use peoples/businesses' credit to obtain gas cards through Exxon, Mobil or Shell. This allowed me to travel around committing fraud without having to worry about fuel expenses. At 18 I used a stolen identity to purchase vehicles off of car lots by using stolen credit cards for the down payment and insurance policy. Once the vehicles were paid off I would sell them back to strawmen I created.

Over the next few years I continued to build my own net worth. By 21 I quit the two jobs I was working, feeling that I had exploited them as much as I could. White collar crime felt like a job to me. I felt it was a victimless crime and that the banks and people I was defrauding would get reimbursed by the insurance companies. I never met the people from the chatlines who committed the fraud with me. I had no girlfriend up through my early 20s –I remained a virgin. Once I quit my jobs I was able to move around the country committing fraud and evading detection, this is probably why I was not arrested or questioned for almost a decade. I would travel to cities, stay for a few days doing fraud through banks, malls, retail stores, and then leave town never to return. I invested in a Jeep Grand Cherokee with an enclosed travel trailer; on these trips I would fill up the trailer with stolen goods obtained by credit cards then return home to Pennsylvania and use my connections to resell the products.

When I wasn't committing fraud I would spend hours on chatlines for entertainment and scouting/recruiting others who were in positions to help me commit more fraud. That's where I met Jason Michael Carpenter who would end up being a future codefendant in my criminal case. Carpenter was from Houston Texas, I met him on Defcon where he was advertising himself as a broker selling thousands of blocks of active credit cards. Usually I would get my own credit cards and not deal with people in this way, but I thought it was quick and easy to deal with him, so we worked out a deal where I would give him $200 per active credit card. He was obtaining credit cards through a new technique called phishing, which consisted of sending out mass emails to AOL customers making them think the emails were coming from AOL and asking them to resubmit their billing information to maintain services. I never met Carter, never gave him my real name or contact info other than an email. I worked off and on with Carpenter for two years, with neither of us knowing anything about the other's personal life. I used fraudulent money to purchase a home in my parents' names in Holiday Florida, which I got through a thirty year mortgage, but paid the 100k home off within months. While in Florida I met Stephanie Costley Doyle in a MSN chatroom, who would also be my future co-defendant. I invited her to my home. She never left.

Stephanie would be my first love and I opened up to her showing her my fraudulent world, and she decided to be a willing participant in it. I was able to provide her with material goods and take her travelling with me around the country committing fraud with pleasure. We were together for about a year in 2002 until the FBI arrested us in February 2003. We had no clue that we were being watched by the FBI –no warning that they were coming. This came about because around December 2002 Jason Carpenter sent me an email saying he needed a way to contact me, which lead to me letting my guard down. I provided him with a number for a clone cell phone. When we spoke, he explained to me how a Mexican had hit his car in a hit and run and he wanted me to look up his information based on databases I had access to. I gave him the information not knowing that he was working with the FBI and that they were tape-recording our conversations.

This now gave the FBI probable cause to investigate me, which they did. For the next few months the FBI was watching Stefanie Doyle and myself commit credit card fraud in stores and cash advances in banks, building a case against us. On February 23rd 2003 I left my house to do cash advances in multiple banks throughout Tampa. Coming out of my 5th bank the FBI swooped in and arrested me in the parking lot. I refused to cooperate. They arrested Stephanie at my home around the same time. She cooperated. We were both taken to the county jail in Hillsborough County Tampa, where they let males and females mingle together during booking. We talked and hugged, but I knew it was over for me.

Agents had a complaint against us from Houston Texas. Jason Carpenter had been arrested for sending fraudulent packages to vacant homes and began cooperating with the FBI against me. I was denied bond in Federal Court in Tampa because the agents found hundreds of identifications and ID making machines at my residence. Stefanie was given house arrest. Within weeks I was extradited to Houston. During the extradition the FBI arrested my parents for allowing me to purchase a home in their names; this was probably done to put pressure on me to plead out.

Once I was in Texas I was indicted with multiple people from all over the country whom I had never met. I was assigned a public defender because I had no money and my parents had to use their own money to defend themselves. I was housed in a Federal Detention Center in Houston, which was very difficult for me to deal with because I had never been in prison before. Our case dragged on for the next fifteen months. Meanwhile I had no contact with Stefanie or my parents as their lawyers were pointing the blame at me.

Eventually I plead guilty to wire fraud and conspiracy. Jason Carpenter, who was the head of the indictment, was given a bond for cooperating but he fled after pleading guilty. He stayed on the run for a few more years committing more fraud along the way. My parents' lawyer managed to have my parents plead guilty to a lesser charge that only entailed probation. Stefanie Doyle received a two year sentence. Other co-defendants received between four to seven years. I got sentenced to ten years because the government argued that I was the ringleader. I challenged the arguments but my attempts were shot down by a Texas judge.

Having already been held in Federal Detention for sixteen months, that time counted towards my sentence. The courts and lawyers will tell defendants they would have to serve about 85% of their sentence, with good time factoring in fifty-four days per year, but in reality if inmates receive all good time it's really 87% of their time, which is 47 days a year. So, a ten year sentence would have gotten me 470 days off that sentence. Federal sentencing judge, Melinda Harmon, also recommended

331

that I participate in the Bureau of Prisons Residential Drug Abuse Program (RDAP) which is a nine month program, and if completed takes one year off of your sentence, plus an additional six months in a halfway house once your sentence is completed.

Once sentenced, I stayed in the Detention Center for a few more months while the Bureau of Prisons scheduled where I would do my time. I was shocked to discover that I was to be sent to Maximum Security United States Penitentiary in Coleman Florida. Bureau of Prisons considered me high risk because one of my identity theft victims had been former Attorney General Janet Reno.

I left FDC Houston in the summer of 2004 and boarded a U.S. Marshall plane and was transported to a Federal Transfer Center Hub in Oklahoma City. I was shackled on the plane. I was held at that Hub for a month until another plane took me to central Florida where I was subsequently bused to USP Coleman. Never being in prison before I experienced a culture-shock my first day on the compound. Races of inmates stayed in their own cliques and ate together at meal times. There was daily violence. I spent my days running in the recreation yard and studying in the law library. I wanted to learn how to appeal my criminal case because I felt that the outcome was harsh and draconian.

I behaved well during my time in Coleman and did not get involved in negativity or prison politics. Within a year's time I realized the Bureau of Prisons had classified me incorrectly as a violent inmate. I brought this to my case manager's attention and was offered a lower level custody if I was willing to go to a medium security facility in South Carolina called Federal Correctional Institution of Bennetsville, which was just opening and needed bodies to fill it. I took the offer and was transferred in 2005. Once I arrived I realized that the correctional guards were more petty and that the rules were stricter than in high security. I began getting write-ups for minor infractions like not standing straight for count or disobeying an order.

These infractions did not effect my good time, but I was sanctioned loss of commissary and visits. At Bennettsville the law library was computerized instead of being contained in books; inmates use the pacer.gov and Westlaw system. Since I had a fixation with computers and telephones I spent as much time in the law library reading case law to appeal my case pro se (without a lawyer).

In the spring of 2006 my name came up on a list of random people for another institutional transfer to another medium security facility in South Carolina called FCI Williamsburg. I didn't want to leave Bennettsville because I had established relationships with some inmates and I was comfortable there making the best of my situation, so I manufactured a story saying that I would face danger and bodily harm from individuals if transferred to Williamsburg. The staff at Williamsburg disregarded it so I filed my first lawsuit in in the Federal Courts of South Carolina seeking an injunction and restraining order against the transfer due to my life being in danger. The courts responded quickly to the motion, dismissing it as frivolous cited with case law. I went to the law library to look up the meaning of "frivolous". This opened up a new chapter of my life: deciding to bombard the courts with frivolous nonsense because pro se inmates don't get any consideration from the courts.

I'd like to say a little more about that first lawsuit (it was a restraining order). I was at the Federal Correctional Institution in Bennettsville South Carolina where I developed a friendship with an anti-government inmate named Dale Martin Jacobi, who was one of the Montana Freeman defendants. The Freemen wanted to eliminate the Federal Government & create their own currency. Jacobi was older than me and introduced me to the concept of what he called "Paper Terrorism" which involved bogging down the Government with claims against them that would force them to respond, along with the belief that the United States was a corporation and our own personal names were strawmen held under contractual law. In short, the Freeman argument claims that U.S. sovereign citizens are bound in a contract that is against our will -this theory holds for both civil and criminal cases. Being around Jacobi for months really incited me to challenge my illegal sentence and attempt to legally hold the people civilly responsible for my incarceration.

Prison officials at Bennettsville got wind that a group of "Sovereign Citizens" were filing tons of paperwork through the Bureau of Prisons, so they decided to split everyone up by shipping them to different prisons with Jacobi the only one to remain. I didn't want to leave Jacobi, so I filed an emergency preliminary Injunction/TRO temporary restraining order with the Federal Court in South Carolina preventing me from being shipped to another prison as I claimed imminent danger & bodily harm would be done to me by other co-defendant affiliated inmates waiting for me at the new prison. The Federal Judge ruled against my suit instantly by claiming it was "frivolous". Well, I certainly was not a lawyer and really didn't know how to draft a lawsuit in proper form, so I felt letdown and bitter that the courts would dismiss a lawsuit at face value from a pro se inmate just because they couldn't draft the lawsuit properly, especially if the suit could have merit.

Nevertheless, I was shipped to a new prison, but once I got settled into my new location I wanted as much time as possible in the prison law library to understand how the Federal

Rules of Civil Procedure worked and about the entire lawsuit process. In order to spend more time on this investigation I pretended I had a leg injury by limping around the prison. The medical ward provided me with a cane & work exemption -all Federal inmates otherwise would have to work.

Since the Federal Judge ruled my previous lawsuit as "Frivolous" I wanted to understand how the judge came to that conclusion. The Prison Law Library was set up through LexisNexus, which provided case law on every Civil & Federal Lawsuit filed in the Country. The library had no internet access. Searching the system I discovered that in most federal districts inmates would file the majority of civil lawsuits and judges seemed to be dismissing these lawsuits "Sua Sponte- on its own motion" as frivolous. The Prison Litigation Reform Act (PLRA), 42 U.S.C. § 1997e, is a U.S. federal law that was enacted in 1996, which Congress had enacted in response to a significant increase in inmate litigation in the federal courts; the PLRA was designed to decrease the incidence of Litigation within the court system. All inmates can proceed In Forma Pauperis (Not paying upfront court costs) if they don't have three or more lawsuits that were deemed frivolous or without merit by a judge. I concluded that judges were ruling inmate lawsuits as frivolous so each inmate would collect strikes and that once an inmate has 3 strikes they would not be able to file future lawsuits In Forma Pauperis and they would instead have to pay the entire cost of the lawsuit upfront (this was $450 dollars at the time). As the prison population was increasing, the courts were getting flooded with inmate lawsuits and needed a way to cut this amount down by finding a way to thwart inmates from filing. If an inmate had three strikes & tried to submit a lawsuit without the full payment submitted, the clerk of court would return the lawsuit to the inmate unfiled.

I found an exemption to this rule. If an inmate claims imminent danger and bodily harm then the courts have to accept the lawsuit. On top of me searching around the LexisNexus system about frivolous litigation and lawsuits that had merit, I concluded that it was next to impossible for a pro se inmate to file a lawsuit against anyone & actually win. Judges will find some reasoning to dismiss it outright or the defendant's lawyers will convince a judge that the suit needs to be dismissed. I made the decision to flood the courts with bullshit suits and waste everyone's time because I felt my own personal sentence was draconian and I wanted to clog the courts to elicit a reaction and in the process get revenge on them. I decided to test my creativity out. I added my name as a Plaintiff and chose George W. Bush as the lead defendant. Then I started listing other Government officials after Bush. Then I added random defendants that everyone hears about in pop culture using newspapers and magazines as a reference. Then I added entities and individuals that were dead as defendants. I was asking other inmates around me for names to include in this mega George Bush lawsuit. I came up with over 700 named defendants, which was almost ten pages in length. Finally I added a complaint that was really short and frivolous. My thinking was that the Clerk of Court that received this lawsuit would have to docket each listed defendant separately. I knew the defendants would never be served. I just wanted to waste the court's time and see the judge's response. I made copies of the lawsuit then mailed it to the Federal Courts in the Eastern District of Pennsylvania along with an attached Informa Pauperis application.[i]

About two weeks later my vision came to fruition: the courts responded back with the judge dismissing the case as frivolous. I took that same lawsuit and switched the court heading on the top to the North District of Illinois and sent it to the Federal Court in Chicago. Again, I got a response back from the judge dismissing the lawsuit, but the judge also said that that the clerk of court spent hours docketing each listed defendant. That left me thinking that that was a good result, maybe somewhere in the process I had prevented someone else from having a court case assigned. In Federal Court the same judges hear both civil and criminal cases. My thinking was that if I start flooding the courts with lawsuits then that will waste the courts' time on me while delaying some other criminal defendant's case. The federal prisons are packed. People complain about prison overcrowding. I thought that flooding the courts with lawsuits and inspiring others to flood the courts with suits will slow new inmates from entering the system. Criminal cases would get delayed. I still think that to this day.

I made an internal commitment to be down for the cause. I told myself I am going to find the way to subsidize the costs of stamps to send lawsuits and I'm going to send as many as possible to courts everywhere. Maybe this is a way to shut it down and a way to get released from prison. I came up with a catch phrase: "I got the balls to fuck with, the halls of justice, the law can suck dick!"

I was eventually transferred to FCI Williamsburg. After a few months I settled down with a routine of running multiple hours in the recreation yard and doing my post run recovery in the law library. I started filing lawsuits in different federal courts to see what would happen. Everything was trial by error. I could file in forma pauperis applications with the lawsuits, claiming that I was indigent or in imminent danger so I wouldn't have to pay the $350 court-filing fee. The prison library had cases of the same names of individuals who would file lawsuits against officials over and over, so I used the same tactics, but instead of suing officials with legitimate claims –claims I knew I would lose- I would pick celebrities instead of officials to sue. I would also try to be as creative as possible, making up far-fetched allegations that made no sense. I slowly learned to tailor my language in intentional ways to target specific courts to see how far the suits could get before they were dismissed.

I remember seeing on the news that Michael Vick was indicted by the federal government in Richmond Virginia for dog-fighting, so I filed a civil suit in the same courthouse against him claiming he had used my dogs for dog-fighting as well as other bizarre allegations, knowing that journalists would find it while investigating the details of his case. This plan worked. My lawsuit against Vick was on the news, which I watched on the prison television. This granted me a certain degree of notoriety and respect by inmates and guards.

I did my next lawsuit against Barry Bonds because of the steroid controversy he was embroiled in; this also resulted in me getting on the news. I had found a new hobby. Something I could do to pass the time, be creative with my writings as a form of art –free of charge, getting a reaction from the courts and sometimes lawyers involved in the cases in the process. My ongoing eating disorder got me cans of Ensure provided by the prison medical staff, which I then bartered for stamps to use for mailing my lawsuits. Over the next few years of being transferred to different prisons, getting kicked out of the RDAP because of my lawsuit addiction, etc., the lawsuit became my life. I would intervene in criminal cases, file motions to be parties' counsel, etc. All this is evidenced by the lawsuits seen here and thousands more that can be found through the courts if you are lucky enough to obtain them.

JLR ©

Made in the USA
Coppell, TX
31 May 2024

32963064R00187